ALIVE AND KICKING

Aberdeenshire Library and Information Service
www.aberdeenshire.gov.uk/libraries
Renewals Hotline 01224 661511

David Bryce with Simon Pia
Foreword by Irvine Welsh

ALIVE AND KICKING

A Story of Crime, Addiction and Redemption in Glasgow's Gangland

MAINSTREAM
PUBLISHING
EDINBURGH AND LONDON

First published in Great Britain in 2005 by
MAINSTREAM PUBLISHING COMPANY
(EDINBURGH) LTD
7 Albany Street
Edinburgh EH1 3UG

ISBN 1 84018 989 4

A catalogue record for this book is available
from the British Library

Typeset in Billboard and Sabon

Printed in Great Britain by
Clays Ltd, St Ives plc

I would like to dedicate this book to the memory of my mother and father and my sisters Moira, Ann and Wilma for all the support they gave me throughout their lives and also my loving wife, Jeanette.

Without Jeanette's support and understanding this book would not have been possible, and the same is true of my three children, Angela, David and especially Stephen, whose continual support for the last seven years as my assistant manager at Calton Athletic has been invaluable.

I would also like to express gratitude to the hundreds of head teachers who were courageous enough to invite Calton Atheltic's Drugs Awareness team to their schools, enabling us to speak to 80,000 young people across Scotland. A special thank you to the recovering drug-addicts who made these presentations and our chairman at Calton Athletic, James Alston.

Then there are our many supporters over the years, not least the Trainspotters and the Robertson Trust. Special support has come from Irvine Welsh and Simon Pia, whose help and encouragement were vital for this book. Thanks also to Bill Campbell at Mainstream for publishing it.

Last but not least a special mention for the families of the 3,000 people who have been through Calton Athletic, especially those who lost someone dear to them. Our thoughts are always with you. God bless you all.

David Bryce

Contents

Foreword

Alive and Kicking is the story of an unusual and highly successful football club. The Calton Athletic Recovery Project is run by, and for, former drug-addicts. So this book is the story of a drug rehabilitation project and of Davie Bryce, the man who has given the last 20 years of his life to helping people conquer their addictions. While an uplifting and inspirational tale, it's also a cautionary one, and in its telling it issues a challenge to us as a society, regarding how we perceive and tackle one of the great social problems of our time.

Davie and I became friends in 1995, during the filming of my first book, *Trainspotting*. The Calton Athletic Recovery Project provided generous and, to my mind, essential assistance in the making of the highly successful motion picture. It was a great experience for everyone involved, the relationship between the cast and crew of the movie and the Calton project continuing to this day. I had been aware of Calton Athletic for a long time prior to this, however, and not just in relation to the exploits of their all-conquering football teams.

I had known people who had passed through the project, and I'd been amazed to see the incredible transformation in their lives, in terms of health, confidence, motivation and direction. This, it has to be said, was in marked contrast to the litany of old acquaintances who had gone through 'the system' of state-managed or sponsored maintenance programmes relying on methadone, and well-meaning but generally useless 'professional' counselling.

The Calton philosophy was, then as now, a purist one: you're either off all drugs or you're still an addict. Instead of merely substituting dependences, Calton Athletic focused on self-improvement through sport and fitness as well as behaviour modification through peer-group influence. The project was amongst the first to truly recognise the importance of peer groups in defining drug users' behaviour, thus it had the potential to help change it. Calton Athletic practised this, and with astonishing success, long before it became fashionable rhetoric in the spheres of education and social work. And this was simply because Calton Athletic grew out of a directly affected and involved community, and had no other agenda except to try to reverse the drug epidemic which was (and still is) sweeping through Scotland.

Despite its astonishing success rate and its often high media profile, Calton Athletic has always been a shoestring operation. Government bodies have generally preferred to squander public money on reliably tried-and-failed approaches or have chosen to line the pockets of ad agencies that have fronted information and education campaigns, which are more often than not counter-productive.

There has been a shabby and lamentable set of excuses trotted out over the years to deny Calton Athletic the access to funds to expand their successful services. The one I find particularly nauseating is: 'You're a sports project, not a social work, education or health one.' Calton Athletic is so self-evidently a life project, and a community project in the true sense of the term. These curious distinctions, so beloved of the administrators, mean nothing to the kid on the streets who is struggling with a habit that he or she wants to kick. In an age of bluster about 'flexibility', 'holistic approaches' and 'multi-agency co-operation' in service delivery, the historical treatment of the Calton project by the authorities is scandalous and to my mind shames us as a nation. Perhaps now that we have our Scottish parliament established, it might be opportune for us to confidently nurture our own proven successes, rather than slavishly import the next (generally failed) fad from across the Atlantic.

So while there have been so many remarkable triumphs and uplifting individual stories, it would be unfair to recount these without also referencing the long and frustrating battles the project

10

has endured, often simply to survive. Throughout two decades of the ups and downs of Calton Athletic, Davie Bryce has never flagged in his commitment. His energy and enthusiasm are really something to behold, and they never wane, even in his darkest moments. I recall several years ago meeting up with Davie in Edinburgh to discuss this book. I hadn't seen him for a while, and I was saddened and concerned to note that his health was failing. Though still blazing with passion for his cause, he seemed tired and concerned. He was looking very ill: slouched, uncomfortable and his breathing was laboured. When he told me of the medical problems he faced, I was even worried that the book might not see the light of day, and I'm sure that in the back of his mind Davie was too. Yet when we met in Glasgow six months later, the transformation was amazing. Davie had stopped smoking and was visiting the gym every day. In the process he had seemingly gained two new lungs, a new spine and lost between ten and twenty years. It was hard to reconcile this barrel-chested Desperate Dan character charging around Alex Morrison's gym in the East End of Glasgow with the exhausted, worried man of a few months back. Additionally he'd also managed to rattle out this manuscript.

I recount this episode as it provides an illustration of the 100 per cent mentality Davie has. Rather than just do regular sessions in the gym, he had a structured programme and diet and was pressing what to me was an unfeasible amount of iron. Similarly, he had recounted his story and that of the project in astonishing detail, producing enough material for several books, resulting in this one, generously and empathetically edited by Simon Pia.

Davie and I have had many lively discussions on drug use and health over the years, and it's interesting how our views have converged. I still feel that the state sponsorship of methadone was essential at the time in order to halt the use of needles and the spread of HIV, but I now feel that this is a bankrupt strategy. It promotes a self-defeating social control, and it has to be challenged. This was pulled into focus recently when I was visiting an old friend in prison. He has been trying to stay drug-free, rather than seeing out his time like so many others by swallowing methadone and burning heroin. This may make life easier for both prisoners and staff in the short-term, but it means that on completion of the sentence, the offender is released into the community penniless, unemployable and with a raging habit. It doesn't take a rocket scientist to figure out what the likely future scenario will be for the individual and the community. My pal had been working out in the gym, rising an hour early every morning. But this popular facility – which also serves as a healthy incentive to a drug-free lifestyle – is now threatened with removal, simply because our overworked, under-resourced and overcrowded prison system does not have the staffing levels to supervise the inmates' gym sessions.

Davie, to his great credit, has always swum against this tide of complacency and short-term convenience. And he's done so because he refuses to stop seeing people as individual human beings of potential, rather than just junkies and jailbait. He wants them alive and kicking, not consigned to the limbo of methadone maintenance. And he's seen the alternatives, what people can make of themselves when they get the proper support and encouragement. I have too, having struggled to keep pace with some of the boys in the half-marathons and been sold more dummies than Mothercare by them on the football field. With their pride and sense of self restored, you really couldn't meet better people, and their transformation is one of the most moving and inspiring things it's been my privilege to witness.

Like most people in Britain today, I want to see an end to the misery and waste of lives that chronic drug abuse promotes. In order to do that, the nature of drug use and abuse has to be understood, as do the practices that are truly effective in prevention and rehabilitation. *Alive and Kicking* makes a huge step towards this. It's more than the story of a man, a community and a project, although it is all of these things. If you want to learn about hope, inspiration and the transfiguring, indomitable power of the human spirit, then read on from here.

Irvine Welsh

CHAPTER ONE

Take Me if You Can

'Take me if you can, but leave my men alone'

These words made a deep impression on me when I heard them for the first time as a very young boy. I immediately took them to heart; they would stay with me over the years and are still with me today. 'Take me if you can, but leave my men alone.'

I was not long at school when I got taken to the pictures to see my first film. It was Richard Todd in *Rob Roy* at the Orient in the Gallowgate. Most weans remember their first film, especially in the days before television: the giant screen, the Technicolor, and all in the dark.

I was in awe of it all, totally gripped, and there was one scene I remember as clearly as if it was yesterday. The Redcoats were trying to capture Rob Roy and thought they had him cornered when he turned on them with his claymore: 'Take me if you can, but leave my men alone.'

There was something about what he said that sank in, and it was to have a big impact on my life. It was to be my motto and code of honour as boy and man, growing up in the East End of Glasgow. These words would stay with me as a member of Glasgow's most famous gang, the Calton Tongs, and even more so when I went on to set up Calton Athletic. I still live by them today. You can take me on, but lay off my people at Calton Athletic.

That day at the pictures I also developed a fascination for the kilt. I wanted one, and for years I would go on about it, greetin' to my ma. My father was a bit wider and knew if you were running about the East End in a kilt in the '50s you'd end up in a lot of trouble. I did eventually get to wear one but it took almost 50 years. Meanwhile I'd be chased by more than the Redcoats: by alcohol, drugs, crime and violence. All of this would drag me down, but I recovered. I was able to change my life and finally even change into a kilt.

A further reason for the film having such an influence was that Rob Roy's mother often visited my school. The actress who played her also happened to be a dentist who covered my school in the East End. Every opportunity I got I would put my name down to see her. I was walking around 'gumsie' by the time I was seven, I'd been in so often to the dentist's. Each time she came to the school, I claimed I had toothache, but it was an excuse to ask how Rob Roy was getting on. She'd always tell me he was doing fine but still on the run from the English. They hadnae managed to capture him.

Rob Roy was a likeable rogue, and I suppose I was a bit of a wee rogue but most people in the community liked me, and I can still say they do today, despite everything. I have been misguided at times and took the wrong path, but I have always tried to look after my own, especially at Calton Athletic.

We've a tradition at the club that when someone shares their experience for the first time we give each other the strength to start from the very beginning, and that's what I'll do. It can be difficult but here goes.

CHAPTER TWO

East End Boy

My name is David Bryce. I was born in 1949, a post-War baby, but I was about 35 when my life really took the shape it is in today. That's when I started Calton Athletic, an amateur football team in the East End of Glasgow that was to gain an international reputation as a football team with a difference: it was made up of recovering drug-addicts. Nobody gave it a hope in hell of success. But that football team was to become the best-known rehabilitation project in the UK, and possibly Europe, thanks to help along the way from the television film *Alive and Kicking*, with Lenny Henry and Robbie Coltrane, and the film *Trainspotting*.

Ewan McGregor joined us at Calton Athletic to do research for the film and to find out what it was really like being a drug-addict. Today at Calton Athletic we are proud of how we helped to give the film its authenticity, something appreciated by a worldwide audience.

But first things first. I should let you know how it all came about. I was the youngest of a family of four and grew up at 132 Forbes Street, which ran through the Mile End quarter in Glasgow's East End. At the end of the street is St Mary's chapel, the church of

Brother Walfrid, the priest who founded Celtic. At one time it used to be three streets but after the War it was made into one. The part of the street that I stayed in was originally called Waterloo Street. On top of one of the tenement buildings there was a big cannon to commemorate the famous battle, but its name was changed as there were two Waterloo Streets in Glasgow.

My earliest recollections are happy ones. My father, William Bryce, and my mother, Annie Morrison, were both born in 1910 in the Mile End. My mother was one of six: four girls and two boys. My father was the oldest of eight children. His family were from Soho Street just off the Gallowgate. My mother's family were from Forbes Street and I grew up in the same close as my grandparents. My parents married in 1931. I had three sisters, who were all older than me. Moira was born in 1933, Ann was born in 1946 and Wilma in 1947. I arrived two years later. Not long afterwards, my mum got a job at the local carpet factory, Lyall's, about 200 yards from our house at the Mile End. She worked there till she retired. My father worked at Rolls-Royce, where he'd started during the War, until 1964. My eldest sister, Moira, had a bad heart and wasn't fit for work, so she looked after me when my mum went out to the factory. In the early days I probably thought Moira was my mum because I was with her so much and she did a good job.

I had good pals who I went to school with and played with in the street. I also went to Sunday school and church and had no real problems. My parents were good, solid, working-class people. We weren't poor and I never seemed to want for anything. When I look back, I can see that, as the youngest, I was spoiled.

My family had known tough times during the War and the Depression but were now in full employment. Life in the Mile End had improved for most folk after the War. In my early years at school there were only two or three in the class who used 'pinkies', the tickets for free meals, unlike today, with so much unemployment in the area. It was a close community, and I have fond memories of my early pals. There were the Kennedys in the next close, the Clarks next door and the McGuires across the road, and then there was Matt MacGregor and Billy McGrath. It was good growing up there, especially during the summer holidays, when we got up to everything that all kids do: going away for the day, building guidie carts and gang huts. I well remember the craze for hula-hoops. A good crowd of boys hung around together in the street and none of us got into bother. And, of course, there was that early incident when I saw *Rob Roy* at the Orient. Coming from an honest family, I knew the difference between right and wrong and I now had my code of honour: 'Take me if you can, but leave my men alone.'

The East End has always had a strong sense of community and my grandfather George Morrison used to refer to himself as an Old Caltonian. Calton was only across the road from the Mile End but as far as my grandfather was concerned it was a separate place. I never saw my grandfather drunk except at New Year. He played the concertina and, as the bells tolled on the stroke of midnight, he would throw open the back window and play 'A Guid New Year to Yin and A'' for the neighbours.

My grandfather worked for 65 years – and I mean worked – at Singer's in Clydebank. He started when he was 12, using his brother Jock's birth certificate to get a job, and he was known as Jock from then on. He stayed at Singer till he was 77. When he reached 65, they took him off machine work and put him in the gatehouse, where people clocked in. He only stopped when he turned blind.

My grandmother Mary Morrison was from Beauly, near Inverness. She was an orphan and came to Glasgow when she was 12 to work in service in the big houses in the West End. They only got a half-day off on Saturday, and my grandfather's sister, who worked beside her, took her home one day and that's how she and my grandfather met. One thing I remember about my grandmother is that she was a beautiful speaker with a lovely accent. She spoke at the Socialist Sunday School. They were guid folk, and my mother always had strong church connections and was a Ranger, the older version of the Girl Guides, right up till she was married.

On my father's side I let the family down after four generations. Maybe it was a sign of things to come. The oldest son had always been called William Bryce. The reason I wasn't was that my mother was 40 when I was born. They didn't think I'd be coming along and had called the last of the three girls Wilma, after my father. So I broke the family tradition. I was also to break it in another way, as the first to get into trouble with the police. I would become the black sheep of the family, but it certainly did not start out that way.

My grandfather Bryce had volunteered in the First World War, although he didn't have to as he had three kids by this time. He spent three years in the trenches for King and country, fighting for a better future, only for the Roaring '20s to collapse into the Hungry '30s. The Bryces were from Eaglesham and, like the Morrisons, also had strong church connections. I remember my mother telling me my father's family were Rachabites, who believed in abstinence. I could laugh about this years later when I finally became sober. In the meantime I was to more than make up for generations of my father's family being abstainers.

There was one question concerning my family that bugged me. Most of the fathers of the other kids at Annfield Primary had fought in the War. I asked my mother what regiment my father was in or had he been in the Navy or Air Force. She told me he wanted to join up but he'd worked in an aircraft factory instead. I always felt a bit ashamed of this. My father had applied to volunteer although he was a bit older than average and had a child already. When he went for his medical, he failed the eye test. On his way out the doctor said, 'Are you sure you'll be able to find the door?' I never remember my father having bad sight, though, and he only ever needed reading glasses. The doctor was obviously on to him and being sarcastic.

Years later, when I was at an Alcoholics Anonymous meeting, an old guy from the Mile End was speaking about his experience in the International Brigade in the Spanish Civil War. When the Second World War broke out, he'd tried to join up but because of his connection with the International Brigade he was considered an undesirable. He ended up instead in the aircraft factory with, as he put it, 'the rest of the fly-men from the Mile End'. They had a great war, and seemingly there were lots of parties, with dancing on the nightshift. The men were heavily outnumbered by the women. It was only then, years later, that I realised my father was wide enough to avoid the War and get a good job at an aircraft factory. That was his War effort. The thing was, by then, my attitudes towards war had changed, and I was no longer ashamed of him.

When I was about ten, something dramatic happened in my wee

world. There was another primary school in the Mile End, called Campbellfield, which shut down. At the start of the new term, their pupils came to our school. As there were so many new people, I found myself in a different class, with only about three from my original class, and I didn't like that. I was amongst strangers. The new classmates brought with them some pressure and a couple of fights. It was then that I met two other boys, one from Campbellfield and one who had moved into Dennistoun. Bill Allan had come down from Hikehill and the other was Donny Bain. I liked these two boys and got on well with them. They made up for being split up from the rest of my classmates, such as Roy Clark. Roy was my next-door neighbour. He was three months older so he was put into a different class, but we'd still meet up at playtime and after school. While I was still going about with the same boys in the Mile End, then, there were a few more added to the crew, such as Bill Allan and Donny Bain.

This was when things started to change. Up till then I had been a good boy and had no problems at school. My pals had been from decent families and we all looked after each other. But one thing I learned I could do was fight, so I was to become the leader of this new group.

Rob Roy and the kilt both played their part. I'd been greetin' on so much about getting a kilt for Christmas that my father – who was highly wary of the idea – got me two sets of boxing gloves instead. One set would have been great, but two sets enabled me to turn the landing on our stair into a gym. I set up the ring and proceeded to take on all-comers. I beat every boy in the street. It established a pecking order and I was at the top. Even though I was only ten years old, my reputation spread and I took on boys older than me. Fighting was part of the culture in the East End. At the school I went to, everybody would look back and remember who was the best fighter or best footballer, not who was the brightest. That did not just apply to Annfield Primary but to schools in schemes and hard working-class areas all over Scotland.

I'd also realised boxing in the stair as a laddie that I had an inner strength. I could take a punch. Often, if someone's nose or lip got bust they did not want to know. If someone bust my nose, I wanted to bust theirs and split their eye too. I had natural ability and boxing came easily to me. I was also a quick learner. When someone stuck the nut on me for the first time, I didn't mess about. This boy claimed me at the cinema in the Gallowgate and, as we went outside, he stuck the heid on me, bursting my lip. I was expecting a punch. I flew at him and burst his lip and his nose and did a bit more than I usually did, giving him a few kicks as well.

By the time I went to secondary, my reputation preceded me even further, as I'd had more fights than Jim Watt had in his career. As I grew older, I found it very difficult to back down. More often than not, it was this that got me into trouble, rather than wanting to fight. Pride and the fear of losing face were what drove me on. In addition, my pals would play on my Rob Roy syndrome. They knew I would sort out trouble for them if anyone was bullying them and they would use me as a threat. Whenever there was any trouble, I would be pushed to the front. My pals were not mugs.

This whole mentality was not just limited to school days. Go along Duke Street today and in the pubs they'll all tell you who the hard men are – who's the best fighter – not who's the mechanic, joiner, scaffolder or taxi-driver. In the East End you gain credibility by being able to look after yourself. People respect you for that and I liked it. But I was never a bully.

However, I was always testing my bottle, and my pals Donny Bain, Bill Allan and Roy Clark were also game. Donny was connected to the Billy Boys, the famous Glasgow gang, as his grandfather was Billy Fulton, the legendary leader. Aye, the guy and the gang they still sing about at Ibrox. His uncle, also Billy, stayed in the Mile End and was the leader of the 'corner boys' in Forbes Street. Almost every neighbourhood in Glasgow had a gang at this time, and they would hang out on the street corner – hence, every neighbourhood had its own corner boys. Billy's uncle was the main man in Forbes Street. There were a lot of them in his gang, and some of them were quite capable. Young Billy had a wee bit of ability himself, although he was never quite the man his father was. He was to have a big influence on my young life, all the same, because he was in charge of the corner boys and we looked up to them.

My first bit of trouble came with Donny. It was nothing serious at first, and part of it was just growing up. Donny's dad was also a well-known character, but he had split up from his ma. Bill Allan's parents had also split up, and one of his sisters was going with Ben Ingles, one of the up-and-coming neds from the Calton area. Ben was an arch-rival of young Billy Fulton, and they had had a few skirmishes. Bill Allan's older brothers had also been in trouble, and here I was now hanging around with Bill, Donny and Roy Clark, the four of us thick as thieves. Even though Bill's and Donny's families were at each other's throats, it didn't bother us.

At the age of 11 I was introduced to smoking by Donny, who showed us how to inhale and told me I was wasting it if I blew it out. I well remember the first time I inhaled. A couple of minutes later I took a 'whitey' and thought I was going to die. I vowed I would never smoke again and staggered over to my sister's house. I went there because I didn't want my ma and da to see the state I was in and find me out. After about 15 minutes I started to feel OK and bumped into Donny the next day, who offered us a fag. I told him I didn't want it because I'd been sick. 'That happens to everybody, Davie. You'll no be sick again if you have one, and you'll enjoy it more.' And I did do it and I wasn't sick again. In fact I never had quite the same buzz again after that first time I properly inhaled it.

I didn't know it then, but I would come to appreciate many years later that you build up a tolerance to tobacco, drink and drugs. It is never quite the same after the first time. Nobody starts off with a high tolerance. Nobody starts off on 40 fags a day. We start off with a loose fag shared amongst pals, and it goes up to two or three fags. Then you keep smoking more as your tolerance builds up. I had been introduced to it by one of my pals and peer pressure took over. However, my father was quite strict and, although he smoked, it wasn't acceptable for us. So I had to keep it a secret and I suppose that's when lying started to become part of my life, hiding things from my family.

I also started stealing to get the money for the fags. Peer pressure led me into doing it. I may have been the best fighter but I was frightened of stealing and felt I had to prove myself. Donny had already been done by the police before I met him – when he was only nine – and he led the way. We used to have the Milanda vans from the local bakery parked right outside the school. The drivers would leave them there after their morning deliveries, with loaves of bread left in them. As soon as school was out, we'd fly over to the vans, steal the bread and sell it to our neighbours. There was always a big demand. Although people were working, wages weren't too clever. A loaf cost a shilling and we'd sell them for sixpence. This became a constant supply of income. There was also another bakery in the district, the Welma, and we'd do the same with them. We'd work out what time the vans arrived and we'd take empty bread boxes with us, fill them up and then sell the loaves. It was exciting, and good money, and was my first taste of criminality.

A lot of buildings were being pulled down in the Mile End, so we'd collect the scrap and nobody really bothered about it – none of the neighbours, anyway – but if the police had caught us we would have been done, so we had to be on our toes. We'd punt it at a scrap shop in the Mile End. When I'd gone to secondary school, I was separated from my pals again because my family left the Mile End and moved to the Easterhouse scheme on the edge of the city.

A lot of the families were starting to leave the Mile End, especially the old families who had been there for years. Glasgow Corporation had opened a housing list and these people had had their name on it for years. I know my family had. My ma was always dreaming of a house with an inside toilet and a bathroom. We were all looking forward to it. But we didn't realise how much we would miss the Mile End. When we flitted, we hated it.

Easterhouse was and still is a massive housing scheme, but there were no shops and no schools. There was nothing except houses, and all the kids who stayed in Easterhouse had to get buses down to their old schools. At first it may have been exciting, what with the new house, but I had no pals there. I was missing the Mile End and, instead of coming home after school, I was staying back down there. My sisters, when they finished work, would just stay down as well, and my father also hated being away from the area. It wasn't so bad during the week, when all he was doing was going to work. He used to get picked up in the morning in Easterhouse and driven down to the Rolls-Royce factory at Hillingdon. It was at the weekend that he hated it, because all of his drinking haunts, Big Jack's or Dougan's, were down the Gallowgate and the Mile End.

With the pressure from us all my mother relented, and we managed to get a new house at Bellfield Street in Dennistoun. When I moved to Bellfield Street, I should have gone to the local school on Thomson Street, where my cousins were, but I didn't want to go there. After all I had travelled all the way from Easterhouse down to Annfield School. Now I could just cross over the bridge and the Gallowgate to get there, and that's what happened; I continued to go to Annfield.

The time eventually came when I was old enough to leave Annfield and, because I didn't live in the Gallowgate, I got separated from my pals. Most of the boys in the class went to Bernard Street. Donny had gone to Whitehill, my pal Roy had gone to Onslow Drive the year before and Bill had gone to Bernard Street Secondary. I had to go to Onslow Drive. I had passed the 'qualie' exam to go there rather than to Dennistoun. But I hated it. You had to wear a uniform. I had thought that Roy was going there but, after a short time, Roy's family pulled a stroke and he got sent to Bernard Street. I started avoiding Onslow Drive. I used to 'dog it', and that's the first time truancy came into play. From my early years at primary school right up to about ten, I had near enough an excellent attendance record. Although we were quite wild, my father was strict. That's just the way it was in those days – not just for me, for everybody. If you carried on at school and your parents were sent for, then you would get it. You also got it off the school. Most of the teachers would use the belt.

But I didn't like secondary school, and my ma was at her wits' end. She agreed to go to the Education Department and tell them I was staying with my sister in Forbes Street. That way they'd allow me to attend Bernard Street. When I got to Bernard Street, my reputation already preceded me. In my last year at primary school, we'd been sent to an annex next to Bernard Street secondary, and there was an incident one day with my sister Wilma. A teacher grabbed her and was shaking Wilma, so I immediately jumped in to help her. Take me if you can, but leave my men alone, or in this case my sister.

At that stage I wasn't due to be going to Bernard Street for secondary, but six months later there I was and they hadn't forgotten me. They had my card marked. Not only that but Donny had left

Whitehill as well and joined me at Bernard Street. Now Donny, me and Bill Allan were in the one class and Roy was there in the year above and we were still as thick as thieves. Within a couple of years that corner in Forbes Street where the corner boys used to hang out was to be our corner.

By now we had a few quid from our thieving, the lassies were good and there were plenty of them. They seemed to come from all over the place to hang about with us down the Mile End and Forbes Street. We didn't realise at the time how lucky we were. Although we were smoking and starting to drink, none of us had gone to 'jail' yet. We were now 14. We had all had brushes with the law and there were some near things. In fact three of us got done together the year before when Roy Clark, Donny and I turned over a bookie's house.

Our criminal careers had been progressing nicely. At first it had just been the bread off the Milanda motors, then we started with the scrap. Next we moved on to stealing stuff off the lorries, then it was breaking into shops. It was never through the front door but through the back walls. We had watched the older ones doing it and we used to practise going through the walls in the tenements that were being pulled down.

We were only 13 when we were caught turning over this bookie's house. We had been told there was a lot of money in it by a pal who stayed next door. Every Sunday morning the bookie and his family went to the chapel, so there was nobody in. Our pal told us where the money was and we waited for Sunday. We were going in a wee window, so we had to pick the smallest among us. We punted Roy up to it but he couldn't get in. We then punted Donny up because he was the skinniest. He got in, opened the door and we found the money and got out. Nobody had seen us and we had got away with a nice few quid. It was that much money we didn't know what to do with it. We knew if we spent it all, though, it would draw attention to us.

Nobody loses that kind of money and accepts it, so the coppers were going to be busy. They would be making enquiries, but nobody had seen us. If we had played it cool, we would have got away with it the same as we'd got away with everything else so far. But the boy that put us on to it was a lookout that day and after we got the money we 'naffed off' and never gave him a cut of it. Because he was only the lookout, it was decided that he got 'bumped' – it wasn't my suggestion – and to justify him being bumped we decided that if we gave him too much money his father would find out and put two and two together. Meanwhile, the police were making their enquiries and, because he stayed next to the bookie's and had been in the guy's house before, he got questioned. A bit of pressure from his father and the fact he'd got bumped saw him crack and give up our names. We were all done, even the boy who shopped us. All of us got two years' probation and had to pay £10 each back to the bookie. There had been no evidence against us, except for our pal's. It just shows you that no good comes from bumping somebody. It wasn't right that he grassed us up, but it wasn't right that we bumped him in the first place, and maybe we deserved it.

However, my life was not all crime. I was growing up and thought I was becoming a man. Just before I left primary school that Christmas, my mum had got me my first suit with long trousers. Italian suits were all the craze then, striped ones. I got one and thought I looked a million dollars. My mother also got me pointed shoes, winkle-pickers, which were just starting to come into style, and a short, light-grey Crombie overcoat. I thought I looked smashing and every time I looked in the mirror I couldn't wait to get to the Dennistoun Palais. That was the local dancing we went to on a Saturday afternoon. The Pally on a Saturday afternoon was an important part of our life then – the dancing was fantastic.

Things were starting to change for Bill Allan, Roy Clark, Donny Bain and me. We were joined by a guy called John Wotherspoon. His family had moved up to Easterhouse from Bridgeton and had hated it and then moved down to the Mile End. John started to go about with us and we christened him 'Spooney' – he still gets called Spooney to this day. We were the corner boys and the birds flocked around from Easterhouse, Calton, Bridgeton and Parkhead . . . and they were all older than us. They had already started to work full-time and I suppose that's what made me start on the milk rounds. At least if somebody asked me if I was working I could say, 'Aye, I work on the milk,' and kid on I was an all-day boy when I was really a part-timer still at school. I couldn't wait to leave school, so I had started on the milk before I left. You had to be up at five in the morning and you had to run from when you started till you finished at half past eight. Then you had to make it to school for nine o'clock. I loved it and the money it gave us for the weekend. I had more in my pocket than people who were working full-time because they had to hand in their 'dig money' (for housekeeping). I wasn't handing in dig money and was keeping the tips, as well as still getting pocket money from my mum and my big sister. Life was good. I had nice clothes, I was ready for leaving school, there were a lot of lassies going about with us and we were going to the dancing regularly. But this was when I started getting into serious trouble.

CHAPTER THREE

Tongs Ya Bass

It was the early '60s and the start of the Glasgow gangs. Most of the folk on Forbes Street went to St Mary's School, which I didn't go to because it was Catholic. The street runs into the Calton, though, so I knew most of them as neighbours. The Calton Tongs had just started at the time – the original Tongs – and I knew most of them because they flew pigeons, as did I. When I'd first met the gang, everyone in it was about three years older than me and it didn't have a name. There was another gang in the Calton at the time called the Toi. This crowd that I knew from flying pigeons had all gone to the pictures one night and there was a film on called *The Terror of the Tongs*. The Tongs were a Chinese secret society called 'The Red Dragon Tongs'. After the picture had finished, they were all going down the road and one of them shouted, 'Tongs Ya Bass!' That was it, simple as that, and the famous war cry would be heard for many years to come.

It wasn't too long before the Calton Tongs were being imitated by the next wave of self-styled gangsters; a sort of 'young Tongs' sprang up. They hung about the Omar café down the London Road next to Arcadia Street. There were probably about 30 of them: guys like big

Bunty, Tam McGarvey, wee Doughnut, the two Jarvises, Brizzy, wee Lonnie, the brothers Semple and a few others. They used to go to the Barrowland, while I went to the Dennistoun Palais, so we didn't have much contact. The Tongs had a couple of battles in the Barrowland, but after that they had nobody to fight with as they were fearsome, and I suppose that's when they turned their attention to us. We were the nearest lot to them and we had girlfriends that went to their school. These girls weren't bad looking, and that was one reason they started fighting with us. So that's how I was formally introduced to the Tongs. When they came up looking for a fight, I was always pushed to the front. This bit of nonsense went on for some time.

I remember one night I saw some of them heading in our direction, so three of us hid behind a wall, waiting for them to pass. There were only six of them, or so we thought. We could hear the voices getting closer and I jumped over the wall, pulled a bayonet out and challenged them: 'Take me if you can, but leave my men alone.'

The only thing was there were now about 30 of them. I hadn't seen the rest that had still been around the corner. They were that astounded and taken aback when I challenged them, though, that none of them rose to the bait. I could have been killed. I was also in a state of shock, but I had the element of surprise. Only later did it sink in to them that there were only three of us and I was the only one who was tooled up. The nonsense continued right up until I was nearly 15, with them out to get me.

One night I was standing on Forbes Street with Benny Ingles, the brother-in-law of my pal Bill Allan, when I clocked the Tongs coming. Benny had a reputation and I told him, 'Here they come.' Benny told me to stay where I was. He'd recognised a couple of them, the McGarvey brothers, who were originally from the Mile End. As they approached, Benny shouted them over and asked what all this nonsense was about. They didn't know. Then Benny asked me. I didn't know either. If we didn't know, Benny says, what was the point in fighting? So we shook hands, and that was that. I joined the Tongs that night. It wasn't long, either, before I proved my worth to them.

During the course of the next few months I was involved in a few escapades with the Tongs where I showed them what I was made of.

I was accepted without a problem. I had witnessed the birth of the Tongs and was a leader of the first gang to fight with them. Now I was one of them. It was September 1963, I was about to turn 15 and I thought I was invincible. Within a few months, though, I would be locked up. The few short months I had with the Tongs were to take me straight to jail, and it all happened so quickly. I had hardly left school and the next thing I knew I was inside Kibble approved school.

I'd had to babysit at my sister's house on New Year's Eve, while she and my ma were out at a New Year's Eve party. I'd decided that me and my friends would have our own party there. To get the booze for it, we were going to turn over one of the pubs that was shut for the New Year: the Brandon Bar, just off the Gallowgate. Although I was barely 15, booze had started to play a big part in my life, and here we were, a bunch of laddies turning over a pub: me, Spooney and a guy called Mick Farrell.

There was an empty factory next to the Brandon and, true to form, we decided to go through the walls, grafting our way in. We got the booze out and transported it over to my sister's house while the lassies had been looking after the wean. We had taken loads of it from the pub, and the intention was we'd keep some of it and sell the rest. Later that night I headed back to my own house, and I was in bed when the police arrived. A guy who had been at the party had got involved in some incident with a lassie out in the street and had been lifted with four bottles of whisky on him. When the police asked him where he had got the whisky, he told them we had given it to him: me, Spooney and Mick Farrell. The coppers came to my house and lifted us. My mum tried to protest: 'It's no him. He's been watching the wean a' night.' So the coppers took me to my brother-in-law's house to check out the alibi.

I was dreading what they would find because we had had the party there, but my brother-in-law had tidied the place up. The coppers seemed happy enough just checking out my story. As they were about to leave, though, they found three bottles of whisky and asked my brother-in-law who they belonged to. He said they were his so they charged him with reset (receiving stolen goods) and all four of us got locked up that night and put on remand. Thankfully, my brother-in-law got out after four days, but Mick, me and Spooney and this character who had shopped us were still on remand.

I'd set about this guy who'd shopped us in the cells, but not too badly because we still had to go to court and we wanted to use him. When we reached court, he got a deferred sentence. Spooney's dad had died while he had been inside and he ended up with 28 days, but Mick and I were sent to approved school, which was a boarding school with tight discipline, one below Borstal on the ladder to prison. I had almost got off. The judge had said he thought I was unlucky to be involved as I had only been done for the bottles of whisky my brother-in-law was charged with. The guy who shopped us had decided not to dig us in at the trial after our wee conversation in the cells, and the Crown was going to drop the charges against me. But I had pled guilty to the reset so they would accept my brother-in-law's plea. They did so and I was expecting only a fine for reset. He had been in approved school before, so he was to be committed again. But, when Mick heard my sentence being handed out, he turned round in the dock and stuck the heid on the guy who shopped us. It was a moment of pure madness and there was mayhem in the court. The judge shouted, 'Approved school. Take him away.'

Just five minutes earlier he had been saying he was prepared to give me a chance, and now here I was joining Mick on the road to the jail. I was just 15 and had only been out of school for a couple of weeks. I was sent to Larchgrove, the remand home, before being sent to Kibble approved school. I hated Larchgrove. The teachers were pure bastards. You couldn't smoke unless you were 16. Larchgrove was a terrible place, and I don't think I've come across a better description of it than in Jimmy Boyle's book *A Sense of Freedom*.

When I did move on to approved school, at least it was better than Larchgrove. I had never heard of Kibble, let alone knew where it was. However, once I got there – my probation officer took me, and it turned out to be in Paisley – I experienced déjà vu, as if I had been there before. Obviously I hadn't, but I fitted into the routine. I thought some of the residents were staff, as they were massive. There were 100 residents and you were given a number. Mine was 47. You had to wear short trousers and everything was modelled on the

Army. It was the strictest approved school in the country. However, there were no East End boys, none of the gang, so I was alone. I soon began to hate it and decided to escape.

When I look back, it was quite an achievement fleeing from Kibble to Glasgow in a pair of short trousers and an approved-school uniform. Kibble was not Colditz, but security was quite tight. Another boy gave me the idea. He told me there was a blind spot behind the toilets in the playground that the teachers couldn't see during the break. You could not take a run and jump at it. You would need a ladder, or someone to punt you over, and then you would pull up the guy who'd given you the footie. We decided to do it the next day. My only mistake was in agreeing to go first. When I was up on top of the wall, he bottled it and ran away to shop me. Although it was his idea, he'd tell the governor I had threatened him with a knife. It was a lie and an early lesson about the agents provocateurs I would come across in the penal system.

Anyway, I was over the wall and free and headed for Gilmour Street station, where I intended to sneak on a train to Central station in Glasgow. I had to hide in the waiting room when I saw a couple of teachers from the approved school searching for me. When they swung the door open, I crammed myself behind it, and when they looked in, they saw no one. I sneaked back out onto the platform after they'd gone and jumped on a Glasgow train. As it took off, I leant out of the window and waved at the teachers still scouring the platform, and they started shaking their fists at me. I soon realised this was not too clever as they'd notify the coppers, who would be waiting for me at Central station. When the train pulled in, I jumped out of the track-side door, made it across the railway sidings and got away.

I was free, but it did not take me long to get drunk and then recaptured. Drink was already playing a central role in my life, although I didn't realise it. I had headed straight for the Gallowgate, where I was eventually picked up, pissed out of my mind. Still only 15 and I was on my way back to court. Instead of pleading guilty to the offence they planted on me, I pled not guilty. If I had pled guilty, they would have taken me back to the approved school. In December I had still been a schoolboy, but by February I had been in an approved school, escaped from it and was now certified 'unruly'. I was put on remand for seven weeks at the 'Bar-L' – Barlinnie – the most famous prison in Scotland.

I couldn't get over it. How could all this have happened so quickly? Only two months out of school and here I was in Barlinnie. My whole world had turned upside down. It is a frightening experience for anyone to be in Barlinnie, even for a night, but I was barely fifteen and remanded there for seven weeks.

When I arrived, a prison officer took one look at me and told them to take me over to the hospital wing. I'd get 'pumped' otherwise. It was the right decision, although I didn't quite understand why at the time. A young boy in prison would be abused before he even got near the showers.

The next morning the governor came over to see me in the hospital wing, and I recognised him. A couple of months before I had been delivering his milk. He was one of my customers. Now I was one of his prisoners in Barlinnie. He arranged for me to be sent up to Longriggend. This was to be the first time I was in Longriggend, but it wouldn't be the last. It held 60 youngsters, mainly from the Glasgow area. There was a big turnover of prisoners at that time, as it was an automatic four days for remand. Every fourth day you would have a new draft of prisoners coming up, and we were all mixed together. While I was in there, I was locked up with murderers and guys who were a lot older than me. There was one particular guy who was the same age as me, though: John Slowey, from the South Side. He was involved with the Cumbie, another notorious gang, and was in for a murder. He finished up getting life. Prison was my first taste of the adult world. Longriggend was high security, and you were locked up in a cell.

After seven weeks they took me back to court and then sent me back to the approved school. When I got there, things were a bit different. There were now a couple of East End boys who had both gone to school with us: John Mackinnon and Alex Williams. John was one of the Tongs, so he was a bit of company. They also had another guy in from the Calton area: wee Stein. Wee Stein was in for attempted murder. He had been done while he was out on bail for three other attempted murders and he was only 15. He didn't smoke, he didn't drink and here he was inside with us.

I found things a bit easier now and decided I'd stay for a wee while. At least I had pals for company. Usually when you escape, the 'donners' (staff) in the approved school try to have a go at you. I was waiting for it to happen, and when it did it was because of my pal wee Stein. He got into an argument with a few older guys. The wee man didn't give a fuck, and I stood by him. A couple of days later I was walking through the smokers' corridor engrossed in a letter from home when a few guys jumped me. They got in a few before I knew what was happening. I broke away and ran into a store room, grabbed a plank and went after them. The first one I caught up with was the biggest, a guy called Slim. As soon as I started laying into him, his bottle went and so did the rest of them. They backed off. From that moment on I never got any hassle in the Kibble approved school.

But I wasn't to stay there much longer. I'd settled down a wee bit and managed to get leave. For your first leave at Kibble your parents had to come and pick you up. You were entitled to it after ten weeks, but in my case I had had to wait eight months. My dad duly arrived, and the governor warned him, 'If he's OK, he will be back here on Monday. If he's aff his heid, he will finish up in Borstal.'

I was aff ma' heid. I never made it back on the Monday, and the reason was booze. I missed the bus because I had been drinking. I phoned the governor to tell him I would be late, and he started shouting down the phone. He was giving me one chance and one chance only. When I heard that, I told him to fuck off.

I thought I'd blotted my copybook anyway, so I put the phone down and continued drinking. I stayed out on the run for a couple of months. I survived by stealing and sleeping rough. There were a lot of horses and carts still around the East End collecting scrap, and there was a stable for them off the Gallowgate. I would climb in at night and sleep in the hay with the horses. It was pitch black and frightening. I'd be woken, startled during the night by a bang, but it would only be horses knocking their hooves against the wall. I would also stay in condemned houses, but the problem was the police inspecting them. In those days they were a presence on the streets and knew the district inside out. That's no myth. They'd check out these old buildings, so you had to be alert. During this period I remember John Mackinnon coming out on leave and I met him for a drink. He passed on a message from the governor. It was to remind me that I was nearly 16, and if I didn't give myself up they would send me to Borstal when they caught me. I laughed it off at the time, but deep down I was thinking about giving myself up, because life on the run wasn't what it was cracked up to be. People didn't really want to know. The only ones that did were the gang, and most were still young and staying at home with their parents, so they could not put me up. It was hard going, and I was on the point of giving myself up, but I never got the chance to as I was caught stealing.

The only time I was happy on the run was when I was drinking, but I needed money, and that's how I was caught 'grafting'. When they took me to the police station and I was charged, they asked me how old I was. I said 15. They asked for my date of birth. 'Fifteen, eh? No, you're not, son. You're 16.' I had turned 16 and did not even know it. I had had no contact with my home or family while living rough. I had also forgotten about the governor's warning, and here I was caught at 16 and put on remand for Borstal reports. The first time I had been in Barlinnie was frightening, but it was only for seven weeks. This time I was 16, and I was a Borstal boy heading for the top floor at C Hall in Barlinnie. I got a hair cut, or rather they shaved your head, which was to humiliate you. There were about 18 of us up there, and that's where I met wee Willie Burns.

He had been to court three days earlier. He too was just 16. I was wee but Willie was even smaller, so the two of us made a pact to stand by each other, and that's exactly what we did. After two weeks we were moved to Polmont, and we went through Polmont together, which was better than Kibble as they treated you more like a man. You never got a chance to sit on your backside. You were either cleaning your cell, at work, square bashing (marching) or at physical training.

During those first three months there was nobody from the East End with us. Wee Willie and I had both been milk boys and his experience was something similar to mine. He came from a decent family as well, but he got involved in a gang, the Shamrock. One of his reasons for going about with the Shamrock was better birds. But Willie was also interested in the drink. Together, the drink, the birds and the gangs led him down the road to Borstal. We had our pact and stood by it. Forty years later we were still to have our pact, with Willie working with us at Calton Athletic.

I was severely tested during my first three months at Polmont. There were guys from Edinburgh, Dundee and different parts of Glasgow. Polmont had inmates as old as 21, so we were up against guys of 18, 19 or 21, but we were still boys of 16 and hadn't had the benefit of the circuit training.

I was about 5 ft 3 in. and Willie was 5 ft 1 in. when we went in, but by the time I came out I was 5 ft 11 and Willie was about 5 ft 8. Physically, Polmont was good for us. In the early days it was testing, and during that first three months we were allocated to Rothesay House. It was considered the best. Rothesay and Wallace House were supposed to be for the hard men and Bruce House was for those who weren't all there, who were considered a bit disturbed.

That first three months I tried to avoid trouble, but I got involved in five fights. However, I was never caught. One of them was with a guy called Kane, from Edinburgh. He had tried to get wide with me in the art room with three of his pals. When I walked back to my cell, I picked up my boots and curled them up in my hand. I walked into the toilet and there he was on his own. I ladled right into him with these big boots.

I had another fight down in the annex. That was the part for the rookies, where it was dormitories rather than single cells. You had to fight in jail. If you didn't, they'd stomp on top of you. I'd learned that much at the Kibble. It hadn't done me any harm, and it got me a bit of respect. Nobody was messing with me.

During the first nine months I was in Borstal, things were going mental outside. This was 1966, and the gang culture had taken off, with the Tongs rising to the top. There was mayhem in the streets of Glasgow as gangs ran amok. But there was a price to be paid for those involved, and a lot more boys from the district started arriving at Polmont: Eddie McQuillen, my wee pal Stein who had been in approved school and my pal John from the Tongs.

John was a bit tasty, a bit special, and the leader of the young Tongs. Nobody disputed that in the Borstal. I had known him from when we were younger. Although he stayed in the Calton, he used to go to the same youth club as us when we were about 13. We got on well and both liked the pigeons. John was quite a character and it was good to have him in beside us. By the time I left, half the guys who were in Rothesay House were in the Tongs. Our leader was there and everything was going fine.

I had also got a job in the welders' workshop. I had always wanted to be a welder, and at Polmont I got my chance. The way it worked was that you had to clean the floor at first, then you went onto the machines, and after that it was onto a welding box. I was dying to get onto a welding box and start practising. Maybe it was to help alleviate what I was missing outside, where I could have been serving an apprenticeship. But here I was serving one inside and getting first-hand experience straight away. If I was outside, I'd never have got near the welding torch until I was about 18. I had two good instructors: big Smudger and McFarlane – two decent guys. I wasn't long in the workshop when one tea break we were having a smoke and this character from Bellshill asked for a light. I passed my lighter over, one I had just had sent in from my mum. It was a Rangers lighter and was my prize possession, especially seeing as how my ma had sent it. But this guy was trying to be wide and did not hand it back. When I asked him for it, he said I wasn't getting it. I just stuck the heid on him right away and followed through with a couple of punches. He fell to the deck and I picked up my lighter. Two screws came running and dragged the two of us down to the 'digger' (solitary-confinement cell). I was sure I wasn't going to let this bam take my lighter and when I belted him he'd 'ponied it' (legged it).

I didn't fancy the digger because you couldn't smoke and it meant more time would be added on to my sentence. When we were up in front of the governor the next day, Mr McFarlane came in to describe what had happened. He did me a big favour, putting a different spin on it. He said the other guy had attacked me and I had done nothing. The boy from Bellshill was bad news and I wasn't the first person he had tried it on with, but I think I was the last. He never came back into the workshop and I never had any more problems with him. I now had a chance to become the shop welder, which meant I was top man in charge. I was getting great work reports, plus the physical training had come easily, as had the marching. I was now a good Borstal boy.

After 11 months, my first liberation date was due, and that was about the quickest time you could get out of Polmont. You either had to be exceptionally good or exceptionally clever. I don't think I was exceptionally good, but I was learning from the mistakes I had made in approved school. I kept on the right side of the screws, worked hard and had good pals. I had my liberation date for August, which meant I would still be 16 when I got out. I thought this was some sort of record, to get your Borstal at 16 and be out when you were still 16. I went out for my privilege visit, which you got just before you were liberated. I went home for a weekend and came back no problem. I was determined I was going to get out, especially as my father hadn't been keeping too well.

After I came back from my weekend, I got another one-day leave on a Saturday. You were allowed out for eight hours, and I was driven into Glasgow. I went to a pub and started drinking. While I was drinking, my pal Tam Nolan and three other members of the Tongs came in. They were telling Tam he had to be a witness for a guy who had been done, but Tam hadn't even seen the incident. I pointed that out: 'He wisnae there.' At that point one of the guys pulled a razor and threatened me. The other two were also tooled up. I had nothing in my hand and I was livid. The three of them then left the pub and I asked the bartender for two screwtaps (bottles of beer) and went after them. I flew straight at them on the street. They bolted and so did I, as somebody shouted 'coppers'.

I continued my drinking, had an alcoholic blackout and never got back to the Borstal. The police caught up with me a couple of weeks later, roughing it in Blairgowrie. I was back in Borstal with extra time added on and a month ahead of me in the digger, all because I had gone on an alcoholic bender.

At least the month in solitary confinement was good for me physically. I got circuit training three times a day and, of course, there was the no smoking rule. When I went down there at first, it took me 26 minutes to do the ordinary circuit. By the time my month was up, I was doing the heavy circuit, which was twice the weight, in 13 minutes. Some improvement. I couldn't wait to get out of the digger, and I was prepared to work hard to do so.

Before, I would have been out in August, but now I decided I was going to try to work hard and get out for the New Year. I had made an arse of my liberation date, going on the run because of booze. One day they were shouting out everyone's dates. All the names were called except mine. I was ready for kicking a table up in the air, but I managed to control myself. Then the governor said he had a special announcement. He had one liberation date for December and it was mine. I was over the moon. I had succeeded in getting out for the New Year. It was only a month away and I settled down, looking forward to getting back out there again. I had gate fever. I had grown quite a bit as well. I was almost 6 ft and had a good physique. I'd been involved in the boxing and was captain of the team.

I was at work in the welders' and I got word that I had to go up to the gate house. Big Stan, the welder screw, took me up and was laughing and joking. He never said what it was about, but when I got into the gate house I was told I had visitors. It was my three brothers-in-law. They had come to tell me my dad had died.

I didn't know how to take it. They did their best, but it came completely out of the blue. He had been ill for a while, but you never think the worst, especially when you're young. I thought I was going to get out and make amends for what I had done, show him I was OK. This was the beginning of December, and I had only two weeks to go. I was due to get out two days before Christmas. The governor allowed me out to the funeral without an escort, even though I had escaped before.

That day I felt ashamed as I stood there at my da's grave. All his brothers were there, my mum and the rest of my relatives. I felt as though everybody knew that I was out from the jail. The funeral passed off without incident and I was taken down to the Windsor Bar after it, where they had the meal and the drinks. I took a few that day, but it didn't seem to affect me. I went back to Polmont at the right time, where I was left alone with my thoughts. I knew my ma was devastated, especially with me in the jail.

The governor agreed to let me out as early as he could, and they released me a few days later. Some of the guys I had met in Polmont I would meet later on in life, as with boys from the Kibble and Longriggend. It was December 1966 and I had just turned 17. In the space of just a few years I had already had all of these places on my CV.

I still remember the questions they asked me when I was 15 in Barlinnie and filling out my admission form. Have you ever had a fine? Have you ever had a deferred sentence? Have you ever been in an approved school? Have you ever been in a Borstal? Have you ever done your Borstal recall? Have you ever done a young offender's sentence? Have you ever done a prison sentence? Have you ever been in a mental institution? The only place I had been in at that time was an approved school, and I thought how could anybody ever do all those things and end up in all those places. Little did I know that, by the time I had done my last prison sentence ten years down the line, I would be able to say 'yes' to every one of them.

Now I was getting out and looking forward to the New Year. I had missed it the year before as I was inside. I was a wee bit older, and hopefully a wee bit wiser. I had no intention of going back to the jail. I wanted to get a job, but once I got out onto the streets things were different and I got done twice in the first month. I was even nearly back in the jail before the New Year.

After the pubs had shut, I was walking down to Forbes Street with a couple of pals and we bumped into this guy, Nimmo, and he had this family, the McNallys, with him. I had got in a fight with one of the McNallys a few days after I got out of jail and this was them trying to 'dig me out'. Big Nimmo slinked up behind me and hit me over the head with a screwtap. Fortunately it had no effect, and I turned round and tore into him. The big cowardly bastard didn't want to know once it was one-on-one. The McNallys didn't make a move to jump in because the police quickly arrived on the scene. We were both dragged away to Tobago Street station, where I got battered in by the police in the cells, but I couldn't hear anything from Nimmo.

I was in court the next morning. I was taken through the custody bit and Nimmo came in through the side. He told me in the dock that his granny had bailed him out. I don't know if he was bailed out or let out – this guy was supposed to be a hard man at the time, but we were later to discover he was something else. I pled guilty, got a £20 fine and was out for the New Year. I swore that was me finished. But a couple of weeks later I was in the Gallowgate on a Friday night standing outside a pub. I was waiting for a girlfriend and there was a crowd of the boys on the other side of the street carrying on. When the police arrived, they came over to lift me as well. I hadn't done anything and told them I was only waiting for my girlfriend. When I asked a copper what he was charging me with, he said breach of the peace. It had only been a couple of weeks since I had last been done for breach of the peace, and there was no way I was going down to the station. I was waiting for my girlfriend. So I stuck the nut on the copper and got involved in a scrap with another. A couple of the boys from the other side of the road ran over and waded in. They were shouting at me to run, so I set off. As I was running, I heard a motor behind me. A taxi had mounted the pavement and was chasing me. It hit me and I landed on its roof. The cops caught up and ladled into me with their batons before dragging me down to the station. But when the sheriff saw the state of me in court, he let me off.

After that I did straighten up for a while: six months, anyway. I got a job and, although I was still going about with the gang, I was trying to be careful. It lasted till July and the Glasgow Fair weekend. I had gone to work on the Friday and had made arrangements to meet my pals that night. We were going to Port Seton for the weekend. We were paid early that Fair Friday and went for a drink. By three o'clock in the afternoon I'd been lifted for breach of the peace. Apparently I'd been bawling and shouting in the street. They held me in custody, and I was up in court the next day. My pals were all there waiting for me to get out and go with them to Port Seton, but I was told I wouldn't get bail. I pled guilty and was recalled to Borstal. I couldn't even finish my year's Borstal licence and that was me recalled. I didn't go back to Polmont to do the Borstal recall but to Barlinnie and the young offenders section in E hall. This was on the bottom floor and you didn't have a 'lib' date; you had to earn it.

There wasn't much activity in the young offenders unit as most of the lads in gangs were now in Polmont. The ones that weren't were out on the streets and just about to get big sentences.

When I finished this recall, there was one change in the gang warfare. The Untouchables had got a new transit van. These were the coppers named after the TV programme of the time about Eliott Ness and his war with Al Capone and the Chicago gangs. But these

Untouchables were ordinary coppers in Glasgow in 1967 who were allowed to wear civvie gear with instructions to break the gangs. I am sure every district in Glasgow at that time had their own Untouchables, but we thought they were unique to the Gallowgate. In fact, the order had gone out to clean up Glasgow, not just the Calton Tongs.

I turned 18 and my first young offenders sentence was just around the corner, after I got involved in an incident in Kirkcaldy. After a day trip I ended up charged with five assaults – me, one guy, against five Fifers. These guys had tried to be wide, and I was done for assaulting them and got three months. They got off, but I didn't. Of course, I was steaming at the time. If I had been sober, I probably wouldn't have been charged. But then again, if I'd been sober, I would not have got into a fight. I was already an alcoholic, but I hadn't realised it yet.

CHAPTER FOUR

The Demon Drink

Once again drink was playing havoc with my life.

Girlfriends were another problem. I had no trouble getting them, but I had difficulty holding on to them because of the drink. My first loss of a girlfriend happened before I went to jail. We'd gone to a party at Barrowfield and had left without any trouble. Just as we got onto the street, we heard a fight starting in the house. She was a decent lassie and urged me not to go back. She was a Bridgeton girl who was about to move to East Kilbride, and if I had gone with her that night who knows what would have happened. But I didn't. I left her there on the street and went back to join the gang in a fight that had nothing to do with me. That was the last I saw of her. Of course, I was under the influence of drink. She was the first I lost through the drink but not the last.

I couldn't see that drinking was ruining my life, because everybody else was at it. The first time I really wanted a drink I was only 13. I was at the Orient picture house in the Gallowgate on a really hot day. The Pathe News was on when it was interrupted by the famous advert: 'McEwan's is the best buy, the best buy, the best buy in beer'. I really fancied a drink and remembered my father had left half a screwtap on the sideboard at home. I left the cinema and raced home to get it, but when I got there it had gone. I think one of my sisters had taken it to get thruppence back on the bottle. I was really disappointed, but the idea of drinking had now taken hold.

The corner boys were having a drink by this time and they started giving us some. We also got our own supply going by buying or stealing cans of beer and half-bottles of wine such as VP, 365 or Rampart. You'd get three of them for a quid and we'd build a fire on the wasteland or drink in empty tenements. One night we got lifted when a group of us were caught staggering home drunk on the streets. This was an uncommon sight then for such young boys and I got a right doing from my old man. It didn't start off as drinking every week, but it got more regular, as I was making money from the milk and thieving. Our parties round a fire on the wasteland became regular events, and, with the booze, fights would break out amongst us.

It was only with hindsight that I would see I built up a tolerance quicker than most of the others. I would still drink way past my limit, though, and I started having blackouts. The first time I woke up in Larchgrove on remand, I could not even remember how I had got there. It was a Sunday morning and I had a hangover. The smell of the breakfast fry-up made me want to boak.

My blackouts were probably hereditary, as my father suffered from them as long as I can remember. He always worked and drank only on a Friday night, but when he did he went for it. He would come home a different man from the one who'd walked out the door that morning. The next day he would ask my mother, 'Why are ye no talking?'

And she'd say, 'You know fine well after last night.'

'Naw, I dinnae,' he'd plead.

I'd be standing there thinking, 'Who the fuck's he kidding after the carry-on last night?' I realised only later, though, that he did not have a clue. Every Friday night was a blackout and he would have a real drouth on Saturday, which would be spent coming down, and I would watch him suffer.

He was a grown man, but here was I, a young teenager, already having blackouts. Some of my pals would conk out or fall over, but

I would continue as if I was the life and soul of the party. The only thing was the next day I'd not have a clue what I had got up to.

I'd think I was the best singer, best dancer and the best bird-man when I was drunk. This would go on for over a decade. As I got older, I'd wake up next to a girl and think, 'Where the fuck did I meet her?' Then there was the embarrassment of trying to suss out her name or where I'd met her without letting on. My drinking was not non-stop, as I was to have so many custodial sentences, but whenever I got out I would drink with a vengeance. I remember criticising some old jakies in jail one time as they'd be let out in the morning and be back in that night, but that was to happen to me for the first time when I was only 23. I'd got out of Barlinnie, but before I had even made it home I was arrested for being drunk out of my mind.

Drinking was in my genes, although my mother and my sisters weren't drinkers. I had also had plenty of money for it by the time I was 14 coming on 15 from my milk run and stealing. I also did not have to give money to the house like my pals. There was only so much you could spend on sweeties, so it was booze and fags, and soon I gave up the sweets.

As the drinking got more serious, the crimes got worse, so the booze took me straight to prison. I missed every Christmas bar one from 15 to 21 because I was inside, and then I received my first full prison sentence.

I had been remanded when I was 20 and put in prison after being charged with doing a turn at this exclusive women's clothes shop in Duke Street. We got a lot of 'swag' and headed off with it to a girlfriend's house. It was two o'clock in the morning and the Gallowgate was deserted. I crossed first and then, as my pal Mark followed, the police caught him in their headlamps. We both bolted. I headed up the stair of a tenement, intending to go out through the loft, but it was padlocked. When I couldn't open it, I hard-necked it back down again, and when I got to the bottom of the stairs there was Mark rolling about on the ground with this copper. I pitched in, but reinforcements were now on the scene and we were captured and put on petition. I was refused bail, although Mark got out. I was 20 but turned 21 during the course of the petition. I went up to court and got 15 months, my first proper adult prison sentence.

CHAPTER FIVE

Gangland

Being in prison probably saved me from getting a heavier sentence, as the gang wars continued on the streets of Glasgow. Some of the boys were getting six-, eight- or ten-year stretches. There was one stage when there were 30 of the Tongs in the young offenders unit at Barlinnie and about 24 of them were doing long-term sentences, all waiting to go to Dumfries to be locked up for years. Around the mid-'60s many young men in the East End were in one gang or another. It was not just the Tongs. There were the Baltic Fleet, Dalmarnock Spur, Barrowfield Torch, Dennistoun Monks, Parkheid Wee Men, Shettleston Tigers, Parkheid Rebels, Nuneaton Street Nunny, the San Toi, Glasgow Cross Shamrock, Maryhill Fleet, and I could go on and on.

To give you some idea of how gangland was the big story around this time, shortly after I'd had that fight with Nimmo when I was 19, some of my boys had been done for chibbin' him. Big Nimmo had shopped them all to the police, even guys who had not been involved. Only one guy had done the slashing, but about 12 of the gang had been arrested and Nimmo had got his family and the McNallys to be witnesses. The slashing had made front-page headlines in all the local newspapers. Meanwhile, on the street, everyone knew big Nimmo had done the dirty.

The two oldest McNally brothers had arrived at a party I was at. I was staying with a lassie at the time and was on the run. The McNallys had started throwing their weight about, but they weren't going to try it on with me. They started on one of my pals, J.D., and I was watching all this with my pal Spooney. We waited until the other brothers drifted away and it was just the two oldest left, the ones who could really fight. Spooney and I waited till the right moment then attacked. J.D. was drunk and joined in, but the damage had already been done, and there was a lot of it. We slashed the two of them to bits. After they bolted, we had to do something because we knew they would shop us. The whole family would grass us. After all, they had been witnesses for big Nimmo.

J.D. was picked up later that night, and when the police got him down to London Road station he took the blame for it. J.D. later swore he hadn't made a statement, but he was cautioned and charged. I had managed to get away that night and so had Spooney. The police later caught up with us, but before they did, my pal John from Polmont, the leader of the Tongs, had put pressure on the McNallys not to dig us in. That meant that J.D. was the fall guy. The only other witness was the lassie that I was staying with at the time. Give her her due, she was sound and never incriminated me, Spooney or J.D. But that was one incident where I was lucky, as it would have made the front pages, what with the climate at the time. J.D. was found guilty only of the lesser charges but still got 21 months.

It was no wonder there was a public outcry, as this was a violent time. When the Tongs had nobody to fight, they'd fight with each other. It was a big gang, with a lot of hangers-on. Getting involved was like serving an apprenticeship, and there was no better way to prove yourself than by cutting it as a hard man. I had done that long ago.

I was still 21 when I finished my first proper prison sentence, and I wanted to settle down. I had already realised that I was losing out on life, but there were other people worse off than me in the gang who had paid a heavier price with the law. However, we all accepted the code, 'If you live by the sword, you die by the sword,' and we took it seriously. Anybody who was deemed an informer would be ostracised. They would also have their face taken off. That's just the way it was. The gang was proud of its reputation and, even though its members got the jail, they carried the gang on while they were inside. Anybody who didn't would be shunned when they came out. But if they did well when they were inside, they would be hailed as a hero when they got out.

Meantime I got a job and had a few new relationships. Prison was behind me, or so I thought, but the main attraction in life for me was still the pub and drinking. My ma's heart was roasted by all this. She had never been in trouble in her life, but by this stage she had been to visit me at Longriggend, Larchgrove, Polmont, Polmont remand, Barlinnie and the young offenders in Edinburgh. She always turned up, never letting me down. The only person letting anyone down was me, and it was through the booze. I had got this reputation as a hard man and hard drinker and I thought I had to live up to it. Deep down I wanted away from it, but because of the booze I couldn't do anything about it. That's the way it was to continue right up to a month before the Jubilee in June 1977, up to when I was 27 years of age – a cycle of booze, violence, crime and prison.

When I started drinking, I didn't know when to stop, and anything could happen. I tried cutting down, but whenever I drank – which wasn't every day – I was a binge drinker. Once I got drunk, I went through about ten personality changes: from the happy guy to the fighting guy, from the fighting guy to the singing guy, to the sad guy to the bad guy and back again. The blackouts were also getting worse. I was no longer getting what I used to from the drink. The hangovers were taking longer to go away and were like comedowns, lasting for days at a time. Relationship after relationship would die a death.

I was also getting careless through the drink, and one night I was jumped. It wasn't the first time I had been jumped but it was the first time I had really taken second prize. I had been involved in a lot of violence and could handle it. That's the way it was when you were part of a gang. If you were dishing it out and you got it back, you had to accept it and keep your mouth shut. But this time I ended up in hospital in a bad way.

The other major pitfall of running with the gangs was that the police would fit you up if they wanted you. Minor set-ups were part and parcel of the gang scene. If you didn't have an offensive weapon on you, the police would often plant one. If they saw you walking along the road, they would say you were shouting and bawling so they could lock you up for breach of the peace. For them the ends justified the means. We could live with that. A lot of the time we were bang at it and deserved what we got, but other times we weren't doing anything. The police had the attitude that if you flew with the crows, you got shot with them.

However, there was an incident back when I was 19 that should have taught me how bent the system was and how you could never win. The life I was leading was for losers, and I should have realised this when I got caught up on the fringes of one of the most notorious crimes in Scotland.

I'd got a job at Butlins in Ayr as a kitchen porter, to try to get away from the scene in Glasgow. At first it seemed to work, but there was nothing to spend your wages on but booze. It was the same old story, and one night, along with another boy from Hamilton, we got into a fight with the bouncers in the dance-hall. The next morning we were called up before camp security and both of us were told we were getting paid off, but first someone wanted to see us. It was the murder squad. I could not understand it. I had only been involved in a run-of-the-mill fight at the dancing. I'd been in hundreds of them. But it began to dawn on us that, a couple of days before, there had been a Tannoy announcement at the camp asking for any witnesses to come forward to a murder that had taken place nearby. An old couple, Mr and Mrs Ross, had been beaten, tied up and robbed. It was 20 hours before the couple were discovered, and the woman had died. The husband had nearly died as well. It was a particularly brutal attack, and the police were looking for the sadists who did it.

I knew I had nothing to do with it but they questioned us and we told them that, at the time of the murder, we had been working in the camp. They asked about our background and what I worked at. I said I was a KP: a kitchen porter.

One cop replied, 'Aye, a KT, as well. You're a known thief.'

They had done their homework on me. I was not going to deny my record, but I was certainly not a murderer.

They were satisfied we knew nothing about it, but, at the end of the interview, they said, 'You are well known in Glasgow and hear a lot of things. If so, give us a phone and let us know.'

This made me angry. Who the fuck did they think I was? I would never associate with cunts that would do that to an old man and woman. I went to Ayr station and got the train to Glasgow. Little did I know that, within 20 minutes, I would be drinking with one of the murderers.

On arriving in Glasgow, I caught a bus from Central station to the Gallowgate and headed straight to the Club Bar. As I walked in, someone I knew ordered me a drink and shouted me over to the company. There were seven or eight men drinking. I'd hardly raised my glass when a newsflash came on television. Someone had been arrested for the murder in Ayr. One of the guys in the company was paying particular attention, and as soon as the bulletin finished he dived over to make a phone call. I didn't know then that this was Ian Waddell, on the phone to his accomplice, William 'Tank' McGuinness. Waddell was checking to see if he'd been nabbed but found out he hadn't. The two guys who had done it had not been pulled, but the police had got someone else. Not only had they arrested Paddy Meehan, an innocent man, but they would make damn sure he was convicted. As Paddy Meehan was protesting his innocence, the guy he'd been with on another job that night – James Griffiths – was tracked down by the police three days later and it ended in mayhem.

They tried to arrest him, but Griffiths was not going to be taken alive. He opened up with a gun and shot 13 people in a mad spree across Glasgow. Griffiths had heard who the killers were, and after Meehan got nabbed he headed for the Gallowgate with two guns and a bandilero looking for Ian Waddell. Luckily for Waddell he never found him, but there were terrible consequences two days later when James Griffiths opened up with a gun trying to escape.

It was acceptable being set up when you were in the gangs, but somebody being convicted for a murder they did not commit, as in Paddy Meehan's case, left more than a bad taste in the East End. Meehan was a 'peterman', a safe-cracker, and was known not to be involved in violence. The murder of Mrs Ross in Ayr just didn't fit, and it was widely known who'd done it. But Paddy Meehan was to serve seven years in solitary confinement before the famous Glasgow lawyer Joe Beltrami managed to get him out. A lot of prominent people took up the case, including Ludovic Kennedy, who wrote a book about it called *Presumption of Innocence*. But it wasn't until Ian Waddell's accomplice, 'Tank' McGuinness, got murdered that Joe Beltrami was able to release evidence of a confession Tank had given him that got Paddy out on appeal.

The whole affair was tainted. Ian Waddell also ended up murdered, as did Gypsy Winning, the guy who killed Tank McGuinness. There was something sinister about the whole case, and it was a real insight into the Serious Crime Squad, or the Serious Fit-Up Squad, as it became known not just in the East End.

I should have realised then where this life was leading, but booze, or, rather, alcoholism, kept me embedded in it. I did not walk away – not yet, anyway. Indeed, I was a lucky man, as through drink I lost total control and who knows what could have happened to me.

One incident a couple of years after Paddy Meehan got set up should have been the final warning. I was drinking in the Gallowgate with a pal and his girlfriend and her cousin. He wasn't a gangster, but, during the course of the evening, someone came into the bar and told me a guy who had stabbed us two years ago was in the Crest. This character had caught me off guard and got me with a big blade. I never got the chance to get him back because a couple of days later he was arrested for a robbery and got done. But he was out now and in a pub nearby. I said to my pal I was going to get him, and his girlfriend's cousin chipped in that he had a gun in the boot of his motor. He was a member of a gun club and had never been in trouble before. It was a legitimate firearm, but I asked him for it and he handed the gun over, even though I was crazed with drink.

We drove round to the Crest and waited for the guy to come out. Then I spotted him at the door, facing back inside. As we started up the motor and began to drive past, another pal of mine just happened to be coming out at the same time and was standing a couple of yards away. With the car still in motion, I put the gun out the window and fired. I missed the guy I was trying to shoot but nearly shot my pal. The guy I was after had not seen me, as he still had his back to us, and we sped off. The pal who I'd nearly shot saw it was me but realised who my intended victim was. Meanwhile, the guy from the gun club dropped me off at a party as he headed back to Cumbernauld, where he lived. The next day I woke up at the party and was soon looking for another drink. You would think if you had tried to shoot someone the night before, you would remember, but I didn't. Not a thing. It was only when my pal Davie, the one I nearly shot, caught up with me that I realised what had happened. Davie told me all about it. Here he was, worried about me although I had nearly killed him. He knew what my true intentions were and, credit to him, he never said a word to anyone. Davie himself, by the way, was to end up in the Special Unit at Barlinnie for murder.

It should have been a wake-up call as to how bad my alcoholism was becoming. I had had blackouts before – lots of them – but never as serious as forgetting about trying to shoot someone. If I had not been drinking, I would not have tried it in the first place. Drink had led me into enough trouble already, but this could have been really serious. Meanwhile, the long prison sentences being doled out were splitting up the gang, and many, to their credit, were settling down. A hard core among us, though, bonded by the booze, kept at it.

A lot of the Gallowgate was being pulled down, so we shifted our drinking quarters up to Duke Street. Apart from hard-core drinking we were still involved in crime, mainly stealing. We were refusing to grow up, but it was not all blood and thunder, and we did have a lot of laughs. One night me, Spooney, wee Bertie, Bunty, Derek Green and big Dennis were going to a party in Springburn and were quietly, for once, walking up the road. That was until I started shouting: 'Bastard! Fuck-pig! Ya dirty bastard!'

'What's up wi' ye, Davie?' wee Bertie says.

'I've stood in dog shite.'

'What are ye shouting about? That's good luck.'

'No' if ye've got a fucking hole in yer shoe and it's come right through.'

Everyone was still pissing themselves by the time we got to the party. I was getting wired into the bevy when one of the boys, big Dennis, says, 'Here, Davie, pit these on.'

He handed me a box containing a brand-new pair of shoes.

Without thinking where he got them, I took off the shitey wans and put on the new shoes. Perfect fit. I threw mine out the window. Sober, I realised they'd been a birthday gift for the guy whose party we were at and Dennis had lifted them, but as I'd been drunk I never asked any questions.

We'd often get drunk and go on massive shoplifting sprees but never got caught. We'd sell the stuff then drink the profits. Most of the thieving was planned in the pub. One time we were going to do a wages heist, but, when we got inside the place and were about to pull our masks on, one of the boys said, 'Haud on. I've left my mask in the motor.' That crime was aborted at the last minute – just as well – but it showed how careless we could be. None of us could afford to be identified, as we would have gone down for seven years if caught.

Another time, we were planning a robbery in my house and I grabbed some jumpers to cut the sleeves to make masks. My ma came in with cups of tea for the five of us: me, Bunty, Bertie, Dennis and Derek.

'What on earth are you doing to ma jumper?'

'We're just making masks, Mrs Bryce,' big Dennis says.

'Well, if you're going to make masks, cut his jumpers up, no mine.'

But the good times, the ones I could remember – and they were fewer and fewer – were coming to an end. One night after a party Derek and Spooney got arrested on their way home. I'd met Derek in Borstal and then again at young offenders, and we'd become close friends. He had been done for a car theft, jumped bail and was hiding out in the East End with us. The pair of them broke into a garage on the way home and got caught on the roof. They were put on petition. Spooney got two years, and was later to join us at Calton Athletic. Because of Derek's outstanding car theft, he was remitted to the High Court. The garage merited no more than six months, but, with the car theft, he got four years. Two years into his sentence Derek hung himself at Barlinnie after a visit from his girlfriend. I couldn't believe it. Derek was a good boy from a good family. But his mother and father had both died while he was inside and he was missing his family. He'd just had twin sons, Derek and Andy, before he went away. He must have lost all hope at what a mess he'd made of his life and finished it. The tragedy increased when, a year later, Derek's girlfriend hung herself, leaving the twins to grow up never knowing their ma and da.

This, as much as anything, hit me hard. It was snide luck that Derek got four years, and while he was inside I had begun finally to get a grip and to change my life. I had given up the booze and was now nine months sober when the news came that Derek had taken his own life. It had a profound effect on me. He was a happy-go-lucky guy with a great personality, but I realised when I became sober that Derek had been an alcoholic, like myself. In Johnny 'Boy' Steel's book *The Bird That Never Flew* he recalls Derek was a pal of his dad's, and his death had a big impact on him. That was the sort of person Derek was. I was very fond of him, as was my mother, who was a good judge of character. She always liked Derek and thought he was a good boy. Derek, though, just like me, loved the drink, but the drink didn't love us.

CHAPTER SIX

Dead End

Derek was inside when I got my serious wake-up call. This was that time when I was jumped and, for the first time, took second prize. I had been out drinking up in the Parkhead area and had had a couple of problems with some guys there. I made it known that I was going to get them. I had been staying in the area with a girlfriend, but she couldn't take any more because of the booze and had moved out of our flat. I was on my own and it had turned into a dive – a drinking den for all sorts of unsavoury characters who were coming and going. One night these guys that I was looking for had heard where I was and had kept me under surveillance, waiting until I was drunk to bang into me on the street. I had a carry-out and rolled it up, ready to have a go at them, but one of them had a brick and threw it at me. It hit me bang on and knocked me out. When I went down, the rest of them waded in. A guy that I knew, wee Maxie, saw the incident and told me about it later, because I couldn't remember a thing.

When the police arrived and saw it was me, they were going to charge me, although I was the one who had been jumped and was in a bad way. They took me to Chester Street police station, but, once inside, they could see they had to get me to hospital. When my mother heard I was in the Royal Infirmary, she came to see me. I was lying on the bed and she walked straight past. I waved to her and she waved back, but she still didn't recognise me. I had to shout after her, 'Hey, Ma!'

She was shocked at the state of me and asked what had happened. I didn't know. I couldn't even remember who had done it. I'd had another blackout, and maybe another couple of kicks that night would have finished me off. I had a stab wound in the back, a scar on my nose and my jaw was broken in three places. The scars were easy, the stitches were in only a week, but this broken jaw was a problem. I was wired up and couldn't eat, and I had been warned not to drink because I could vomit. I never paid any attention and, during the course of the next eight weeks, all I did was consume booze. I was constantly hungry. I couldn't eat but I could drink. I never choked, but I don't think I was ever quite right about drink again after that. Drink would never taste the same after boozing for eight weeks steadily on an empty stomach.

Not long after I recovered, I was done by the police and was back in jail. I was appearing in court the next morning and when I got my charge sheet it read 'No Fixed Abode'. I was devastated. I had no fixed abode. I knew I had to do something. When your mother won't even say you stay with her, you know you've got problems. I was ashamed of it, but I'm glad it happened. This was part of the process that got me off the booze.

At one time I could have been a contender. I had always been able to handle myself on the street, but drink had robbed me even of that. I could not even look after myself. I couldn't see a way out. This was May 1977, the Jubilee year, and I remember the last night I had a drink. It was a Monday, and the next day the Queen was due in Glasgow. Hung over on the Tuesday I went along to Glasgow Cathedral with my brother-in-law and nephew, who was named after me: David Bryce Martin. We were waiting for the Queen to come along with the Household Cavalry. There were thousands of people and there was a holiday atmosphere, with families and people of all ages enjoying themselves, but I was feeling terrible.

I was in a bad physical condition. The drink wasn't working, and

I was hurting. I knew I had to do something, but I didn't know what. As the Queen passed by in her carriage, accompanied by the Household Cavalry, with the crowd cheering and waving, I turned to my brother-in-law and told him I was ill and was going to the doctor's.

I walked into the doctor's and he took one look: 'You will need to do something about it this time.' I was in such a state that he wanted to put me into a detox facility at a psychiatric hospital, and I was prepared to try it. There was an ambulance strike that day, which meant he couldn't send me straight there from the surgery as he wanted. He asked me if I could manage to get there myself and gave me a letter for Gartloch Hospital.

It dawned on me that I was going to a mental institution. I didn't know what lay ahead. When I was a boy and we moved up to Easterhouse, we stayed just over the loch from Gartloch. It had big, imposing towers, and we wouldn't go near it because we were told that was where the 'loonies' were and some of them might escape and do us harm. I was terrified of that place, but here I was years later going to Gartloch. I had ended up as one of the 'loonies'. I had been one for a long time, but only realised it now.

CHAPTER SEVEN

Junkie

Gartloch was to be my introduction to sobriety. After leaving the doctor's surgery that day, I went round to my mother's house and packed a few things. I told her where I was going. I expected her to be shocked, but she wasn't – far from it. She thought that I was in drastic need of help. I had not realised how other people must have seen me. I don't think anyone who knew me at the time, including my mother, could possibly have predicted or believed that I'd had my last drink.

One of my pals, big Dennis Curran, came to the bus station with me. I hadn't eaten for about three days, but that wasn't unusual. This was the sort of thing that booze was doing to me. I didn't know what to expect, but big Dennis told me his brother had been in Gartloch and when he came out he'd looked great. That was a bit of encouragement, and I duly arrived at the admission ward and presented the letter from my GP. They took my gear and I got changed and ready for bed. They put me in an observation room and told me I would spend the first night there. I don't remember too much about it, but three days later I was still in that wee observation room where I was told I would be for only one night. After the third day they released me into the general ward. Everything was fine until it was time for medication.

People would get up to have their breakfast, then the staff would come round with the medication and everybody would turn into zombies. This was my first experience of being controlled with drugs, and I didn't even realise it. I wasn't drinking but they had me on Mogadon. It was making it easier for me not to drink, but I didn't fancy these pills much. I was just taking them because that's what the psychiatrist prescribed for me. In the general ward I was allowed to listen to the radio or watch TV. I sat down next to this guy in his housecoat – you weren't allowed to wear your own clothes. I asked him what would happen now.

'You'll be all right,' he told me. 'You will probably go to the recovery ward, the convalescent ward, Ward 8. It's a good ward. I'm just waiting to go myself.'

I asked him how long he had been waiting.

'Three years.'

A wee character from the next bed butted in, showing me that some patients at least hadn't lost their sense of humour: 'Aye, three years that he can remember.'

He had been in a lot longer than that.

I was weighing everybody up and thinking that I wouldn't want to end up like them. But the reality was I had a wee bit of them in me already and I couldn't see it yet. After a week I was moved out of the convalescent ward, which meant I could wear my own clothes, have access to the grounds and could go down to the bookies if I wanted to put a bet on.

That summer of 1977 was beautiful. The first day I could I sat outside on a deckchair. I had only been out for about an hour when I needed to go into the toilet to wash my face because it felt hot. When I looked in the mirror, I was like a lobster. Nobody had told me that the new medication I was on had an adverse effect when you were in the sun. Anyone who was on it was supposed to wear strong protective cream. I had a shower and the pain was like being stabbed all over with pins. I asked the doctor to be taken off it as I wanted to go out in the sun. I wanted to be as healthy as possible and look good.

By this time I had started eating. When I first arrived, they asked me when was the last time I had had something to eat, and I told them it was three days ago. They told me they would bring something down. I told them not to bother because I couldn't eat it anyway; I was feeling terrible. They gave me a five-day course of massive vitamin injections – one a day on alternate sides of my bum. I turned my head away when they stuck in the needle, and about ten minutes later I was starving. Over the next five days I was like a Tasmanian devil, devouring everything they put in front of me.

Meanwhile in the ward I had found some information about Alcoholics Anonymous and had been reading it. Other people were going to AA meetings, but nobody had ever invited me and I wondered why. I thought it was maybe because I was considered a bad 'un or I couldn't take it a day at a time. I did find the AA's motto 'one day at a time' confusing. I thought this was for people who couldn't stay sober for more than a day and here I was four weeks without a drink. Looking back, it was purely down to chance that I was never invited, and also maybe luck, because if I had been invited, I would have got out earlier and my life would probably have been different.

In Gartloch I recognised that drink had caused most, if not all, of my problems and maybe, if I stopped, my life would be different. Things were already starting to improve. I had a reasonable suntan, I was looking well and had put on weight. After six weeks free of booze I was determined I was going to make it. However, I still wasn't prepared for the outside world and the harsh reality of what it would take to stay sober. Sobriety is different from stopping drinking. Up to then all I had done was put the cork in the bottle, and unfortunately that's the way it continued for the next five years.

I met my wife Jeanette shortly after leaving Gartloch, and she would stand by me all the way through my addictions. In an effort to make a proper go of things, I got a job right away. It was hard work, but things were looking good. At this point I still didn't know about change and didn't know if I could do it. All I knew was that I had stopped drinking, but around this time I was smoking a bit of dope. It wasn't the first time I had tried it. Back in the '60s I'd had a few blasts, but it had done nothing for me. I'd tried it again a few years later in the Crest one night, when all the mob were there. A couple of them were up from London and had brought some dope, and when I walked into the Crest they were smoking it. I asked them what were they smoking that shite for, and they said I should have a draw. I had several long ones, as I could take it. I smoked Capstan Full Strength at the time. I passed the joint back and told them, 'Fuck that shite.' The next minute I had a 'whitey', and I thought the pal I was with was being chibbed in the toilet. I panicked. I thought I was dying and this was just with a couple of blasts of a joint. When I pulled myself together, I said, 'Fuck that, it's not worth the hassle,' and carried on drinking. My poison was the booze. I wasn't interested in drugs.

During my time in prison I never saw a joint, but I remember taking a couple of 'black bombers' (amphetamines) when I was in Barlinnie doing my first sentence with my pal Mark. After about ten minutes things started to feel brighter. I was feeling the 'up' side. It felt great, but I couldn't sleep for three days. As I came down, I tried to light a fag, but the wick in my lighter turned into a snake and I threw it away. I had another experience with drugs in Barlinnie when I was sent down to trial at Airdrie Sheriff Court for a case of assault and robbery when I had been out on bail. We were in the dock and a guy passed me a parcel. I felt it and put it in my pocket. It was quite soft and I thought it was tobacco. He passed me another parcel with a letter tied round it and I heard it rattling and thought it might be matches. I was found not guilty and was taken down to the cells before being taken back to Barlinnie. I started reading the letter, but it wasn't addressed to me. It started off 'Dear William' and I thought who the fuck's William? Why had this guy given me a letter to 'William' when he knew my name was Davie? I opened the box and discovered it contained pills. Without knowing what they were, I popped a few. What the hell? I thought they would work instantly, but when they didn't I popped some more. Then I heard the prison van coming and I tried to pull myself together. I was later to discover that these pills were Mandrax and the letter was meant for William 'Tow' Elliot, a known gangster who was in for murder. Somebody was giving me the parcel to pass on to him, but I'd just thought the guy was giving me some sort of magic pills. On the journey back to

Barlinnie in the van I started gibbering. When we arrived, I nearly fell out of the van, but managed to pull myself together and climb into one of the dog boxes. When they opened it up, I was lying there singing. One of the dog men went away to tell the screws, and I got up and started wandering about the reception area, singing ma heid aff. I vaguely remember the screws arriving, jumping on top of us and shouting, 'Where the fuck did he get the booze?' They thought I was drunk.

There was nothing like the drug culture there is in prisons today, and any drugs that did come in would be downers and black bombers, and these were supposed to be passed on to Peterhead for the long-termers. The characters up there would take them for a couple of days, and there would be mayhem. Then it would settle down until the next batch arrived. But here I was gobbling down some pills with no idea of the effects. I was taken up to the observation cell in the hospital and was told later that I'd drifted into a coma. They stuck needles in the soles of my feet but I wasn't responding to pain. If it hadn't been for the prompt action of the prison staff in reception, who sent me to the hospital rather than putting me straight into a cell, I would probably have died. I got caught in reception and maybe this was the luck of the alcoholic – lucky to be alive. When I woke up in hospital, I couldn't remember how I had got there. I realised I should be in jail, yet I wasn't, and I could not recognise the place.

I thought I'd been certified during the night and I was in Carstairs, the secure mental hospital. But I wasn't. It was Glasgow Royal Infirmary. I tried to get out of the bed, took a couple of steps and fell on my face. The nurse and the screw came running. 'Just take some water,' the nurse said. 'You've got to drink as much as you can.' She handed me a tumbler. I tried to put it to my mouth but missed my face, pouring it all over myself. These drugs had had some effect. I'd nearly died with a drugs overdose and the funny thing was I wasn't even into drugs at that time.

It was only much later that I really got into them. I'd smoke a wee bit of dope at the weekends but was still making the odd mistake of going down to the pub, sitting with my old pals with a Coca-Cola. That wasn't good for my sobriety, but I didn't realise it at the time. I started to feel demented, and I was wondering why. I got a job with a construction company working on a tunnel, but lost it when the contract ended. The money had been good, even if the shifts had been long and hard, but foolishly I thought I deserved a break when it came to an end. It was now that I got into speed. Just a wee bit at first, but I liked the feeling, especially if I was going to the pub. I could handle being there better as I didn't feel so bad about everyone drinking except me. So the speed and a bit of dope made it a bit easier being off the booze. But the problem was you couldn't get much dope at this time. By the end of 1977 if you wanted it, you had to travel, and even then the quality wasn't too clever. One night I went to score from a pal and he told me there was hardly any about. There was only a wee bit on the table. I asked what were they going to do if there wasn't going to be any about for a while. He said they had found this other stuff called smack.

When I asked what it was, he told me my first lie. He said it was a mixture of cocaine and something else. I can honestly say at this point he never told me it was heroin. This guy who was now offering me smack wasn't a stranger. I knew and trusted him. I asked if it was addictive.

'Don't be stupid. We wouldn't be taking it if it was.'

That was the next lie. He started putting lines out and asked if I wanted one. I said yes and snorted it up. In a very short space of time it wasn't such a big deal having hardly any dope in the house. They had that wee bit that was on the table and we had a couple of joints, which seemed to bring on the strange and hard-to-describe effect of the other stuff. I was finding it tough being sober, suffering daily trials and tribulations. But when I took a line that night, all of a sudden it was easy, too easy, the big easy. And I remember thinking: Christ, if I had discovered this all those years ago, I wouldn't have been in all those jails.

This stuff didn't make me want to fight and hang out with the gangs. It made me feel contented and different. Maybe if they had told me it was heroin, I wouldn't have taken it. I don't know. But I took this stuff called smack, which was heroin. Smack was just a street name, taken from the sound of junkies hitting their arms trying to find a vein, but I was totally unaware of this at the time, and you never get an honest answer from junkies. It was not unusual that I didn't know much about heroin as, although I was streetwise, these were early days and heroin wasn't a problem in the late '70s.

Needless to say I was back to see my pusher a couple of days later. I'd felt a wee bit iffy and a bit seedy. I didn't know it at the time but I was coming down off the heroin. He told me, 'You'll be all right. Just take a couple of these,' and gave me Valium. I did start to feel OK, although I couldn't believe that pills would do the trick. I was never a pill man. I was a booze man.

After he gave me the pills, I said to him, 'See that stuff I had the other night. Do you think I could buy some?'

'Aye, but it's expensive.'

'I don't care. I'm just going to take a wee line to feel OK.'

So I gave him the money for a quarter of a gram and we did a line each. Then I went home, taking the rest with me, and never told Jeanette. But it wasn't too long before the quarter-gram was finished. I went back again and got more. Three weeks later I was 'in' big time and I didn't even know it. I also decided I was going to go back to being a thief. I kidded myself on I was doing it for Jeanette and the weans because I wasn't working, but it was to get money for heroin.

That's how cunning and insidious it is. You become addicted and you don't even know it. Within a very short space of time I was paying £100 a day for that powder to feel normal, to try to feel half the guy I used to be before I ever took it. During the next three years I was to drive all over the country to get heroin and earn the money for it. Of course, it was not legit. Sometimes I was stealing seven days a week to feed my habit.

At the beginning I was staying in a council house we'd got in Easterhouse and driving a banger, but I was justifying to myself I needed £700 a week to live on. This was the late '70s and early '80s. The reality is £100 would have been enough to live on. In the East End the only way to get that kind of money if you were not working was crime. However, I had started to become ashamed of what was happening to me. I was using different dealers as I didn't want to let the first person know how much I was spending. I was also becoming scunnered with the people and the lifestyle. At least when I was involved with the Tongs there was honour amongst thieves, but there was none among junkies. I didn't know that when I started, and I never realised I was going to end up as one of them. After all, I'd been told you only became addicted if you injected. I never put a needle near me. I didn't like them up at Gartloch, even though in that case they'd done me some good. One thing I am glad of, at least, was that I was never one of those junkies who robbed their families. Somehow I didn't sink that low, probably because I was already a villain and knew how to earn money.

I'd already crawled through a personal gutter with the booze that almost destroyed my family; how had I got myself into this situation again? I had to recognise that my own personality played its part. As my wife Jeanette says, I am an extreme person. When I drank, I took it to extremes. When I gambled, that too was to extremes. When I joined the gangs, I took fighting to extremes. Now that I'd moved on to drugs, I was a full-blown heroin addict. Jeanette says the only thing I do in moderation is sex.

This time, though, I was determined I wasn't going to let it destroy my family. I would turn this aspect of my personality into something positive and take my recovery to extremes. I wanted off it and was sitting in a pal's house one night. We were all still snorting, and one of them asked, 'Do you think you'll start injecting?'

'There's no danger of me injecting,' I said, turning to my pal Willie Burns, who had also got into heroin. The two of us had started on smack at the same time, but not with each other. When Willie was asked, he said he wouldn't like to think so, but he couldn't say it with the same conviction as me, but he believed me when I was saying it.

The other guy then said, 'But there'll come the day when you'll no get anything out of the heroin by snorting it.'

'What do you mean "come the day"? I've no had anything out of it for the last 18 months. I'm taking it to try and feel normal. I'm taking it to feel half the guy I used to be. I hate giving these informing bastards o' dealers my money. I'm ashamed of what I've become, and I'll tell you something: I would rather lift a drink before I stuck a needle in my arm.' I swore there and then to him and Willie: 'I'll never inject or take a drink.'

I did not stop there and then on the smack, but I was determined I was going to get out.

CHAPTER EIGHT

Cold Turkey

The first time I got off it I had my withdrawals at home. It was straightforward cold turkey. The withdrawals only lasted for five days, but they were hellish. I used the same reasoning that had seen me go nearly five years without a drink and said to myself if I don't take the first line of heroin, there is no way I can take a second one. For seven months I stayed completely off the smack, and, slowly but surely, I started getting better. Terribly, though, I fell back into it after I got in a fight one night and broke my toe when I kicked a guy. I went to the doctor's. My own doctor wasn't there, so his stand-in gave me painkillers with morphine. I threw them away. My brain was screaming out for heroin. I had the perfect excuse as I had a broken toe. I was just going to have one bag for the pain and that would be it. But that one bag took me back in, and five months later I was worse than I had ever been, and I was faced with having to go through those awful withdrawals all over again. I lost out on another Christmas, as I was under the influence of heroin. If I wasn't full of it, I was strung out trying to come off it.

I knew I had to do something, and my wife saw an advert in the papers: 'Drugs: Looking for Help?' She phoned up only to discover they were gathering statistics. My wife told them straight, 'Look, we are looking for help.' Eventually we got given a number for the St Enoch's Society in the Gorbals. A group of volunteers over there had got together and set up a project backed by Jimmy Wray, the local MP. The place was in a dilapidated state, and an old guy invited me in and asked me to sit down. I did so and told him I was sick and tired of it. I had money in my pocket for smack but I didn't want to use. He told me that he understood: he had two sons in the back who were both addicted to heroin. He looked at me and thought there was something else wrong with us apart from my heroin addiction. My physical condition was that bad he made an appointment for me to go to the Southern General the next day.

I went along with Jeanette, and in the waiting-room I recognised a guy I knew from jail. He came over and told me he didn't think he was going to get his 'script' (prescription), but he had a sawn-off shotgun at home. If I wanted, he could go and get it and we could do a chemist. I told him to get to fuck. I was serious about going clean, but everybody else was there to fuck about to get a prescription for more drugs. I got called in and the doctor put me on a methadone prescription of 40 mg. I told him how much I had been using and he offered me more. I didn't want more. I wanted to come off. I wanted out of the scene. I was sick and tired of the whole scummy business. I'd left booze behind and now I was determined I wasn't going to let smack kill me. What was the point of being sober and not drinking if heroin was doing this to me? Still I got my methadone prescription and was told to come back in four weeks.

I took the methadone and never cheated or went out stealing. After four weeks I went back and saw another guy I thought was a doctor. I was talking to him about the previous visit four weeks before and told him I hadn't been cheating.

'You are still in a bad physical condition,' he said. 'I can get it put up.'

'I don't want it put up. I want to come off it.'

'OK, I'll recommend for you to come off it in two weeks, but I'm not a doctor. I'm the same as yourself, only I'm off it.'

I'd never met anybody who'd done that before. He'd been off a couple of years. I'd thought he was a doctor because of his English accent, but he was just working at the project as a volunteer. I never saw him again after that day in 1982, but it was him who gave me hope that it could be done. If things had worked out for this English guy, they could maybe work out for me.

I finished my methadone prescription and thought, 'Christ, that was easy; they should give everybody methadone and that would get them off it.' That was day one. The second day I was more convinced than ever they should give it to everybody, and I started telling people about the project. On the third day the withdrawals started from the methadone, and I mean withdrawals. Nobody had told me you have to withdraw from methadone. I'd only been on a six-week programme, with gradually reduced doses each time, but that had been enough to get me hooked. I'd just come off a £20,000 heroin habit from the previous year. That was a lot of money then, probably equivalent to about £60,000 today. I had been a man possessed, robbing all over Scotland to get it. And here I was now withdrawing from the methadone, and this time it was worse. That's another thing no one ever tells you. Withdrawals don't get better.

I was having a horrendous time, vomiting liquid poison that kept coming up for hours. I thought it would never end. At the height of it I didn't even have the strength to crawl to the toilet but lay there in my own vomit on the floor, retching and spewing, my body in spasms. It lasted five days. Vomiting for five minutes takes a lot out of you. Try doing it for five days. I still felt terrible and now weighed about 8 st. I was mentally undone, but I'd got through my withdrawals. I knew this was just the start.

I had to change and make it up to the people that I'd hurt. At least I'd never injected drugs and had never robbed from my family. I suppose I wasn't a total scumbag. But I had neglected them, as I was too busy out stealing for drugs. Now I had done cold turkey for a second time and got through it, and two weeks later I was looking in the mirror and realised I was finally prepared to change. I decided to go to Alcoholics Anonymous.

CHAPTER NINE

Why Me, Lord?

My first AA meeting helped me begin to confront my life. I looked back on the person I had become and how I could change. A key part was to get away from the users and the drinkers, although I must say there were a lot of good guys among my old pals from the Tongs. Many of them went on to do good things and I've still got a lot of dear friends from those days. However, I was prepared to ditch the scumbags I had hung around with in the drug scene. I was determined to start again.

When I went to my first meeting, I was worried about who would say what to me. The first person I met was J.D., one of my old drinking partners. He had stopped drinking nearly five years after me, yet, in a few short months, he looked smashing. All the people there had something I wanted: contentment. AA was to give me skills that I would need for the rest of my life. The people there, and I can't thank them enough, helped me in a way no other people could. They identified with us and I could empathise with them. I attended as many meetings as possible in 90 days. This was before dedicated drug-treatment places had really got going. In fact there were very few facilities around. But I already knew about AA. Drink had led me to drugs, and both were addictions. If I could properly see off the booze at AA, it would help me with my drug problems. Staying sober was the same as staying clean, and I was to use the basic tools that AA gave me as the basis of our programme at Calton Athletic.

During the first few months I did one thing that I found very hard to do. I admitted that I had been – and therefore always would be – an alcoholic. Once I said it, I started to feel a wee bit better. I liked the meetings and the idea of challenge and change. The physical element was a good start. I got my first joggy. For the uninitiated, that's a tracksuit. I started going down to Glasgow Green at night and running. I did it at night because I didn't want anybody to see us. It's stupid, I know. I was doing something positive about myself and I didn't want anybody to see me, yet in my bad days I didn't give a fuck who saw me. I was also a wee bit ashamed when I went to the first meetings. I'd look around in the street to see if anybody was watching. I was still struggling to throw away this image that I had of myself as a Glasgow hard man. With time it would go and I didn't give a damn who saw me. I needed help. I wasn't hard. I wasn't strong. I was weak. But I could change and become a really strong, decent person, somebody my family would not be ashamed of, and things did start to come together. This time I did change.

The first year in recovery flew by. I'd stopped drinking for six years, but when they presented me with an anniversary cake at an AA meeting it had only one candle on it. There's usually a candle for every year that you're sober. I pointed that out to the guy with the cake. I was six years sober. He said, 'No, Davie, you're six years without a drink. You've only been sober for a year. Your sobriety started the minute you walked in the door of AA. Before that you'd just been off the bottle.'

He was spot on, and that cake with one candle made me the happiest man walking on two feet. If you had given me a million pounds instead, it wouldn't have made me feel any better. I hurried down the road, eager to show the cake to my wife and weans. This was the first thing I'd ever really achieved in my life that I could be proud of. The satisfaction was tremendous. Looking back, that gave me the courage to stand up and be counted.

I was sure I had kicked drugs for good but felt I needed to achieve more than just my own recovery. I needed to make amends. Many things were probably coming together inside me that gelled one night. I am not a sentimental guy, nor prone to flights of fancy, but it was a spiritual experience. Call it an epiphany. I'd always liked country and western and was a big fan of Kris Kristofferson, Johnny Cash and Willie Nelson, all guys who had walked on the wild side with alcohol and drugs. This night there was a Kris Kristofferson film on TV, but I fell asleep. I was still not in the best physical condition and it was a cold, bleak winter's night.

I woke up when Jeanette was going to bed, and I was cursing I'd missed the film, but she told me she had taped it. With the family in bed I wrapped a blanket round myself and put it on. Something happened that night that was special. When Kristofferson was singing 'Why Me?', the words began to resonate. He was asking the Lord if there was a way he could repay all he'd taken from him, perhaps by showing someone else what he'd been through.

I had never been particularly religious, but I felt a spiritual awakening. I was still down and feeling low, but the room seemed to light up. Deep down something inside me must have been moving in this direction, but hearing Kristofferson's lyrics clarified for me what I had to do. I knew I had to go out there and show people I was not using. I had to stand up and be counted. I had to tell others they could change and help them.

After watching the film, I got up and looked out of the window across the dark, silent streets of the East End, which were being devastated by heroin. I decided I was going to start a branch of Narcotics Anonymous in my community. This was 1983, and, with the help of a few old friends from AA, we would soon have Calton Narcotics Anonymous (CNA) up and running.

I believe I was to be directed along the way by a greater power than myself. Over the last 20-odd years too many things have happened and there have been too many coincidences not to believe in fate. I was not a clever enough guy to achieve what we would without help and guidance.

I had heard about Narcotics Anonymous – a 12-step programme that was very successful in America – through AA and wrote to them. They sent me their literature, and five of us from AA started

CNA, with the first meeting held in Calton Youth Club. The group comprised Kate, J.D., John the Plumber, Andy McKinlay and myself. AA gave me the tools to go on and do what I did, and showed me that my dual problem of alcohol and drugs was not, as I'd previously thought, unique. I realised that I was able to identify with others, as the four people who joined me in CNA had similar problems to mine.

CHAPTER TEN

Chasing the Dragon

When we started CNA in 1983, an increasingly high number of young people were using drugs and the East End was awash with heroin. In the '50s there had been only about 50 registered drug-addicts in Glasgow who were prescribed pharmaceutical heroin from their GPs. They were mainly amputees from the War or social drop-outs. When the hippy movement came along in the '60s, drug use began to seep into all sorts of different social groups across Britain, encompassing drop-outs, students and anyone who considered themselves bohemian. It was mainly cannabis and pills such as French blues, speed, black bombers, purple hearts and some LSD. Timothy Leary was the guru, with his mantra 'Turn on, tune in, drop out'. This did not happen on a large scale in Glasgow, though, as the hippy movement never really took hold here. There were perhaps only several hundred hippies indulging at the time. Young Glaswegians were tuned in to alcohol and gang violence, much the same as their fathers. The gangs had taken off at the same time as the hippies, with the Tongs, Toi and the Cumbie, etc. attracting nationwide fame. The crooner Frankie Vaughan was so shocked by the level of violence when he came to Glasgow that he held meetings with the gang leaders and a weapons amnesty was set up.

It was only in the late '70s – when heroin began to come in – that a noticeable proportion of Glaswegians rejected alcohol as their no. 1 drug. By the early '80s there had been a massive explosion of the drug on Glasgow's streets. The heroin epidemic was strange for several reasons. First, it did not involve students or musicians and took off in the schemes and the inner city. There are many theories that this was due to social deprivation, unemployment and Thatcherism. However, I disagree. It coincided with a time in the '70s when many Glaswegians had been turned on to cannabis and had begun to score a bit of dope each week. The dope scene had been taken over by the gangsters. They realised there were big bucks in it and the hippies had been edged out. By this time the bevy for a proportion of punters was no longer necessarily their first choice. Then all of a sudden the supply of cannabis dried up, and the dealers who had previously sold cannabis started pushing heroin, only they called it smack. Most started snorting it or chasing the dragon: smoking it. I did both. But your tolerance builds up. A wee line of heroin gets you stoned, and soon it's a bigger line, then a quarter-gram, and before you know it you need a half-gram a day. That's a lot of money, so it is cheaper if you inject. It's sound economics, but soon you develop a tolerance to injecting. I still thank God that I never tried injecting it.

Before the authorities knew what had hit them, there were thousands, rather than hundreds, of young Glasgow boys and girls addicted to heroin. The authorities were hopelessly at a loss as to how to deal with it, as they had no previous experience. By the early '80s there were 10,000 addicts injecting in Glasgow. This is the situation we faced when setting up CNA, but what lay ahead was worse. After 1985 the supply of heroin would dry up, but there were still 10,000 addicts injecting, and Glaswegians are masters at improvisation. The first official response was to prescribe methadone to reduce the numbers on heroin, and it was only consultant psychiatrists who could issue a script. They were inundated, but as they were not seeing people coming off, they stopped it.

Addicts were to start using Temazepam, which was prescribed by GPs to cure addiction. Temazepam was taken orally, but junkies would crush it, liquidise it and inject it. It was horrendous, as a lot of people lost limbs through shared needles and septicaemia, and then there were those who lost their lives. Heroin would return to the market but was not as high quality. Drug-addicts would mix it with Temazepam and other sedatives and painkillers. These were not supposed to be injected, but people would do anything to relieve their cravings.

Glaswegians wanted maximum value from their drugs, and that led to injection. When someone told a junkie it was cheaper to inject, it was music to his or her ears. When you snort, you have to wait 10–15 minutes for it to hit you. It's the same chasing the dragon, waiting for the stone to come on. If you inject, it's instant karma. But the day you stick a needle in your arm, you are opening yourself up to infection.

The problem that lay ahead for CNA was in standing up to the government and telling them that 'harm reduction' – their policy of administering methadone and clean hypodermic syringes – was good in theory but not in practice. There is no safe way to inject. That is a fact of life. Meantime, infection was running amok. Edinburgh had been the HIV capital of Europe but Glasgow would take over. The official policy was deluded. You can't stop spreading infection by stabilising addicts. Ask any former junkie. Nobody wakes up on a beautiful summer's day and says, 'I think I'll start injecting,' and trots off down to the needle exchange to get nice clean needles.

Young people start injecting in company. Fellow junkies tell you that it's cheaper and there's an instant hit. What they tend not to tell you is you could also become infected with your first shot. Between the late '70s and 1997, when the New Labour government came in, people were injecting a whole cocktail of drugs, but at least there had been a steady increase in people coming off them and a decrease in their availability. The cost and stiffer prison sentences also played their part. Heroin was becoming harder to get, and not many doctors were into prescribing methadone back then. Not everyone wanted to go down the prescribed route, anyway, so they needed a different way out of heroin. That's why I started Calton Athletic. I recognised that people were crying out for a cure for their heroin addictions, and we would prove we could get people off. As I say, this was all prior to 1997, and the official policies that the Labour government would bring in.

CHAPTER ELEVEN

Kick-Off

As the first wave of heroin hit Glasgow, CNA was set up, and we started attracting young people from the area. They came under a lot of pressure from drug-dealers, who started throwing stones and bricks through the window, trying to disrupt our meetings. This only made me more determined to carry on. I'd already had more than a few bricks thrown at me in my time. Unfortunately a lot of the youngsters were too intimidated, and CNA was only to last a year, but it gave me the chance to come into contact with young people. I also heard about a new rehabilitation centre that had opened up down the Clyde at Cardross run by a guy called Willie Blaney. He told me if young people came looking for help I could take them to Cardross. Not long after this I took the first youngster down there to have a look at the place.

The idea was that one recovering drug-addict would help another. Somebody who had been in for three months was helping somebody who had been in for two months. Somebody who had been in for two months was helping somebody who had been in for a month. Somebody who had been in for a month was helping somebody who was just in the door. The differences between somebody just in the door and somebody who's been a month off drugs can make them seem a lifetime apart. When you come off drugs, you just can't see past that first day. The first week seems like a month away, while a month seems like an eternity. Cardross was good. It gave that young person a chance to get out of the community and away from the hostility of people who didn't want him off drugs. It was an environment that was drug-free. Willie Blaney had an aura about him and began to show a bit of interest in me. Whenever we visited with the boy, Willie would always ask, 'What are you on to?'

One day I told him, 'I'm toying with the idea of starting a fitba' team.'

'What kind of fitba' team?'

'One made up wi' recovering drug-addicts.'

He laughed. 'That'll never work, Davie.'

But I told Willie I was going to give it a go.

'OK, if you gie it a go, I'll gie ye the first set of strips.'

And that's what he did. Willie gave us our first set of strips. The team was made up of boys that I'd been involved with during the previous year, boys that had come to the CNA meeting and were intimidated but fancied the idea of a game of football. I'd been watching the CNA boys having a kickabout and noticed quite a few of them had a bit of talent. They also looked happy and relaxed, more so than I'd ever seen them. It made them feel good and there was a bit of camaraderie. I thought that this was an obvious way to get them physically back in shape and to help them bond as a group. A team would also mean meeting up every week, rather than once a month.

Most Glasgow boys can kick a ball, to one degree or another, and a big new sports complex with beautiful football pitches, Crown Point, had just been opened up in the Gallowgate. The time was ripe for starting up a football team, one that was going to be different from any other football team, one made up of people recovering from drugs. Nobody gave us a hope in hell of surviving, let alone winning anything, but that team went on to prove people wrong.

Our first ever game was a friendly against a team fielded by Cardross rehabilitation centre. They were coached by big John Hughes, the former Celtic player who was working there at the time.

The centre had about 60 boys, and they'd all been there for a while. Our boys from the Calton had never been in rehab. All they'd had were their CNA meetings. And when the CNA meetings finished, all they had was me. But they were doing well in recovery, and I had 13 to choose from. There was a lot of natural talent here. Tam McLafferty, for example, was one of our players who, if he'd behaved himself, could have been a pro. We played Cardross at Crown Point in Willie's strips and beat them 5–3. Some of these Cardross boys, such as Stevie Lynch and Hugh O'Neill, ended up joining us when we entered a league. Hugh O'Neill was probably our best ever player.

That was the day Calton Athletic was born. We were looking for a name for the team and didn't want to call it Narcotics Anonymous. That would bring NA into controversy, and the traditions of both AA and NA are about avoiding controversy. We came up with Calton Athletic. Why not? Most of my drug use had been in the Calton district of Glasgow, and I lived there, so I thought, well, Calton Athletic, let's go for it. Most folk laughed when they heard about us and said, 'See the junkie team? They'll probably needle ye.'

We went on to play 18 friendlies before our game with Dennistoun Thistle, after which Willie Barnett, their manager, suggested we join the Glasgow Welfare League. Dennistoun had been on the go for ten years and were a good team. They'd got to the semi-final of the Scottish Cup and had won the Welfare League, and now we'd drawn 3–3 with them. Willie had a word of advice. Success would be holding things together for a year, one season. Anything else would be a bonus. Well, we're still on the go in 2005, and that football team that nobody gave a hope in hell was to go on and win the Scottish Cup twice, in 1992 and 2001. To me that first time was the equivalent of Berwick Rangers winning the European Cup.

While I managed the team to begin with, I recognised my shortcomings. Training, physical fitness and discipline were not a problem and neither was man management. There's no great secret to that, and it's something that came naturally to me. I could establish a common bond and ensure the players stood by each other. But so much of my time was being taken up with more and more people approaching us and I had to deal with families, doctors and statutory agencies, like the Health Board, Social Work and the police. So I got Jimmy Faulds, a Dalmarnock guy who was a bit of a lad and came from a well-known family, to coach the team. Jimmy had a bit of experience with football and added the skills equation to the team. Unfortunately Jimmy's recovery fell away, so I then approached John Jarvis, who had a bit of background in football and knew Tommy Burns. He was 38 at the time, but he still played and was an old heid for the team. Another bonus was that John had never drunk in his life, so he would be a good example. I would remain the overall manager, but John took the training and coaching of the team and worked on tactics and ball skills. John was still with us more than five years later when we won the Scottish Cup in 1992.

Following Willie Barnett's advice, we joined the Glasgow Welfare League and saw our name alongside famous Glasgow institutions like Govan Shipbuilders, John Brown, Rolls-Royce and Tennent's Breweries, who all had teams. It was a good test to see if Calton Athletic could hold their own with them. We did and we too became a Glasgow institution. In an early game Tennent's beat us 10–4, but in the dressing-room I told the boys we were the only team that had managed to take four off them. Calton Athletic was all about being positive. We had no other choice.

Joining the league set standards for us to aim at. This gave our players an extra incentive to stay clean and get fit, and I would watch John Jarvis take the training to see how their recoveries were progressing.

When we started the Under-18s in the mid-'90s, we would take our coaching to a higher level. That's when I got in Gerry Collins, a seasoned and respected pro who was at Partick Thistle and who would go on to manage them. Gerry had grown up in Soho Street and I'd known him since he was a boy. Gerry would come down and take sessions, but his professional commitments were increasing as assistant manager at Partick, so he put Davie Farrell onto us. Davie was a Thistle player and East End boy. He did a marvellous job and we won the Under-18 league, but when Davie was signed by Hibs he could not continue.

When Gerry left, I got in contact with Bobby 'Wee Rab' McCully. Wee Rab had been at school with me and went on to be a pro with

East Stirling when Alex Ferguson was manager. He also played for Falkirk, Ayr United and St Mirren. He had been the smallest player in Scottish football at the time, and the *Sunday Post* once did a feature on him with the 'Girvan Lighthouse' Peter McCloy, the Rangers goalkeeper who was the tallest player in Scotland.

Bobby took the Under-18s to the Scottish Cup final and two semis. His technical know-how was tremendous, and he did such a good job that the senior team got jealous, so Bobby ended up taking both teams. He'd coach them on a Tuesday night, and on a Thursday another local guy, wee Ricie, a former sergeant and Army PTI (physical training instructor) would put them through their paces. Ricie drove them hard, but the boys learned to love it. They were like paratroopers, they were so fit. What with Bobby's technique and Ricie's fitness, 1996–98 would be our most successful period. It coincided with the club being well resourced and by then running a day programme, schools projects and a women's service, which included marathon running, aerobics and general fitness training separate from the men's.

When we went to France in 1998 to watch the World Cup, people thought the boys were legionnaires, they were so fit. We would also go on to sponsor the West of Scotland Under-21 league, and under us it expanded from two to four divisions. There was to be almost a decade between our two triumphs in the Scottish Welfare Cup, which proved we were no flash in the pan. Calton Athletic had indeed become an institution. For our first Cup glory in 1992 we beat Yarrow Shipbuilders 5–1 at Camelon Juniors, near Falkirk, and Davie Main lifted the trophy. Davie would become a legend in amateur football in the west of Scotland. He'd been on Celtic's books and played for Scotland Under-16s in Italy. When we won it again in 2001, Davie was still captain and scored the winner in extra-time. In some ways this was a bigger achievement as we had lost so many resources and our funding, as well as wee Bobby and Ricie. Despite setbacks, though, we proved we could still attract and retain individuals, and Eddie Roxburgh, who had come through our ranks, would become player–coach.

From the outset Calton Athletic was always more than a football team. If somebody did not have the talent to play for the team, they would still do the training. It was all about camaraderie, discipline, getting fit and showing commitment. Some boys never played, but, like all the girls and women who were with us, they were encouraged to do half-marathons and aerobics. Physical fitness was the key to getting the body back into shape after all that drug abuse. Regaining mental health would take longer.

CHAPTER TWELVE

Cardross

When the team first started back in 1985, I began working with Willie Blaney at Cardross. He'd asked if I fancied coming to work in a voluntary capacity. I agreed because I was impressed with Willie. If it had been somebody else, I may have refused.

Cardross didn't have a catchment area and took in some lassies, but it was mainly boys, mostly under 25. I discovered that a lot of people that got off came back, and the main reason was booze. Cardross was drug- and alcohol-free, but when the recovering addicts went back to their own communities, nothing had changed. They would go back to their old lifestyle and pals. They wouldn't use at first, but they'd maybe take a drink, and one thing would lead to another. I realised that people needed something after they left.

I spent two years at Cardross, and the wisdom of Willie Blaney taught me a lot. It was from him that I heard the word Aids for the first time. I had used drugs for five years, but had never come across this disease, and I didn't know anybody who had died of taking drugs, either. When Aids first started to hit the news, Willie Blaney wanted to find out as much about it as possible, as the main groups threatened by it were the homosexual community and intravenous drug-users. The homosexual community was well served by the Terence Higgins Trust. These people had started to implement changes in their lives, but how could drug-addicts do likewise? When you're addicted, you've lost control, and you can't regain it until you've stopped using. We knew drug-users were a high-risk group, but this was a new phenomenon. I didn't know at the time what an impact it would have over the next 15 years, and that many youngsters I knew would die from it.

Willie Blaney proved to be a pioneer. He travelled widely to find out as much as he could and started to get drug-addicts in who were infected. I had never met one before. I had seen people with hepatitis B, as that was quite common and it was easy to identify them because anyone with it turned bright yellow. But Aids was different, as it didn't have immediate tell-tale signs in the first stages.

The first boys Cardross took in who were infected came from Edinburgh. They were intravenous drug-users, not homosexual and would go out of their way to make sure you knew: 'Mind, Davie, I got it using, no the other way.' Their attitude was it was better to be an infected drug-addict than a non-infected homosexual. Just shows you the mentality that prevails in the drug scene. But I could empathise with it as that had been my way of thinking at one time. You can't change your attitude until you open your mind, and I had done that. Every bit of information we were getting about Aids was doom and gloom. People were frightened, and ignorance makes you even more so. I even remember thinking in the early days I could catch it from any contact with an infected person, so I used to stay clear of certain people. But with Willie's help and encouragement, and the information he gave us, I realised I was safe. At least I knew what not to do. I'd never injected and I knew I was lucky. Meanwhile it was bleak times, as the infected boys didn't seem to have any hope.

After about a year we started getting our first young HIV-positive Glaswegians. The Edinburgh boys were saying that Aids had started in their city through one American drug-addict who was HIV positive and had been sharing drugs and needles. Only 18 months later it had spread across Scotland. Glasgow is only 50 miles away from Edinburgh, and Willie was very worried. A lot of people at that time thought he was going over the top. Some said he had done his nut in over it, but he hadn't. Willie was ahead of his time. He foresaw what was happening. He also realised that the only way to stop it was to get people to change their lifestyles and their attitudes, but he was fighting a losing battle. He didn't have much in the way of resources, and the Health Board was not interested and the Social Work department was only interested in the people in Cardross who were already infected. Willie was always opposed to the Health Board and Social Work taking over. He had to do things his way. At the time I thought he was being awkward, but I would come to realise he was right all along. I'd ask him what he had against Social Work.

'Davie, as soon as you take anything aff them, they want to control the place, and if they control the place, the place widnae work.'

With the benefit of hindsight I'd realise how true Willie's words were. I knew now it was more important than ever that I had to get the message out there to people in the East End about the threat from drugs, HIV and Aids. Cardross was doing a job as a residential unit, but most of the people using were out in the schemes. Somehow we had to get a service to them. Cardross worked for some, but it wouldn't have been any good for someone like myself. Residents had to stay there nine months, and I couldn't have contemplated that when I was coming off the drugs. I had a wife and a young family. Many other married people or single parents found themselves in this position when they came off drugs. They couldn't go away and leave their kids.

Calton Athletic was working as a football team in which one recovering drug-addict supported another, but we could do so much more, and we needed facilities in the community. When I left Cardross, I went to Denmark Street, a Greater Glasgow Health Board community-based project. Willie Blaney was one of my referees, but he did warn me, 'You'll come back – you'll no last.'

My contract was due for appraisal in two weeks' time, but it never got renewed. It was my turn to naff off. But when I left, most of the Possil people I'd met there who were serious about recovery left with us and came down to Calton Athletic.

I was now finding out that boys at Calton Athletic sustained their recovery longer than boys who had been in rehabs or had gone to the Health Board or Social Work services. We were now attracting boys not just from the Calton, but Possil, the Southside and Sighthill.

Meanwhile I began to apply one of the best things I took from Cardross at Calton Athletic. It was marathon running. I was inspired by another volunteer: Robert Barton, who came from Dennistoun and stayed round the corner from me. I had seen him around, trying to get involved with young people to show them the right direction, and one day he'd stopped me and asked about Cardross. He was interested in doing a bit of voluntary work, so I set a meeting up with Willie Blaney, who liked what he saw. Now Robert had a hobby of going out jogging, and he got to speaking to the residents about marathon running and the medals he had won. The boys were having a laugh as they couldn't picture Robert as an athlete. He had specs as thick as Coke bottles and was a comical character. But gie Robert his due, he had good patter.

The next day he brought in his medals and showed them to the boys. He really was an athlete. Robert told them about the benefits derived from distance running. As well as encouraging people, he led by example, and that was the key to the success of Robert Barton at Cardross. The Glasgow Marathon was coming up, and he managed to get 14 residents and me to enter. Getting just one of the Cardross boys to enter would have been some achievement, but with the support of Willie Blaney and Robert's determination we had 14 runners. I was so busy with my work at Cardross and Calton Athletic that I'd not been training, and Robert had to remind me a month before the race, 'Davie, you'll need to get some training in.' So I tried to do a bit. I had gone running in the early days of my recovery, but that extended to only about three miles. My first training run was from Cardross to the gate house and back, a distance of a mile. On the way back, just at the top of the hill, I had to stop because I was knackered, but four weeks later I finished in the same group as the others in the Glasgow Marathon. It was a tremendous experience. Above all it set a record: 14 recovering drug-addicts in a marathon.

When he was training, Robert took people out with him. He didn't just talk the talk, he walked the walk – or, rather, he ran it. He led by example and his enthusiasm spread among the residents. That marathon has stayed with me to this day. It was my first, but it wasn't going to be my last. Cardross and Robert Barton taught me the therapeutic benefits that running could bring to people in recovery.

CHAPTER THIRTEEN

East End, Dead End

Three years on from our first football match Calton Athletic formed a management committee to fight for resources to provide a rehabilitation service. Till now we'd been running on money generated mainly by myself, and it put a big strain on my family. I knew we had something here that worked, but there was only so much you could do through voluntary effort. So we put a submission in to the Scottish Office for a community-based drugs rehabilitation project. We got help from Ken Murray, the regional councillor at the time in Scotstoun. Ken had been a former prison warder and was a key man in setting up the Special Unit at Barlinnie. He came highly recommended from Jimmy Boyle. Ken did everything in his power to steer our submission through all the necessary committees. We also had to solicit the support of a statutory agent, so we went through the local process with community councillors and area liaison committees, and then took it to the next stage, which was Strathclyde region's social-work committee. After two years' campaigning, I was convinced that if the resources were there and we had the right people managing the project and delivering the service, an awful lot could be achieved.

I'd seen what Cardross could do in a limited capacity as a residential unit and this was an opportunity to do it in a community setting, where we could reach more people. We gave the submission to Ken Murray, who liked the look of it. I got a phone call a couple of days later from Ken, saying that he'd received another submission that was almost identical. It had come from the Social Work department and the other family-support groups in the East End.

Ken knew that only one submission would go through and that maybe we should liaise with these other groups, because their aims and objectives seemed to be similar. No wonder – they'd managed to get hold of our copy and submitted it as if it was their own, using our statistics and the hard work we'd put in. After a lot of debate I agreed to meet these other groups. They were family support groups, and most of the people who ran them had kids using drugs. Their lives were chaotic, and we were being asked to form a management committee with them. Nevertheless, we did it, and after a lot of campaigning the Scottish Office offered a record amount of funding for this project – £240,000, with the primary aims and objectives of getting as many people off drugs as possible and preventing as many as we could from falling into the drugs trap. It sounded good in theory. It was what everyone wanted. Just maybe this would be a way forward. We were prepared to go down that road, and when the Scottish Office granted the money, they came to select staff for the newly instated East End Drug Initiative (EEDI).

Most of the Calton Athletic management committee, because of their experience, would have been ideal candidates, but the EEDI committee was to be made up of two from Calton Athletic and four from the family-support groups. This was despite Calton Athletic now having about a hundred members, while the other four groups had about twenty between them. But with the right will we could work together. During the couple of years of fighting for the resources I had come in contact with these groups constantly and found myself overrun at times with demands from them. Could I help their daughter? Could I help their son? This is the last time; they're definitely serious this time.

A lot of work had been put into these families and groups, and we hoped a sort of mutual respect would build up, but it didn't turn out that way. Social Work had ensured they had a management committee they could manipulate. When the time came for jobs, things didn't work out how we would have liked it, either. Only three members of Calton Athletic were taken on as staff: myself and Bobby Jamieson as counsellors, and Tommy Toban as a development worker.

This project, which was going to be different from other projects and had received the biggest funding to date, went on to become the biggest disaster in the drugs field. Within a couple of months I was sacked from my job at the EEDI for arguing with the project leader. EEDI was now in charge of all resources from the Scottish Office for the East End, and there I was, dumped after campaigning for it despite impossible odds.

Social Work employed people who couldn't get addicts off drugs and only knew about prescribing drugs. This was the start of the new policy of harm reduction, then called 'minimalisation'. EEDI should have been a breakthrough for the East End, and it should have given hope to Calton Athletic five years after we had started from scratch, but I was out of a job, and Calton Athletic were excluded from the resources.

This disaster, though, turned out to be our salvation, as when we were on our own we stuck to what we believed in: getting people off drugs. Things went from strength to strength.

Meanwhile, EEDI was degenerating into madness. My wife Jeanette attended one of the management-committee meetings with representatives from the four other groups. Jeanette was trying to chair the meeting when she noticed that this woman – a big, butch lesbian – was under the influence of drugs. Jeanette says to her, 'Can you no have a bit of respect and come to a meeting straight?'

'I've no had any drugs. All I've had is six pints. Is that all right, everybody?'

'Well, I can see different fae your eyes,' Jeanette said. 'You might have had six pints, but you've also had something else.'

The woman pulled a knife and lunged at my wife. Luckily others intervened, and, in some ways, I'm glad I wasn't there. I don't know what I would have done. But Jeanette was fine. She's a strong woman. This, unfortunately, was part and parcel of the management-committee meetings at EEDI, which, at the time, was the biggest-funded drugs resource in Scotland. It was a farce, but also a tragedy for the East End.

CHAPTER FOURTEEN

Jimmy Boyle

I was angry and frustrated about what happened and visited the Gateway Exchange through in Edinburgh, run by Jimmy and Sarah Boyle. I was very impressed.

I had first crossed paths with Jimmy Boyle at Barlinnie. I'd seen him around, and everyone knew who he was. The man was a legend. He'd fought the system and they had been unable to break him. We met properly in 1985, when we were both out of prison. We were at a meeting of the Glasgow Association of Family Support Groups. We hit it off immediately and it was as if we had known each other all our lives. This was hardly surprising, as we had a lot in common: the gangs and the whole penal experience. We'd had an almost identical journey. We'd both been at Larchgrove remand home and Longriggend approved school, then Polmont Borstal. We'd even been in the same house there. The next step was young offenders and then prison.

Now we were at a similar stage in our lives, both wanting to put something back into the community, only it was in different cities: Jimmy in Edinburgh with the Gateway Exchange and me in Glasgow with Calton Athletic. Jimmy stayed in touch with his Glasgow roots, though, and was keen to help out where he could.

I liked what he had to say at the Gateway Exchange and was impressed with the way he conducted himself. Jimmy and Sarah had already given us great moral support, but now, when I was really down, Jimmy said he'd finance Calton Athletic for a year to allow us to get into premises and to put the dreams that we had into practice. Jimmy had seen what HIV was doing in Edinburgh, and he had a vision of what could happen in Glasgow.

So, with the support of the Gateway Exchange in 1991, I got twenty volunteers from Calton Athletic who had been with us over the last six years and we set about making our dreams into reality. Opening the premises was our first attempt to try to stop the spread of HIV and Aids in the East End. Finding a place that would have us was not easy, as we came up against the NIMBY (not in my backyard) factor. Everybody wants to help drug-addicts, but nobody wants them on their doorstep. As luck would have it, there was a group called the Calton Support Group who were struggling with their premises in London Road. The owner, a big guy called Ian Storey, let the place out to us for a year in 1992. A lot of hard work was put in to renovate it. We painted it bright red outside, with the bold words above the door 'CALTON ATHLETIC'. Anybody passing along London Road would see it, and crowds coming to the Barras at the weekend could not miss it. People could see that Calton Athletic were alive and kicking and weren't just playing football.

Once the place was renovated, we set about putting the structure together with a management committee of tried and trusted people, people such as Davie Main, Archie McCormick, Lorraine Fraser, Ann Main, big Archie, Jeanette and myself and Joe. These volunteers had life experience, but they had no practical experience of working on rehab projects, so I had to pass on mine. I started to put my vision into place. We'd try to take the good from the other places I'd worked at and get rid of the bad. We set up a programme of rehabilitation, so we had the ability to take somebody who was using drugs, put them through cold turkey, with someone appointed by us to closely monitor them through this traumatic time, then into an after-care service and from there into full-time employment. It was a vision and a dream, but I believed it was achievable.

From 1985 to 1991 Calton Athletic had been run from my house.

It had not been ideal, and I've got to admit my wife and my kids suffered. We never even had a telephone line in the early days, and when Jimmy Boyle wanted to contact me he would phone my mother. She was 80 at the time and stayed at the back of us. We worked out a system where she would pull the curtain back whenever Jimmy called and I would go and contact him. Good job I was straight and living well at this time, the same as Jimmy, because if the police had been watching they would have thought there was something suspicious going on. But it was an effective way of getting a message to us, and my ma was probably the best secretary I've ever had. She never got a message wrong.

I can't ever thank Jimmy Boyle enough for the support and the encouragement he gave us and the opportunity to open our first premises. I've an awful lot of respect for him, and over the years I've tended to think of him as a member of the family. Sarah Boyle was very supportive to Jeanette from day one, because she needed it. It wasn't easy being my wife in those days. I was trying to do my best, but it seemed to generate a lot of resentment and even hatred towards us. This was not from everybody – most people in the community and on the streets supported us – but some in the EEDI and statutory agencies did not. The resentment came from people working in the drugs field, or, rather, people trying to work in the drugs field. They were jealous of the success we had achieved so far and the attention we were receiving not just in the East End but across Britain. Meanwhile we now had a golden opportunity to see what we could do with volunteers.

CHAPTER FIFTEEN

Gordon, Lenny and Robbie

While I had been campaigning for funding, I was invited to attend a Labour Party meeting down at the Tron Theatre at Glasgow Cross to talk about drug abuse and the danger of infection. There were two young MPs there: Brian Wilson and Gordon Brown. I was asked to speak and quickly got onto the subject of HIV, telling them it was a bigger threat to our communities than anything else. But if we tackled the drug problem in a sensible manner, getting people to change their lifestyles and attitudes, then maybe something positive could come out of it. Brian and Gordon contacted us shortly after the meeting and asked if we could meet them privately down at Marco's, the new fitness centre on the site of the old Templeton's carpet factory. We had a cup of coffee, and both of them subsequently wrote articles about Calton Athletic in the papers. Brian's was in *The Herald* and Gordon's appeared in the *Daily Record*, in which he had a column at the time.

This helped us gain further credibility and wider recognition, as the name of Calton Athletic spread outside the East End of Glasgow. I hadn't gone looking for them; Brian and Gordon had sought me out. It had been a good meeting, and I liked both of them. Brian was to go on to become a government minister, while Gordon, of course, became the Chancellor, and who knows, maybe Prime Minister. I've still got their articles to this day.

One day while I was still doing my short spell at the EEDI, Gordon Brown phoned and asked if it would be OK if he could come and see me at the office in Barrowfield. When he arrived, the receptionist called up that there was a guy called Gordon Brown to see me. The project leader thought it was some addict but just about fell over when Gordon came in with another guy, who was the editor of *The Observer*. We chatted for about an hour and a half, and Gordon went on to write a great article for *The Observer* magazine.

As chance would have it, Lenny Henry spotted it that Sunday morning as he was sitting on the toilet. He told me later that he went through the article in a oner. They were banging on the cludgie door to get him out, as they thought something had happened to him.

It had. He'd been gripped by the story of Calton Athletic. Lenny phoned a pal, the writer Al Hunter. 'Let's do something with these guys. This is a great story. It could make a good film and it could get a point across.'

Not long after, I got a phone call from Al Hunter. He told me he was a writer who was in contact with Lenny Henry, who had read the article. He asked if he could come up and see us. I said sure and arranged to meet him at Crown Point, where we had a game. We got talking on the sideline and then he came to visit me at the EEDI. He asked if it would be OK if he came back again. He was starting to get a picture in his head about how things could work out as a TV drama. I was in the office at EEDI when I got a call from the receptionist. There were two gents to see us. Was it OK to send them up? 'Aye, send them up.'

The door opened and Al popped his head round: 'How are you doing, Davie?'

Then another head popped round behind him. 'How are you doing, Davie?'

It was Lenny Henry. I was a bit taken aback, but the rest of the office was flabbergasted.

Lenny's a huge guy, and immediately I took to him. I found him so likeable, charming and caring. Meanwhile EEDI was buzzing. It hadn't taken long for word to get round that Lenny Henry was in the building. Lenny and Al suggested that me and Davie Main – who would become my deputy and you'll hear more about – go for a meal with them. First, we picked up my wife. I called Jeanette: 'We'll be up in 20 minutes. We're going for something to eat. I've got a couple of guys with me.'

Twenty minutes later we were at the house, and I got Lenny to chap the door. Jeanette opened it and nearly died. It took her quite a while to pull herself together. She also recognised Al, as he'd been an actor in *Crossroads*. She was fair thrilled as we all headed for Coia's café in Duke Street, an East End institution that has been there for 75 years. When we got there, it was mobbed, and we were about to leave when Nicky Coia shouted, 'Hey, Davie, haud on.' He got a table and dragged people out of their seats. That's East End hospitality for you. We sat down and got talking. It was at this stage that Lenny declared he couldn't play football but he was mad keen to do the film. It would be his first serious role. He was famous as a comic but he wanted to break into drama. This was his opportunity, and it was also a story he believed in. Lenny would play Davie Main, the young guy who would go on to be my deputy at Calton Athletic, and Robbie Coltrane would play me. I was delighted. I liked Robbie a lot. He could definitely do it. I was well known for calling a spade a spade, and Robbie could carry that off. That night Lenny and Al came to watch us playing at Crown Point. There was a big crowd and they attracted a lot of attention. We heard later it was the first time anybody could remember that no cars had been broken into or nicked. The neds were too busy gawking at Lenny.

I trusted both of them and was happy for them to go ahead. One problem was Lenny has many talents but he just couldn't master a Glasgow accent. It was supposed to be set in Glasgow but it had to be switched to the Midlands. I had a lot of contact with them during filming, and when it was finished I was invited down to London with Jeanette to see the film, *Alive and Kicking*. It was strange sitting in an empty auditorium, just the two of us, watching a TV drama about Calton Athletic up on the big screen. It ends with the team of recovering drug-addicts playing their first game, and as the credits rolled it said, 'This is a real story based on Calton Athletic in the East

End of Glasgow.' I went back to the hotel they'd booked for us with Jeanette to talk about it. We were really pleased, and were sure that everyone at Calton Athletic would be too. That TV drama is still shown to this day in Scottish prisons as part of the drug treatment process. A lot of guys over the years have come out of Barlinnie and told me they'd seen it inside.

The name of Calton Athletic had gone nationwide thanks to Lenny, Robbie and that inspirational article by Gordon. Lenny, Al and Robbie were also to prove they weren't fair-weather friends over the coming years. They were to nominate me for the Unsung Hero Award from the Celebrities Guild of Great Britain. Robbie Coltrane was to officially open our first premises in London Road, and he was there to give moral support when our School Drugs Awareness team gave its first presentation to the great and the good, officials from Strathclyde region and the Scottish Office.

I still consider Lenny and Robbie valued friends, even though big Robbie ensured I would never work for anyone again, as in the film he went about sticking the heid on people right, left and centre. Anyone who got in his way or disagreed with him got the nut. I've tried to explain this was artistic licence.

However, all this publicity did not go down well with some of the EEDI staff, particularly the project leaders. Nearly everybody who was coming to the EEDI wanted to join Calton Athletic, so jealousy and envy had already begun to creep in. It had never been Calton Athletic's style to be meek and mild. We were gallus. We came from gallus people and would have lacked credibility in the East End if we weren't. It was part of our success. But I was already finding out all too well that people hate it when you succeed, especially if they are failing. This attitude would haunt us over the next decade and is still there today, but we would never give up our principles – principles that had won us respect in the community and further afield.

CHAPTER SIXTEEN

Italia '90

Scotland had qualified for the 1990 World Cup in Italy, and we decided we would be there too. After all we were a football team, and not only could we watch the matches over there, we could also play some of our own. It was a great idea, but how would we do it? Jimmy Boyle once again was a tremendous help. He was doing a documentary at the time, and part of it included Calton Athletic, so he got the producers to donate a few quid. We also had a fundraising dance in John Lynch's pub in the London Road, and Jimmy arranged a surprise guest of honour. I was standing up the stairs in John Lynch's, collecting tickets at the door, when I saw this woman coming up. I couldn't see her face, only the top of her head, and when she got level she had this beautiful voice: 'Is this the Calton Athletic dance?' It was Glenda Jackson.

'Oh aye, hen,' I blurted out. 'Delighted to meet you.'

I took her in and Glenda was tremendous and made a great speech. She'd also brought me a gift, *A Rough Guide to Italy*, and she signed the book. She also danced with everybody. It was a night to remember and was such a turn-up for the books. Five years after we'd started and now we had an Oscar-winning actress at our party.

Glenda was not yet an MP and had come straight from the Citizen's Theatre that night, where she was appearing in *Mother Courage.*

So, with a little help from our friends, and our own efforts, we raised the money for 17 drug-addicts in recovery to make it over to Italy. We got a bus from Glasgow to London, then the train to Newhaven and the ferry to Dieppe. Next it was rail all the way via Paris to Genoa, where we found ourselves in a place called Pele – as good an omen as any for a place to stay at the World Cup.

As we were setting off to go to the World Cup, we had been approached about a documentary based on the club and our trip. The guy making it was Ray Stubbs, who was then a TV rookie. Today he's never off the box. Several years later at the Great North Run we'd meet up again, and Ray told me he'd been watching the video and reckoned it was one of the best bits of work he'd ever done. Italia '90 was to be our first World Cup – but not our last. We were to make it to USA '94 and France '98, and also down to England for Euro '96 and Portugal for Euro 2004.

Back in Italy in 1990, we ran into the Rab C. Nesbitt crew and Jonathan Watson, who were making a World Cup special. We were in the bank cashing our traveller's cheques and looking over at the Rab C. crew, and they were looking at us. The one nearest was Jonathan Watson, and I started to chat away. He was a smashing guy: 'Davie, what a coincidence. Before I came to the World Cup, I went to the dentist and I picked up a magazine and in it was an article that Gordon Brown had written about Calton Athletic. The night before I was ready to fly out, I was watching the news on TV and it shows you lot, Calton Athletic, going away to the World Cup, and I thought to myself, "I wonder if I'll meet them over there" and sure as hell, here we are bumping into each other in a bank.'

But there was a serious side, and Italia '90 was to be an important part of our learning process. We were naive and setting out on an adventure, but if we could pull this off it would be a major achievement. We also had one additional member, a Roman Catholic priest. I'd asked Father Willie Slaven, then coordinator of the Scottish Drugs Forum, for a bit of advice, as none of us spoke Italian, and he arranged for a young priest, Father Archie, who was a friend of his, to come with us. Father Willie didn't know what Father

Archie was getting into, but I've got to say that, without him, I don't think we would have made it the success it was. I say success because we got everybody back home and nobody got the jail. It was part of the process, learning about booze and recovery. Everybody who went was definitely off the drugs. They wouldn't have been going if they weren't. There were three lassies with us: Anne-Marie, Tracy and Michelle. Anne-Marie was a great lassie, the leader among them, and she had a great World Cup. Tragically, after she got back from the World Cup, drugs took her life: a great lassie from a smashing family who had supplied us all with Italia '90 towels.

We made it to Pele and booked into our campsite, which was mainly populated by Swedes and Brazilians. We didn't know much about Italy, but what we quickly found out was that it cost more for a cup of coffee than it did for a bottle of wine. With a west of Scotland attitude to a bargain it was almost a disaster, but the young priest Father Archie was invaluable. He would come up to the camp every morning, see if we needed errands done and arrange to get us tickets for the matches.

The first game was the infamous one against Costa Rica, and every one of us got there. That's what you go to the World Cup for, to see the football, and we all made it. We didn't have much money available and were running on a tight budget. The whole trip cost three and a half grand for seventeen people. The actual game was a disaster and enough to put everybody off the next one, but I made sure I went. Most thought if we couldn't beat Costa Rica, we had no chance against the Swedes. But we got a result off the Swedes and I was there. I was elated, and the Scottish fans as a whole were tremendous. They're a breed apart, as are Calton Athletic.

It wasn't too long, though, before some of our group succumbed to the booze. It was so cheap, after all – about 50p a bottle – and they were so skint, but still I was raging. I tried to avoid the drunks, but I couldn't as I was in charge of the camp. Straight away there were personality changes, and arguments broke out. I noticed that people who had been initially friendly to us on the campsite started avoiding us because of the drinking and rowdiness. The pressure got to me and I was on the point of gubbing a couple. I sent two home, and one of them eventually came back and is still a member today. I had to make a stand or else booze would have ruined the trip. I knew then that alcohol was a gateway back to drugs and offending. After Italia '90 it became a strict rule – no bevy.

About three-quarters of the group in Italy had hit the booze at some time, but it did not go too far, as at least nobody was stabbing anyone. When the problem was confronted, the majority fell in line. But even the old ones had joined in with the youngsters, including my mate Spooney. The campsite had a shop, and behind it was a cliff, and at the bottom was the wine store. It wasn't long before some of our boys found a rope and were abseiling down the cliff to get to it. I thought, 'What the fuck is this? The Milk Tray advert?' Spooney was doing it too.

The trip taught us about the bad apple affect. If two start drinking, it will spread. Italia '90 was special because it was the first opportunity I'd had to spend a long period of time with some of those in recovery, to wake them up to the reality of their situation. One person in particular really stood up to be counted: Davie Main. He'd shown a lot of quality in times of trouble. Things would be different at the next World Cup, although getting there was a tall order, as it was in America. It had been hard enough getting to Italy; how would we manage to get over there?

CHAPTER SEVENTEEN

Opening Time

The official opening of our first premises on London Road back in 1991 was a great event. As I've said, our old friend Robbie Coltrane did the business. He brought his new girlfriend, Ronnie, with him – a wonderful woman. They didn't have kids at the time, but I was delighted they went on to have a family. Robbie's sparkle and patter was magic, while Ronnie got her sleeves rolled up and mucked in with the rest of the lassies, helping with the catering.

Robbie was also joined by Charlie Nicholas and Tommy Burns. Charlie, who was at Celtic at the time, is a smashing guy, and I still see him now and again. Tommy is an East End boy himself, who was brought up round the corner from us. He was managing Kilmarnock at the time and was always a good friend to Calton Athletic. Fred Edwards, chairman of Strathclyde Social Work, also made an appearance. The media were out in force and we made the BBC and STV news.

The place was mobbed that day and everybody was full of enthusiasm. We were going to give it our best shot. We were going to do everything the EEDI should have been doing but wasn't. It had been our submission that was accepted by the Scottish Office, our vision and dream of how we would tackle things. We'd been let down, but now we were going to get a chance to put our vision into practice in our own premises.

Jimmy Boyle had given us £20,000, and that was a lot of money for us. Although Calton Athletic had been going six years, we didn't have two pennies to rub together. Money or donations never poured into Calton Athletic in the early days. Up to this time it had been supported by me, with a little bit of help from my mother. Jimmy would give us the odd few quid as well. Jimmy also set us up with a residential weekend at Newbattle Abbey, for our volunteers to go away and start to get a business plan together. That weekend was tremendous. We set out in stages how we were going to achieve things. By the time the official opening day arrived, we'd already been providing services for nine months. It had taken that long to renovate the place and to get our big event in place. This meant that, when it did come, not only was it a grand old day down at London Road, people could already see the proof of the pudding. Some of the people who had been through the programme shared their experience with the visitors.

The location appealed to me on a personal level. Our base was 20 yards from the place in which I used to stay in the Calton, where I'd sunk to my lowest with heroin. Here I was returning several years later and opening up a service next door that would help people get off the drugs. When I was using, whether I like it or not, I was probably encouraging other people to use drugs. Not that I was forcing them into it, but people would say, 'If it's good enough for Brycie, it's good enough for us.' I still regret those days. These premises were going to give us an opportunity to make amends. If I did influence anybody in the wrong way, I would now try to make my influence for the good.

We had a name for ourselves by now, and we were on a main road, both of which deterred petty drug-dealers and others from smashing our windows in like before. The drug-addicts knew where we were and what we were: a service for men and women, whether you kicked a ball or not. This was important as, from that day onwards, about a third of the addicts coming through the door were women. All we wanted to do was to help people, and even the gangsters stood back and let us get on with it.

CHAPTER EIGHTEEN

The Main Man

The first year in the premises gave me a chance to see how the volunteers operated on a daily basis. Some were inconsistent. The place needed a structure and I knew I needed a deputy. Most of the volunteers were on the management committee, and I realised we had to split this up to prevent a conflict of interests. I was chairman, so I resigned from this post when I became project leader. Meanwhile, people providing the service had to step down from the committee as well.

I'd assembled the team of volunteers and told them I was going to appoint a senior counsellor. I'd been taking a long, hard look at them. Some of the older ones did not respond the way I thought they should, and some other good people had other problems to deal with.

Someone who stood out was Davie Main. He had stayed off the booze when others hadn't in Italy. He had come through to Edinburgh with us to see Jimmy Boyle at the Gateway. I was supporting a lot of people, but I needed a bit of support myself, and although this guy was young he had a lot of real qualities, and he's still with us today. When I announced to the staff that Davie Main was going to be the senior counsellor, it caused a few problems. Davie was only 22, and some of the older ones thought he was too young. They thought they knew better, and slowly but surely some started drifting away, or their commitment slackened. But Davie's commitment became stronger. He had the ability to lead by example and was already captain of the football team.

I had first come across Davie when I was visiting a residential facility in Possil called The Place and I noticed this young boy slouched in a corner. He looked as if he weighed 9 st. if he was lucky, although he was a big lad. The reason he caught my attention was I'd noticed the woman he was with. She had gone to school with us. She was Davie's mother, and I spoke to her. She was heartbroken. I looked at Davie and he didn't know where he was. He just had that lost, dejected look that addicts have. I later discovered that Davie ran away from The Place a couple of days later. He thought he had to run away to escape, although he was there in a voluntary capacity. He climbed out the window and hurt his back, when he could have walked out the door and got a bus. That first meeting didn't create too much of a stir in me. I was more interested in his mother, who was at her wits' end. I came across him again in Robinson's House, a Social Work facility. I was working in the EEDI at the time, and his mother had come to see us to say that Davie had been asking for us. I went to see him. This time he was 14 st. He'd been in the rehab for about ten weeks and was looking good, but he was still frightened and confused about what would happen now he was ready to leave. I told him he could come and see me at the EEDI in Barrowfield. He could also join Calton Athletic if he wanted. I hadn't seen him playing, but I'd heard a bit about him. Davie had been a schoolboy international, as well as on Celtic's books, and had looked as if he was going to have a bright future in football. One night he had been on his way to training when he met his pals sitting in the close smoking dope. Usually he walked past, but this night he stopped because he thought he was missing out. It might not have been as bad if it had stopped at dope, but he was young and impressionable and got sucked in. It doesn't matter who you are, you're susceptible. At 16 Davie had had a bright future, but when I met him in the rehab he was 20 and finished. During the course of the next couple of years, though, he had started to show a lot of promise, both at football and in other areas. He didn't say much. He preferred to walk it rather than talk it. And I think to walk it we had to have a programme, a structure whereby people could develop their communication skills and grow in confidence. Davie had all the raw materials, and I recognised that.

I've got to say that without Davie things would have turned out differently. He'd probably tell you a different story, but I have to put on the record how much I appreciated him and still do. The role model he went on to become was a tremendous example to the many young people who have come through the door and managed to get their lives together.

CHAPTER NINETEEN

Tough Love

Not long after the official opening we got a call from Glasgow Health Board. They had a surplus at the end of the financial year and could we think of anything we needed? Where did we start? We didn't have any computers, transport or heating. We asked for a van and some equipment to help make the premises better. Having our first computers made a big difference, and we started recording everything we did: how many people were coming through the door, how many people were going on the programme, how many people weren't going on the programme. We started to learn from our mistakes. We discovered that some people were coming along and using the credibility of being with Calton Athletic to sell their 'drugs'. By drugs I mean their prescriptions, because by this time the harm-reduction ethos of the EEDI was starting to kick in. A lot of young people had stopped using heroin and had turned to the National Health Service cures. Temazepam was getting sold on the black market, and somebody who got a prescription could make themselves a nice few quid by selling it. We started noticing this, and the people who were doing it weren't going to make it anyway. If you want to start off with that kind of attitude in recovery, forget it.

Along with no booze another golden rule was introduced. As part of the assessment procedure we told people to come back with a letter from their GP telling us they weren't getting any prescribed drugs. When they'd ask why, I'd say 'There's two reasons. When you're with Calton Athletic, you won't be using any prescribed drugs, and the second reason is when you're with Calton Athletic, you won't be selling any prescribed drugs.' This turned out to be one of the most significant things we did. It was our way of separating the wheat from the chaff. If somebody was serious, they would bring that letter back. If they weren't, they wouldn't come back. This was good for us because it was an intense programme at Calton Athletic, and only people who were serious were going to make it. I'd like to think that over the years we've taken at least 1,500 of these prescriptions off the market. They would have been sold to younger people who couldn't get prescriptions themselves. And the addict who was selling the prescriptions would be using the money to buy the drugs he wanted, rather than the prescribed drugs he was getting.

Anyone who was still using was quickly sussed out and sent away. They got a chance to come back in maybe three or four months' time, but only if they were clean. We couldn't run the risk of people who had stopped using looking at one or two who still were and thinking it was OK. This policy helped to raise the standards and quality of Calton Athletic. Drug-addicts may do a lot of stupid things, but they aren't daft. If they think they're going to get caught, there's less of a chance they'll do it.

But they were allowed to get away with it at all the other projects. We were different. We were going to make it as hard as possible for anybody to mess about. We didn't just operate from nine to five, because people are in recovery twenty-four hours a day, seven days a week, and if we can keep them busy for seven days a week, they have a better chance of success. And this is exactly what happened. We didn't perfect it right away at London Road, but we set out to learn from the mistakes and started to change things.

I couldn't believe how quickly things started picking up in terms of people coming through the door. The management committee met once a month, while the group workers would handle the rehabilitation programmes daily, and the counsellors the assessments as and when they were needed. Assessments examined the needs of people coming in, committed them to the programme and explained what it was about. It was trial and error at first, but we could see things were beginning to work. Once we were satisfied an individual was drug-free, we'd put him or her onto the day programme.

The day programme was three days a week: Monday, Wednesday and Friday. Apart from this, we used to have a Monday-night recovery meeting. This would also be for people who had finished the programme, to help sustain their recovery and for them to pass on their experience to other individuals. Just about this time I got in contact with Marco's Leisure Centre, the place where I had met Brian Wilson and Gordon Brown. Marco's allowed us to use their facilities, which I was grateful for. We also had Tuesday-night training up at Crown Point sports centre, and we introduced an aerobics class because by now we had so many female members. It wasn't just for females, though; aerobics was for guys too. Some were put off and one told me, 'I'm no goin' in. I'm a hard man, Davie. Hard men dinnae dae aerobics.' But I persuaded him to give it a try and five minutes later he was doing aerobics. We introduced Thursday-night training as well, and also a Sunday down at Marco's. Meanwhile, Saturday was taken care of with the football. So we were up and running seven days a week, totally in a voluntary capacity. It wasn't just daytime either. We'd have people coming down in the evening to get assessed, and we started to provide a facility for families, because we believed the families had to recover as well.

We didn't know at the time which method would be best for parents. It was generally accepted by the Glasgow Association of Family Support Groups that parents should meet together in a group setting with counsellors. Later I changed my mind about this. I think the best thing you can do for parents is to give them advice and information on an individual basis. Then it's up to them whether they want to take that advice and information on board. If they don't, there's nothing much you can do for them. That support system works when the kids are in recovery as well. I've seen an awful lot of parents over the years who went to groups with the best of intentions and thought they would help to get their son or daughter off drugs but it never happened. The Glasgow Association of Family Support Groups seemed to believe in unconditional love being the best healer of people's problems, but our policy was that you had to get off the drugs and that people would only get so many chances.

I believe in tough love, where the key element is being tough because you love them. If you're tough, there's a chance they'll come off the drugs. If you're not, they'll probably stay on drugs and maybe go on to pay for it with their lives.

We weren't part of the Glasgow Association of Family Support Groups, but we were probably seeing more parents than the whole lot of them put together. We also made it clear it was not acceptable for our members to have one face for Calton Athletic and another at home, and that's why we had to include families. If the family see someone's not quite right, they can tell us, then we can maybe nip things in the bud.

But we made mistakes. One of the biggest was allowing a parents' support group to start on the premises. Parents in a group situation would start to lie to protect their son or daughter, rather than have them put off the programme. This was creating the bad-apple effect, because the others could see who was messing about. We tried to get it through to parents how important it was for them to be honest with us. But some would rather lie so their kids could stay. So that's how we came to the conclusion that the best way to deal with parents would be on an individual basis. You can't offer more than the best advice and information you've got. They're the ones who have got to put it into practice, and if they don't, nothing is going to alleviate their situation. When parents have got somebody using drugs in their house, they'll always be demented, worrying whether they're going to find them dead from an overdose or their purse stolen. I'd also seen parents in the group resenting other kids getting off while theirs was still using. Then it starts: 'Who do they think they are just cos their son or daughter's aff the drugs?' That's the insanity of drug abuse. It doesn't just affect the addict, but eats up the people around them.

Everybody I've seen at Calton Athletic, including myself, didn't start to get better until recovering was forced on them. It only worked when loved ones – like my Jeanette – started getting tough and weren't prepared to put up with it any more. For the rest of the family's sake, those in a position to help have got to get tough. I believe that's what gets more people off drugs than anything else. I've no problems about that.

Sinking into a personal gutter also gets people off drugs, but in a more desperate, last-ditch way. Then you've got to take a look at yourself. The rest of the people you're out there using with, they're not your pals, they're just acquaintances, and if you've not got drugs, they don't want to know you. The people that do care are your family. All the rest of them you use with don't give a shit. It was important that we really got our service together to prevent people from hitting rock bottom, and started giving both addicts and their families the best information we possibly could. I'm delighted to say we still do that today.

CHAPTER TWENTY

Lord Jamie

All sorts came to London Road, and one day we got a phone call from the *Daily Record*. Would it be all right if they brought Lord Jamie, the Marquess of Blandford and heir to the Duke of Marlborough, down to the premises to have a talk with us? I didn't have any problems with this. The hand of friendship's open to anybody, no matter who they are. Lord Jamie Blandford had been front-page news when he got into trouble with drugs. When he arrived, he looked every part the officer and a gentleman. He was about 6 ft 2 in., a big handsome guy. He was articulate, and I got on very well with him. I've got to say, above all else, he was straight that day. He was to have relapses, but I've not heard anything for a long time now, and in this game no news is good news. Jamie told me he was born with a silver spoon up his nose. I liked that.

I told him about the role physical fitness played in Calton Athletic and our ethos that the healthy body leads to the healthy mind. Jamie chipped in, 'I've got a mountain bike, Davie.'

I raised an eyebrow. 'I know, I've seen you going scoring on it.'

Jamie liked that. He was a decent big guy, and I hope he's doing well and has found his recovery because he was looking hard for it.

If you keep looking and keep working, you'll find it, and I hope Jamie has.

Shortly after Lord Jamie, a young professional footballer turned up. He was in a hell of a state through heroin, but was still trying to keep up a front that everything was OK. He seemed ideally suited for Calton Athletic, as he needed help and would be a bonus for our football team, but it never turned out that way. When heroin gets a grip, it robs you of your natural abilities and gives you nothing back in return. Sad to say this big guy never made it on the programme. However, his sister did. He left, as he thought he could do it himself. Soon after, I noticed his name in the papers a few times for housebreaking and other offences. It's sad, but whatever your status in life it can't protect you when you're into heroin. That was the case with Lord Jamie Blandford and now the professional football player.

I've met very few people who have tried heroin and just chucked it as quick as that. Once you try it a couple of times, you're in. Most people don't realise that. Heroin is cunning and baffling. It's evil and insidious. And the people who fall into it – hooked before they even know it – come from all walks of life.

London Road was proving too small for our ever-growing requirements, so, in 1993, through the greatly valued help of Lenny and Robbie, we applied to Comic Relief for funding. We made up a submission based on acquiring the old Calton Club in Green Street, which had lain derelict for years. We got a firm of architects who costed it, and we put in a submission for £300,000 to Comic Relief. I got a visit from their director, Maggie Baxter, and showed her the Calton Club. Comic Relief granted us £100,000 but they put pressure on Greater Glasgow Health Board to match it and to give us recurring revenue, as that's what they rightly believed we needed. We'd had a bit of dialogue with the Health Board in the previous two years about expanding and received some capital money at the end of their financial years. We'd bought a minibus one year and the next year they had helped to refurbish London Road. Now we needed to put more pressure on them as things were getting drastic out on the street.

By 1993 there was an unheard-of level of drug deaths. The statistics had been getting higher each year and the harm-reduction policy that the council, Social Work and the Health Board had dreamed up was turning into harm production. This idea of giving addicts prescribed drugs and hoping that would stabilise them wasn't working. So we organised a march to the Health Board premises in Ingram Street. That day 150 of us turned up outside with banners and handed in a petition. The media arrived and the Health Board granted me and Davie Main an audience. The senior management asked for a couple of days to think about things. When Davie Main and I walked out of the Health Board, I told the reporters that the Health Board would be meeting us again in three days' time at London Road. Three days later we thrashed out an agreement that they would give us recurring revenue of £106,000 for three years. We were very careful during these negotiations, as we'd already been burnt with the EEDI.

Calton Athletic management committee wanted to insure the policy and to control the resources. The Health Board had no problems with this. They had stipulated that three full-time staff would be required: a project leader, a senior counsellor and a development worker. They also gave extra money via the Social Work for a part-time clerical worker. The rest of the money, the core funding of £40,000, was left to the discretion of the management committee. This would pay rent, electricity, postage, programmes and activities. It sounds quite a lot, but when all these things had to get paid, there was very little left. From day one in 1985 we had raised money on our own, but at least now after eight years we had recurring revenue. Just after they had granted this, the money from Comic Relief came through.

In the meantime, vandals had set fire to our proposed new premises, but we hadn't yet bought it and we managed to find an alternative place in Dennistoun. We would still be based in London Road for the day programme, but Dennistoun would serve as a day centre which would run until 2002, even when funding from the statutory agencies was stopped in 1998.

CHAPTER TWENTY-ONE

USA – All the Way

I'll never forget that day at Camelon's ground in 1992 when we won the Scottish Welfare Cup. I'd had the feeling at the beginning of the season that this was going to be our year. Davie Main was showing great form, and we had a lot of good players. Sure enough we reached the final to face Yarrow Shipbuilders, which is down at the Scotstoun area, near Clydebank. They'd been on the go for years and thought that all they had to do was turn up that day, but we knew differently. I can honestly say that nobody was going to beat Calton Athletic that day – not even Rangers or Celtic. I believe not just that history was made in Falkirk at that final, but that a miracle took place. I ain't that clever and I had hardly set out to win the Scottish Cup back in 1985 when I started getting boys to kick a ball instead of using heroin. But here we were eight years later. We showed tremendous enthusiasm, courage and skill to win 5–1, and our supporters – a few hundred who had followed us through from the East End – were ecstatic. It was a tremendous day that nobody can ever take away from us. We'd won the Cup. We'd also set a precedent on the football park. This was the standard we were capable of achieving. Gone were the days when it was just about turning up on a Saturday. Calton Athletic were getting a reputation for fitness and determination, whether it be football or half-marathons.

What better way to celebrate the Cup than for everybody to save up and go to America for the World Cup 1994? Shortly after, everyone was sticking ten quid a week into a bank account. But if anybody messed up, started boozing or using, they weren't going and they weren't getting their money back either. That's the way we did things. We'd provided a facility and a platform for people to go through the door to recovery. Some had gone on beyond their wildest dreams. Some of them kicked the ball in that final, and some of them scored in that final. Now they were going to USA '94 with 22 other recovering drug-addicts and everybody had to be on their best behaviour. This kept everyone on their toes for that full year beforehand, and the build-up was tremendous. A couple of weeks prior to leaving I was having a chat with Jimmy Boyle, and he said, 'Have you thought about what you're going to do at immigration in America?'

'What do you mean?'

'Well, you need to fill a visa in on the plane, and it asks questions like have you ever been in trouble? Are you a drug-addict? Are you an alcoholic?'

'Christ, I hadnae thought of it, Jimmy.'

'Well, I'm going to America shortly, Davie.'

'What are you going to do?'

'I'm gonna be honest and fill in the questionnaire.'

'I'll wait and see what happens,' I said.

Jimmy went to America with his wife and kids and filled in the visa honestly. But when he touched down at Kennedy airport, immigration would not let him into the country, although they let Sarah and the two kids in. It even made the papers. What were we going to do? A week before we went to the World Cup, a group of guys from the East End of Glasgow had saved up the same as ourselves and I'd seen in the news that when they'd got there half of them were turned back for being criminals, a couple for having drug convictions. They'd also brought attention to themselves with a wee bit of carry-on on the plane. They were drunk, high-spirited, nothing major – but it drew the attention of the immigration officials. What a disaster.

Hopefully things were going to be different for us. We hadn't decided what we were going to do. We had two options. We could maybe apply to the American government and they could turn us down flat, or we could just hard-neck it through. We needed to make a decision. We'd hard-neck it.

The great day arrived and we had to be at Glasgow airport for five in the morning. There were 22 of us, including big Archie Main. When his son Davie got clean, Archie got sober, and he'd been doing a bit of voluntary work with Calton Athletic for the past couple of years. This was his first trip abroad and his first time on a plane, and for weeks beforehand he had been terrified. He talked about it all the time, and as soon as I walked into the airport the first person I clapped eyes on was big Archie. He had a pair of shades on and his hat was hanging over to the side. He looked like Cheech or Chong. He raised two fingers in the peace sign: 'How you doing, Davie?'

He was that nervous the night before, his wife had put Valium in his tea. It had such a calming effect that he wasn't even worried about the flight, but I was because I don't like flying either. During the build-up to the World Cup I had tried to reassure big Archie, 'I'm mair worried than you,' and he'd always say, 'No, you're no.' But it turned out on the day of the flight that Archie was fine and I wasn't. We got through immigration at Glasgow airport and were making our way towards the departure lounge when one of the boys, Neilie McCrimmon, got pulled up. Big Davie Main went over and asked what was wrong, and by this time the Customs had called the police over. They had discovered Neilie had an outstanding £250 fine for something he had got done for before he came to Calton Athletic. They led him away, and Davie went with them. The police, true to their word, let him out as soon as Davie handed over the £250. The boy couldn't pay it because his money was in traveller's cheques, but Davie took it out of his own money and got it back once we got to America.

When Neilie McCrimmon was getting interviewed by the police about the fines, they told him, 'We knew you were coming here; you're part of the Calton Athletic group.' So there was us thinking we'd been secretive when the police and the Customs knew all along we were heading off to America.

We thought this would maybe cause problems if they contacted the American authorities. Now we had a bit of a sweat on. We left the departure lounge and boarded the flight. Our base was Orlando, because Ireland were playing one of their games there and that's who we'd decided we were going to support.

After the plane took off and everybody got settled down, big Archie asked if he could take the window seat. This was somebody who had been terrified of the thought of even being on a plane, now wanting to look out of the window. However, I was still sitting there white-knuckled. Maybe it's because I'm always sober that I don't like flying. I hear all the noises. I wouldn't have a problem if I was drinking. If I was drinking, I would want to fly the plane. I would probably want to join the Mile High Club. But sober, it's a different kettle of fish. You hear and see everything. I turned round and looked at one of the boys, and he'd ordered a drink up. Alarm bells started ringing in my head. About two hours into the flight one of the boys, John Plotts, came up and sat next to us. John was a real character from Renfrew, who had been at the club a year. He'd been everywhere trying to get sober before he came to the Calton. He was about 25 and was full of enthusiasm. His main goal when he first came was to get straight for a year, stay sober and then start a project in Renfrew. He was single-minded about this, and we encouraged him. We knew he would gain a lot of experience with us and get the support of other people at the Calton.

But when John sat down next to me, he said, 'Are you having a drink, Davie?'

'What do I want a drink for, man?'

'It'll make you feel a bit easier.'

'No, John, it'll no make me feel any better. I'm quite prepared to tough it out.'

It's not just about staying sober when things are easy – when the going gets tough, you've got to stay sober, and I couldn't afford to start finding reasons to drink. I turned back to him: 'How, what made you ask?'

'I was thinking of taking one myself. I don't really like flying, and I see one of the other boys has taken one.'

This was the bad-apple effect at work. John had clocked the same guy as us. By now there were a couple of them drinking. John said, 'How are you no gonna take one, Davie?'

'Well, quite simply, John, if I take one the noo, and I wake up the 'morrow morning with a hangover, I'll only be one day sober and straight. I'll have thrown away all thae years, and it's no worth it. But it's up to you what you want to dae. You're a year sober the now. If you take a drink, when you wake up the 'morrow you'll be only one day sober.'

John had a wee think about it. He never took that drink, and I don't think he's taken one to this day. John was to go on and start his group with the financial support of Jimmy and Sarah Boyle at the Gateway Exchange. Now John's still doing his best down in an area where it's really tough. There have been a lot of drug wars down in Renfrew and Paisley. John's right in the middle of it, and he hasn't got the same kind of support that I've got at Calton Athletic, but he's determined to see it through.

When John Plotts first arrived at Calton, everybody thought he was a bit strange. He was very honest and up-front, so much so at times he was a bit over the top. He was going through a desperate struggle coming off the booze, but with the help and support he got from Calton Athletic he started to settle down. He told me early on about his plans to form Renfrew United and some day they'd be bigger than Calton. I told him, 'Fair play, John, and good luck, son.'

There was something about John I liked. He was the sort of person who always had strange and remarkable things happening to him. A prime example of this occurred during the early days, when he was pretty troubled and was seeing other people as well as us for advice, including a young priest. This somehow gave him the idea that going to Rome to see the Pope would help him: he might get some sort of a sign. So John duly went to see the Pope.

Now the papal audience is always a big event, and thousands of people come to it, but John was convinced the Pope was going to pick him out of the crowd and touch his hand. We all had a good laugh about it, and John took a lot of kidding. Off he went, and he came back five days later. He told us he'd gone to St Peter's and the

Pope was saying mass. When the Pope was walking through St Peter's Square, he ushered to one of the Swiss Guards to open up the very aisle that John was in. He walked over to John, breaking away from the procession, and reached out and touched him. We were all amazed, not sure whether to believe him or not. Finally I said, 'Christ, that's some story, John.'

He said, 'It's no' finished there, Davie. On my way back from Rome I had to change planes at Orly airport in Paris. I was going from one plane to the next, and I needed the toilet. I went in, and I came walking out and bumped into this guy. As I bumped into him, his hand touched my hand and I felt a strange sensation. It was Pelé.'

'Pelé! Christ, John, that's amazing.'

We were still not sure whether to believe him. Anyone else and you'd know they were waffling, but there was something about John. But he wasn't finished: 'The reason I got a special feeling off Pelé was because he's a faith healer. I've read about it before. I felt different after I banged into him and spoke to him.'

The doubters had stopped smirking and were even beginning to have second thoughts. John then pulled out these photographs. Sure enough, there was a big beautiful photograph of Pope John Paul II reaching out and touching John's hand. It was as plain as day. I'm convinced that the bit at Orly airport was true as well. Everybody just sat there.

Not long afterwards about 50 of us went to the Glasgow Pavilion Theatre to see Lenny Henry in a one-man show. He'd stood by us, and we were just returning a little bit of support. Big Alex Goldfarb was winding John up a bit about the Pope and Pelé. 'Seeing we're up at the Pavilion, John, do you think Lenny will come walking off the stage and touch your hand?'

'Fuck aff. Naw, I want to meet Muhammad Ali.'

'Muhammad Ali?' Alex says.

'Aye. Ali's a prophet. He could see things years ago.'

And just as John said this, we turned the corner and there was a big poster: 'Muhammad Ali – book signing at W.H. Smith's, Glasgow – next week'.

John turned to big Alex: 'I'll be there to meet him.' They had a good laugh at that.

Above: LITTLE BIG MAN: That's me far left, back row next to Miss Moore, who's making sure she can keep an eye on me.

Inset: BORSTAL BOY: Believe it or not I was a good 'un and enjoyed activities like camping.

Below: WOMAN IN LOVE: With Calton Athletic, that is. Glenda Jackson, the Oscar-winning actress, had a starring role at our Italia '90 fundraiser with me and Jimmy Boyle at John Lynch's pub in the Gallowgate.

Top: OPENING NIGHT: Robbie Coltrane cuts the ribbon of our first premises, aided and abetted by Celtic's Charlie Nicholas and Tommy Burns.

Above left: BBC BONUS: Ray Stubbs did a documentary on us and told me years later: 'One of my best pieces of work, Davie.'

Above right: LENNY HENRY: A big guy with an even bigger heart.

Top: MY ROLE MODEL: I was proud to have Robbie Coltrane (here with my son Stephen) play me in the TV drama *Alive and Kicking*.

Inset: MAY THE FORCE BE WITH YOU: Obi-Wan Kenobi points the way forward to Calton Ladies' Jeanette Bryce (the wife) and Lorraine Fraser.

Below: TRAINSPOTTING: Danny Boyle, the film's director, and its writer, John Hodge, with me and Davie Main.

Above: EWAN McGREGOR: Getting to grips with Calton Ladies at Craigpark.

Inset: MAIN MAN: Irvine Welsh is a great writer, but more than that he is a great friend.

Below: STARSPOTTING: Our *Trainspotting* pals Danny Boyle, Andy Macdonald and Irvine Welsh got a few of their pals to play in our fundraiser, among them: Nick Hornby, Johnny Lee Miller, Bobby Carlyle, Ewan McGregor and Peter Mullan.

Top: THE PLOTTS THICKENS: Who's the guy in white with
John Plotts in St Peter's Square?

Above left: PEER PRESSURE: Lord Jamie Blandford was a genuine guy.
He told me he was born with a silver spoon up his nose.

Above right: DANI GIRL: Ms Behr gets to meet Eamon Doherty and
Andrew Macdonald after she has presented me with the
Unsung Hero Award at the Dorchester.

Top: CARRY ON CALTON: Barbara Windsor tickles her fancy – our boys Davie Main and John Gibson – at the Celebrities Guild awards.

Inset: MUMMY'S BOYS: Two people who gave me so much support: Jimmy Boyle and my mother. She loved what I did with Calton Athletic.

Below: THE GREAT WALDO: Walter Smith invited us to Ibrox and Everton. I've always told him if he ever needs a job, he can be my assistant manager at Calton Athletic.

Top left: SUPER-ALLY SUPPORTING SUPER-CALTON:
Coisty opened our Academy.

Top right: EAST END BOYS: Tommy Burns grew
up round the corner from us. Like Walter he's a bit special.

Above: BAILLIESTON BOYS: Scottish football's finest turned
out for us, including Tommy Burns, Gerry Collins, Jim Traynor,
Alex McLeish, Chick Young, Stuart Farrell, Jonathan Watson,
Jimmy Boyle and mascot Robbie Coltrane.

Above: MARTIN & ME: Sinn Fein leader Martin McGuinness
also believes in the power to change and he invited us to Derry.

Below: ANGEL, ANGELA AND ME: Robbie Williams may have been top
of the pops but he demanded he get a game for Calton Athletic. So here he
is with me and my daughter Angela in our Scotland strip.

Of course, Lenny didn't come off the stage and touch John's hand, but a few days later I was sitting watching the six o'clock news. There was Muhammad Ali in Glasgow signing autographs for his book, and I don't need to tell you who was standing beside him shaking hands. John's vision of meeting Ali had come true as well.

Naturally, then, while we were on the plane to America we were all saying to him, 'Who are you going to meet over here, John?' For a month he'd been saying it was George Foreman. 'How are you going to meet him?'

'Don't worry,' John says. 'I'll meet him, the same as I met the Pope and the same as I met everybody else.'

So at the World Cup, his main goal was to meet George Foreman, because of his conversion to Christianity. John picked his targets because they were special, and he was convinced he was going to meet big George.

One day when we were at Daytona Beach, John was out looking for him with just a pair of shorts on. He walked along the beach for miles, and when he came back several hours later he was crimson. He had sunstroke, and we put him to bed, filling him up with liquid. He looked at death's door, with his skin ready to peel right off his back. The next morning John chapped at my door looking as right as rain. He was pure white, as if nothing had happened the day before. I couldn't believe the colour of his skin. He'd been burnt red raw ten hours before and was now as fair as snow. The Lord moves in mysterious ways, and so did John Plotts.

John wasn't finished, either. A couple of days later we went to the Mexico v. Ireland game, and we were standing outside the stadium. We discovered we weren't the only Scots there, as we heard chants about Calton Athletic. It was a lot of characters from the Tartan Army we'd met at Italia '90. Davie Main and I had seats together with a wee guy called Colin Nelson, and we asked John if he was coming in beside us. 'No, I'm away tae meet George Foreman.' We tried to persuade him he was unlikely to bump into him, but he insisted, 'Naw, I'm going to meet George Foreman. I have a funny feeling about it.' And off he went.

He had just gone when a big white stretch limousine drew up. It had blacked-out windows, and I looked at big Davie. 'I wonder.' But it wasn't George Foreman. After the game we met up with John Plotts. 'John, you were just away and a stretch limo pulled up – where did you go to?'

'I went up to the officials and asked them where George Foreman was sitting. They says he wisnae on the guest list. Ah says, "Are you sure he's no' on the guest list? I was convinced he was gonna be here." They said, "No, he's not." I says, "Who else is on the guest list, then?" And the official says, "Pelé." I says, "That'll dae. Where is he sitting?" and they put me next tae him.'

It seems the pair took up where they left off at Orly airport. John, son, you helped to make America special.

Eleven years on I was watching the Live 8 concert at Murrayfield, and Bob Geldof's on stage with a familiar football strip telling everyone he was going to wear it in bed that night. It was Renfrew United, the team that John Plotts had indeed gone on to start up. John had got through to Sir Bob. Geldof called John up on stage, and he was ushered to the front. The papers reported it all the next day, and John didn't let them down. He told them that when Bob gave him the call, 'the crowd parted like the Red Sea'.

When we were about five hours into the flight to Orlando, they started handing out the visa forms. Everybody was looking at me wondering what I was going to do. I had my two sons with us and I was racking my brain. So I started to fill it out.

Have you ever been in trouble with the police? No.
Are you an alcoholic? No.
Drug-addict? No.

I marked every one of them 'No', otherwise I would not have got in. Once I filled it in, I passed a copy to big Davie. He filled his in likewise and passed it on, everybody copying it. When the plane touched down at Orlando, we duly marched through Customs. I was the only one who got stopped, but it was just a formality. They asked me what the purpose of my visit was. I told them I was there for the World Cup. They asked me where I was staying. I told them the Quality Suites in Canada Drive. They asked me how much money I had with me. I told them £3,500 in traveller's cheques. (This was the group's kitty.) The immigration official just smiled and said, 'Have a nice day,' and that was me in. Welcome to America.

We picked up three space cruisers and were ready to head off for the apartments when someone pointed out you had to pay insurance. I reached for the traveller's cheques. Panic. The £3,500 was missing. I was frantic looking for it, but we had to do what we had done with wee Neilie: Davie paid it and we'd square up later. Christ, what a start. When we got to the apartments, I phoned home to break the bad news to my wife. I was taken aback at her calm reaction. 'Where did you look for it?'

'I've searched everywhere. I've emptied my bag, Jeanette. It's no' there.'

'Nae wonder,' she said. 'I put it in young David's bag. It's in a zip bit at the side.'

I dived over, grabbed the bag and there it was: £3,500. That lifted my spirits immediately.

The apartments turned out a treat and there were five guys in each. You got a free buffet breakfast every morning where you could eat as much as you wanted, and that kept us going all day. What I hadn't known beforehand was, as part of the deal, you got an hour's free drinking every night between 7 and 8 p.m. The alarm bells went off immediately. Anybody else with a group of 22 Scotsmen hearing about an hour's free drinking would be doing cartwheels, but I knew it could jeopardise everything. I was determined we were not going to have the problems we had in Italy. Too many people had put too much into it. The slip-up by some on the plane was just a one-off. I put the drink on the plane down to people being a bit scared and in need of something to calm their nerves. It was only about four who'd had a drink, and they weren't long-termers. But still, they knew the rules about the trip – it had to be drug- and alcohol-free. We were in America representing Calton Athletic. We were proud of our history. This was our second World Cup, and I was determined that booze wasn't going to ruin things.

On the third night in Orlando I got word that a couple of them had been down for the Happy Hour. The next night I went down 15 minutes before the free drink was on and positioned myself outside the door. Just approaching 7 p.m. the usual suspects came down. The four of them were laughing and joking, but when they saw me they nearly dropped dead. They made some excuse that they were down for something else and went away. At least I'd spoiled that night's drinking, and I thought they would take the hint. Unfortunately they didn't. The next night big Davie Main told me they were at it again. We sat down and discussed what we were going to do about it. We were going to Universal Studios the next day on a trip out of the kitty, and we made a decision there and then that they wouldn't be going.

They came crawling out of their apartments in the morning as the vans were ready to leave, and we told them they wouldn't be going. They were pissed off, but we told them we'd see them when we came back. We had a marvellous day, but when we got back the other four were half-bevvied. We told them we were going to put them all into the one apartment and called it the 'Alkie Billet'.

Within three days the boys in the Alkie Billet were coming up to us greetin' and asking to get out of there. They didn't want to be cut off from us and trapped with the other drinkers. Some had been pissing their beds. Big Davie Main had to go and practically look after them, and after about six days in the Alkie Billet they all quietened down. The next day we'd decided to go and see Ireland train. We set off on our convoy minus the Alkie Billet – they still weren't up out of their beds. Orlando's a big place, and it was a shot in the dark that we'd find the training camp. We were driving for about an hour and appeared to be lost. I asked big John, the driver, to pull in. As we stretched our legs, I said to one of the boys, 'Away ower to that building and ask if they know where the Irish are training.' As the boy was walking across to the entrance, who came walking out the door but Roy Keane. We had our banners with us and our Scottish gear on. Roy did a double-take as big Packie Bonner and a few others joined him. Packie was still at Celtic and just about to join Tommy Burns at Kilmarnock.

Packie shouted over, 'Oi, lads, the Calton boys are here.' It was great to hear that. He came over with Tommy Coyne, who had his Opal skip hat on, and he gave it to my boy Stephen and autographed it. Andy Townsend and Paul McGrath joined us, and we had a great time chatting and getting photos taken. Unknown to us we were

132

being filmed, and it would end up on the news back home later on that day. Our families couldn't believe it when they saw us back in Glasgow. But we were oblivious to it all, as we were engrossed in meeting all the players. Big Jack Charlton had joined us. It was the first time I'd met Jack, and I was impressed. He's a huge guy, and when I shook his hand it felt like a shovel. You could see that he was the gaffer and the players weren't going to mess about. I don't think that squad would mess anybody about. They'd done exceptionally well, and had beaten Italy up in New York. Nobody gave them a hope in hell, but they had a special team spirit that big Jack had built up. Hopefully some of that could rub off on Calton Athletic.

Ten minutes ago we were lost, and now we were inside the Irish training camp. One of the boys came up to us and said that Ray Stubbs of the BBC was filming and had asked whether I could come over to see him. He was about 100 yards away. I mentioned earlier that Ray Stubbs had done a documentary about Calton Athletic just before we went to the World Cup in Italy. Four years later we were banging into each other again at another World Cup, and it was great to see Ray.

Then I heard a voice asking, 'Is that Davie Bryce there?' I turned around, and it was Tam Dempsey from the Calton. He had been one of my drinking partners when we were younger. I hadn't seen him for a long time. He had his son with him, so I got my boys over to get our photographs taken.

Tam told me, 'I've seen you a couple of times in the paper, and I've always wanted to meet up with you again. I'm seven years sober.'

I thought this was a real coincidence. Here were the two of us sober at the World Cup with our kids and we'd banged into each other. And the only reason we'd met up again was that we were sober. This is what I call the gift of sobriety.

Orlando was fantastic, and the only blip was again the drunks. When we had trouble from this quarter, I went for a session in the multigym to calm down, and my son David came in. He was 15 at the time and Scottish boxing champion for his age group. He asked me about the Alkie Billet boys.

'What are you gonna dae, Da?'

He thought I was getting pumped up in the gym because there was going to be a bit of trouble. I assured him that everything was in hand. Davie Main and I had got it sorted out. But young David says, "Cos I'm wi' you, Da, if you want to set aboot them.'

'Don't worry, son,' I laughed, 'we'll handle it different.'

He couldn't believe the way they were behaving. Thankfully there were guys on the American trip that were tremendous, like big Archie, wee Walter Smith, Davie Main, young David, young Tony and J.J. – the vast majority, in fact – but there were four that were doing damage and embarrassing themselves.

People may think we were harsh in the way we treated them, and maybe we were, but we knew the damage the booze can do. Once they saw they were missing out, the Billet boys started to change and came to the Irish training ground the next time we went. When they went out at night-time, big Davie went along to look after them. Big Archie was tremendous in that respect as well.

Everybody's relatives were waiting at the airport. The Alkie Billet boys tried to put on a brave face and not show their families they had let them down, but they were still shocked after I'd told them on the plane that I didn't want to see them again. The four of them played for the football team and two of them had played in the Scottish Cup semi-finals, but they were out, even though we had two finals to play and one game for the league. Meanwhile, as our Britannia Airways flight was touching down at Glasgow airport, we burst into 'Rule Britannia, Britannia rules the air!' Although there had been a couple of incidents, USA '94 was a 100 per cent improvement on Italy.

When we got back, there was trouble ahead. About four weeks before we flew out, a friend had visited us – one I hadn't seen for years. He was going through a bad time. During our conversation he said something that shook me: 'You realise you've got two camps, Davie?'

I was taken aback. 'What do you mean, two camps?'

'Well, I was up at the other place and I could sort of sense an atmosphere, things that weren't quite right.'

I hadn't a clue that we had two camps, but when my friend mentioned it I started to look into it and found out he was right. A group wanted to split away and get funding for a methadone programme from the Health Board. It took the wind out of my sails.

These were people who had come to Calton, had seen people getting off drugs, had been involved themselves in getting off drugs, yet they were going away to set up a methadone programme that would keep people on drugs.

They were setting it up with the idea they would get people on methadone, reduce their level, then get them off and into rehabilitation. But that never materialised and their project only ran for six years.

Again, this was a learning process, but it hurt because I knew most of them well. I'd been involved in getting a lot of them off drugs and had given everyone an opportunity to do some voluntary work to see what they could do, even if they weren't a great asset to the club. This voluntary work was for their benefit. I believe that they were manipulated into breaking away and their loss was Calton Athletic's gain, as it helped us to streamline things further.

The people now with Calton Athletic were all totally committed. The split didn't destroy us because we had a management committee that was solidly behind us. It is still here today, and if they hadn't been so strong at that particular time, Calton Athletic could have been sold out.

It was a lesson, but it opened up the path to the most successful part of our history. We'd now moved into Craigpark, Dennistoun, and Davie Main and I set about restructuring. Jim Alston was the chairman at this time, and he was tremendous. He'd come as a young man to Calton, played for the team and appeared in the Scottish Cup final. He was loyal and committed at a tough time. I call him Dan now, but James is his real name – Dan the Man – and what a man he's been.

You could now only be a member of our management committee if you'd been at Calton Athletic a year, been drug-free during that year and accepted by the current committee. After three years as a member you could then be considered for the management committee if you had something to offer. The management committee was elected by the members. It was important for Calton Athletic to have a like-minded management committee, and you can't get more like-minded than former pupils, people who have come in the door as heroin-addicts, got a service and gone on to become members because they believed in Calton Athletic and what we were doing. This was to be so important in the struggles ahead against pressure from the Health Board, the Social Work and the Scottish Executive to change our policy to harm reduction.

Some in the breakaway group were after jobs and thought they could get them on methadone programmes, which would get funding. Calton Athletic wasn't about jobs. It wasn't a gravy train. With the split the Health Board and Social Work had failed to get control of our management committee, but they still had control of our core funding.

CHAPTER TWENTY-TWO

The Robertson Trust

We were back to just one camp now, and it was as if a burden had been taken off my shoulders. Meanwhile, a seed had been planted by young David that day in the gym in Orlando. He had asked me, 'How can you no' start a club for my pals and people our age and take us to the World Cup?'

He was noised up about the ones who were boozing and ungrateful. I wound him up: 'Take your pals? You're all too busy getting into gangs, shoplifting, fighting and drinking.' That was because we stayed in the East End. Young David went to a school where you'd have thought it was compulsory to smoke dope as part of the curriculum.

He knew I was joking but insisted, 'No, Da, if you and Davie Main were in charge, everything would be OK. Everybody respects both of youse.' Although still a boy, he appreciated what we were doing. 'If it wasn't for you and Davie Main, the other ones would have spoiled everything for everybody.'

It was true that there was nothing for the youngsters under 18 at this time. After school and in the summer they would sit on the bottom of the wall smoking dope but thought they would never end up junkies like the older ones. Just by being there around the fringes of the drug scene, they were being drawn in.

The seed young David planted began to germinate. It was great to get 100 people a year off drugs, but it would be much better if we could prevent thousands starting. The ones on the trip who'd caused the problems were all around 30. They had had their chance at the club. We also had to ensure that infection did not spread among the younger generation.

We were not long back from America when I got a phone call that was to change the face of Calton Athletic. It was from Sir Lachlan Maclean of the Robertson Trust. The Robertson Trust was set up by three sisters whose family had made their fortune in the whisky industry. It is mainly an educational trust to help deprived people. Sir Lachlan wanted to know if we did anything on the prevention side. When we moved into London Road, we got a call from a school in Campbelltown. They wanted us to do a presentation for their senior pupils on leaving day. We drove up, with Father Willie Slaven as our guest. The Red Cross was there, as well as Amnesty International and Alcoholics Anonymous, who were also giving presentations. Unknown to us we were getting evaluated, and a month later I got word back from Campbelltown School telling us the presentation that made the biggest impact with the pupils was Calton Athletic's. That was the first school we'd ever been in, and it wasn't to be the last.

We started to get other invitations to schools, as news of our presentation spread by word of mouth across the country. Unfortunately, at the time, none of them were in Glasgow, although I'd already had our work evaluated by Professor John McBeath at Strathclyde University, who had given it a positive report.

I explained this to Sir Lachlan, who said, 'Thank God – I've been phoning all sorts of agencies and drug projects today asking them if they have ever done anything on the prevention side, and none of them have.'

I invited him down to Dennistoun to show him around the premises and explain the format of our school presentations in more detail. We did a series of three workshops. One was called 'From Cannabis to Chaos'. We were not trying to insult anybody's intelligence; cannabis was just a possible starting point – it could quite easily have been Ecstasy to chaos, amphetamines to chaos, or, more likely, booze to chaos. Most young people drink before they ever take drugs. A very high percentage of young people take drugs while under the influence of booze. So this workshop, although it was called 'From Cannabis to Chaos', was really about where it all starts and how drugs change your life. The other workshop was called 'The Life of a Drug-Addict', which was fairly self-explanatory. The third workshop was called 'The Effects on the Family'. When people use drugs, they think they're only affecting themselves, so what harm are they doing? The reality is that they're affecting a web of other people – their mother, father, sisters, brothers, grandparents. They're all at their wits' end.

We did an introduction before the workshops to let the pupils know we were there to deglamorise something that can appear attractive to young people. I think that's the best thing you can do. If kids think it's 'uncool' and adopt the 'I widnae dae that' attitude, they're more likely to stay away from it. We started doing research on this, and after the workshops were finished we'd get feedback from the pupils. I invited Sir Lachlan to come along to one. Here was somebody who was prepared to listen to the vision that I had for the future, who agreed that prevention was better than cure. We believed that what we were doing worked. Thank God I made an impression on Sir Lachlan, as not long after we got the backing of the Robertson Trust.

A short time later we received a cheque for £80,000. Till then we had been using Calton Athletic workers to do the presentations. (The Health Board had allowed us to take on another three volunteers as staff.) The main qualification you can have in this game is experience, and the only way you can get that is if somebody gives you a chance to go in and show what you can do. We were the only project prepared to give people a chance to show what they could do without a Social Work or a Health Board qualification. I'd known for a long time that the only legitimate qualification in the drugs field is experience. The rest is just bits of paper. Those bits of paper are no good until you've got experience, and unfortunately in most places you do not have a chance to get it. We gave people the chance and they could pass it on to other people. We gave them an opportunity to volunteer at Calton Athletic and the best among them, the tried and trusted, would get better if they kept doing the right things and maintained their enthusiasm. Part of what we believed to be the route to recovery was 'you've got to give it away to keep it'. The more people you help and the more you're prepared to share, the more you'll get out of it. Life works in funny ways.

The only condition set by the Robertson Trust was that they wanted to remain anonymous. I had no problem with that, although I wanted to tell people that somebody had been extremely good to us.

I believe in my heart and soul that Calton Athletic helped to change attitudes towards recovering drug-addicts through doing presentations to schoolkids. We were the people who started it in Scotland, at that school in Campbelltown, and, through word of mouth, we had taken it to this stage where we had £80,000 from the Robertson Trust. I had to think how I was going to get the most out of this money. It would all be directed at a word people don't want to mention – prevention. I believed in prevention, and when I spoke to Sir Lachlan that day I must have convinced him of this.

The first thing I did was employ a schools coordinator, Elspeth Hirst. Elspeth had been the Calton Athletic aerobics teacher for the previous seven years. I'd first met her several years before in the Calton area, where she was involved in youth work. I hadn't seen her for a number of years, until one day I bumped into her down in Marco's. She told me she was an aerobics teacher. Seven years down the line, she was ideal for the schools team, as I knew she was a qualified schoolteacher as well, and that would lend us extra credibility. We also got nine volunteers who we were going to train for the new service. The Robertson Trust helped with expenses for the training, as we wanted to train the people on the schools team seven days a week.

Our 'School Drugs Awareness' team didn't have to look for work – we were still getting requests. The volunteers were doing more hours than full-time workers elsewhere and getting job satisfaction. There was still some money left from the Robertson Trust, and I thought, 'What can I do with that?' I remembered the conversation

140

I'd had with young David about him and his pals. They were 16 now and had been playing proper team football. Their team stopped at Under-16s, though, and they didn't have an Under-18s. I asked him to bring some of his pals up, and he brought five: Steven, Alan Mitchell, Derek Colquhoun, Sceptre and Paul Collins. I told them that if they were prepared to do the right thing, we could maybe start a football team for them. Doing the right thing meant their participation wouldn't be just about football; it would mean staying off drugs and booze. They were keen, so by the start of the 1994–95 football season Calton Athletic had an Under-18s team. They were an instant success, and nearly won the national trophy in their first year, following in the footsteps of the more established team. I couldn't know the full significance of it at the time, but this was to be one of the best moves we ever made.

The Robertson Trust had given me £80,000 and let me be flexible with it, and that's what I was doing, not putting all my eggs in the one basket. Four of the boys in the Under-18s went on to become professionals; two of them – Alan Mitchell and Derek Colquhoun – with Stranraer. Two of the other boys – Barry Connell and Willie Limmond – went on to become professional boxers. This idea of prevention was working. Apart from those four that became professionals, the rest of them were all good boys who had got jobs or were serving apprenticeships. After six months the Robertson Trust broke their cover and over a five-year period gave us £600,000.

CHAPTER TWENTY-THREE

Euro '96

Scotland had qualified for Euro '96, and it was being held in England, so there was no way we were going to miss it. This time we were taking the Under-18s with us too. They had just lost in the semi-finals of the Scottish Cup, where we were very unlucky to succumb to Dundee Newryfield. The score finished at 2–1, and in the last seconds we'd hit the crossbar. I believe we would have won in extra-time and probably won the final. These were talented boys who accepted the same conditions as the older team. These boys weren't recovering drug-addicts but young boys who were growing up in drug-infested communities, and we were giving them the chance to be involved in something that would be drug- and alcohol-free. In doing so, they got to come to the European Championships with us, as they were able to save up with us as well.

My cousin Norman in London arranged accommodation at the Travel Inn in Romford. A room was £35 a night, and we had four people in each room, which was very cost-effective when you consider we were near London.

Everybody was expecting trouble in the European Championships, with English fans up against those from Germany and Holland. We were going to be based near London, so sobriety was essential. Another major worry was in getting tickets, especially as England were in our group and you couldn't get Scotland v. England tickets for love nor money. We had to turn to the SFA, but we'd joined their travel club too late. Just prior to Euro '96, though, I was approached by Tony Higgins of the Professional Football Players Association. He had been commissioned by the SFA to do an anti-drugs video for the players of all the professional clubs in Scotland, and he asked Calton Athletic if we'd get involved in it. Davie Main and I did a bit in it and the video was sent to every senior club in Scotland. It was actually not bad, and we were delighted to be involved. Now I wrote to Jim Farry, secretary of the SFA, and told him that 32 of us were going to Euro '96 and were looking for tickets. We didn't want them for nothing. We'd pay. We knew it was late and there was a big demand, but could he do us a special favour? And, to give wee Jim his due, he came up trumps.

We travelled up from Romford for the first game against Holland in Birmingham the day before to collect the tickets from Jim Farry at Villa Park. Our three minibuses arrived to find the police had the place surrounded. They were not letting anybody near it, but I explained the situation and the police took us over to the UEFA official. He told us, 'We will let you into the car park if you promise to behave yourself.' We had no problems about that. We were representing Calton Athletic. While we were down there waiting, people like Derek Johnstone and Hazel Irvine from the BBC were walking past, and people were getting autographs. Then we noticed an awful lot of photographers around this guy, so we walked over to find out who it was.

It was Kubilay Turkyilmaz, the Swiss hero who had scored against England. Turkyilmaz caught sight of us because we were all in our kilts, and he asked me if he could wear my kilt for the photographs. I duly obliged – luckily I was not a true Scot that day – and Turkyilmaz appeared on TV and all over the papers in my kilt, surrounded by Calton Athletic. The Scotland squad duly arrived in their bus and we were singing to them and got their autographs. This was the first time we had met up with the Scotland squad, but it would not be the last.

The SFA sold us tickets for the Holland and Switzerland games, but they couldn't help us with England tickets because there was such a demand.

The next day we all got up early, got our gear on and painted our faces with the Saltire. I must say it looked very impressive, 32 men, all fit-looking in our Scottish gear, bursting to give our hearts and souls to support Scotland. We had travelled down to Birmingham town centre to soak up the atmosphere. As we were getting nearer the square, it was mobbed, and as we turned into it all we saw was a sea of orange. There must have been 10,000 Dutch fans singing, but when we arrived the place went silent. With all the hype in the media about the threat of violence, maybe they were expecting trouble, but knowing about their rivalry with Germany we started singing, 'If you hate the fucking Germans, clap your hands.' The Dutch started clapping, then they started singing, 'If you hate the fucking English, clap your hands,' and we started clapping. Then we started, 'If you love Dutch football, clap your hands.' The experience we had there was unique. I know it wouldn't have been the same if the 32 of us had been drunk – but we were sober. The Dutch could sense the friendliness from us, and that was a great start before the game. We marched down to the match singing our hearts out, meeting people outside the stadium that we had met in America and Italy. The Tartan Army are a unique mob. They are proud to be ambassadors for Scotland. They feel good about behaving themselves better than the English, and we were no different. We loved it. Scotland got a draw, and we still had England and Switzerland to play.

We went straight back to London, as the next morning we were heading to Jersey for three days to play a couple of matches. An old school pal of mine, a boy called Jim McFarlane, had arranged it. I hadn't seen him for years, and we had missed each other a couple of times when he had been in Glasgow, so I was looking forward to seeing him. When we had been in Italy, I'd met a guy from Jersey at the campsite. He and his wife were over there on their honeymoon, and they knew my old pal Jim McFarlane. The boy told me that Jim was doing well in Jersey. He had his own business and was running a football team. I had subsequently contacted Jim a few months before we went to the Championships and told him we had a wee bit of time between the Dutch game and the Wembley game, and it would be nice to play a couple of games of football. Jim took care of all the arrangements in Jersey. He got us cheap crossings on the ferry from Weymouth and accommodation at an old Pontin's camp. The chalets were fantastic, and we got our breakfast, dinner and evening meal all for £8 a day. I don't know how Jim did it, unless he paid for it himself, but I couldn't thank him enough, because Jersey was tremendous.

On the last day Jim said to us, 'After the game, Davie, I'll take you boys back to the club and we'll have a drink.'

I told him, 'The boys don't drink, Jim.'

We went back to his club anyway, and Jim had provided a buffet. 'I'll tell you what, Davie, I've fixed it for all the young ones to go to a disco next to the club, and you and I can have a chat with each other.' And that's what happened. The boys got into the disco for nothing, and Jim and I reminisced about old times. I suggested we go and collect the others, as the disco was ready to come out. Jim said, 'Davie, the boys are on holiday. They've been great when they've been over here; they've not caused any problems, and they're in a disco. I've been in it – it's full of lassies and beautiful-looking women. Maybe some of them's had a drink. But you cannae blame them.'

I agreed that would be all right.

'Are you sure?'

'Aye, it'll be OK.'

Finally he took us back to the disco and the boys were all up on the dance floor giving it yahoo, all looking great, and Jim couldn't believe it. None of them had had a drink, yet they had taken over the dance floor.

Back in London we couldn't get tickets for the England game. In a way I was pretty glad, because when the Scots and the English meet, anything can happen. The boys had all been sober up to this point. This was better than expected, because before we went some of the older workers were casting doubts about taking the young ones, saying they were young and irresponsible and wouldn't behave. But I knew differently. I had spent the last year with these boys, and I could see how they were responding. I felt quite comfortable about it, and we had no problems whatsoever. It was a big test going up to Wembley to soak up the atmosphere on the Saturday morning. It was a great experience, and we met a lot of people, but an hour before the game we headed back to our accommodation to watch it on TV.

We were just going into the Tube down this massive flight of stairs, when coming down towards us were about 500 English supporters. It was the National Front team, all skinheads and about 17 st. But there were about a thousand police surrounding them. Thank Christ, I thought, as we got past them. Back at our accommodation we watched the game. Scotland did well, although they ended up losing 2–0. People can speak about the penalty which Gary McAllister missed, but they gave it their best shot and we still had a slight chance against the Swiss. At least we could maybe beat them. That would salvage something out of it.

We enjoyed the Swiss game in Birmingham – Scotland had given it everything they could. It had been a good competition for us.

On our final night in Romford my cousin Norman had arranged a night for us in this rockabilly place which had an Elvis Presley theme night. After the meal the staff started the music and were coming round the tables with a microphone. I got up to sing as I knew all the words because I'm an old Elvis fan. We'd had our problems in Italy and America, but this time, with 32 and half of them under 18, it had gone perfectly. Everybody had stayed sober. The young boys were proof that prevention was working.

The Under-18s were demonstrating exactly what they could do if given the right support and encouragement. A lot of good things were happening, but the most important one in terms of putting our name on an international stage was *Trainspotting*.

CHAPTER TWENTY-FOUR

Trainspotting

I had just arrived back from my holidays on a Monday morning when Davie Main told me, 'I've got a smashing book, Davie. My girlfriend gave me it. It's called *Trainspotting*. You've got to read it.'

A couple of hours later I was sitting in my office having a chat with Elspeth Hirst, the school coordinator, when she mentioned a book. 'Davie, my friend phoned me up last night and told me she was reading a great book called *Trainspotting*, and that I must get it.'

Then I joined Eamon Doherty, our group worker, for a cup of tea, and he was reading a book. 'What's that you're reading?'

'Aw this, it's brilliant, Davie. You've got to read it.'

'Don't tell me,' I said. 'It's called *Trainspotting*.'

'How dae ye know? Have ye read it? If no', I'll gie it you efter us.'

I told Eamon that within the space of a few hours three different people had told me about this book. It gets even better. About half past four that afternoon I got a phone call from a guy called Danny Boyle. I'd never heard of him but he explained to us that he was a director. He had made a film called *Shallow Grave*, which I had seen and liked. Danny explained he was working on a new project, and had I read a book called *Trainspotting*?

I told him I hadn't read a book called *Trainspotting* and had never heard of it till that day, but it must be bloody brilliant because he was now the fourth person to tell me about it. I told him three of my staff had recommended the book. Danny told me they were having difficulties turning the book into a film script and capturing the reality of being a drug-addict. Could he come and see us? I told him I would be delighted to see him. Danny came and saw me the next day, and we spoke at great length. I told him about the club. I let him come to our Monday-night meeting and he sat there and listened. The Monday-night meeting is an important one at Calton Athletic.

If I didn't like the look of Danny or had the slightest misgivings, he wouldn't have got in the door. But as I said, we'd spent a bit of time talking about the club and the book and I told him we were prepared to be involved. I had faith in him. After the Monday night meeting he arranged to come back. In the meantime I read the book. I thought Irvine Welsh did a smashing job depicting how things were. It was very accurate, had a lot of black humour and caught the tragedy. I thought it was possible that as a film it could actually deglamorise drugs.

I felt that's what Danny Boyle, Andrew Macdonald, John Hodge and the production team of Figment Films intended. There was a government advertising campaign at the time, but it was having a negative effect. Instead *Trainspotting* went on to become the best anti-drugs message the country had produced. The next time Danny came to Calton, he asked if he could bring someone with him. He arrived with a young man with a skinhead, hair cut down to the wood. I thought he was maybe Danny's nephew and had a drug problem and needed help. It was Ewan McGregor.

They were about to start shooting at the old Gallagher's cigarette factory, which was handily about 100 yards from our new premises. I invited Ewan to the Monday-night meeting, along with Danny Boyle for a second time. Ewan just sat and listened, taking it all in. I never really asked him how he felt about the meeting, and I shook his hand afterwards. That night's meeting made quite an impression on me, and I'm sure it must have done on Ewan and Danny. From then on *Trainspotting* involved us at every opportunity. Near the beginning of the film there is a scene in which the Trainspotters are playing football against a team in blue shirts. That team was Calton Athletic, and the players were all recovering drug-addicts.

They also had to reshoot a scene more than a dozen times, as one of the boys was supposed to get blootered in the face by a football. All of our best players kept missing, until our worst player, wee Colin Nelson, insisted on having a go. Colin got it right first time, and it went straight into the film. I like to think those players have got that memory for the rest of their lives. Quite a few other people at the club got used as extras, and we built up a great rapport. One night Danny Boyle came down to our Tuesday session at Crown Point, where we did aerobics and football training, and we spoke at length. He asked if there was any possibility we could lend him one of the boys from the club as an adviser on the set when they were doing drug scenes. I told him I'd think about it. I got back to him in ten minutes. Eamon Doherty would do it, and he went on set and did a smashing job. Eamon showed them the right way to inject, and all a junkie's other habits.

At the end of the filming the Trainspotters had a farewell party. I didn't go, because I knew the booze and everything else would be flowing – after all, they're actors – but big Davie took the rest of them and they all enjoyed themselves and nobody got drunk. I was also not feeling too well, and I didn't want to put myself under pressure. I met Andrew Macdonald, the producer, before the party and wished him all the best. He told us they would keep in contact and they were going to give Calton Athletic the proceeds of the premiere. I thought this was a great gesture. The club had done well by them, with the extras getting themselves a couple of quid. *Trainspotting* never caused the club any problems. They were genuine people and I'm still friendly with them today.

This was only early days with the Trainspotters. The film went on to become the biggest success the British film industry had had at that time, and I was not surprised – these guys had talent. They also hadn't forgotten where their old arses came from, and they had a bit of humility, particularly Danny Boyle. I was really impressed with him. Danny is one of the nicest and most genuine guys I have met. He kept in touch and went on to play in a couple of Calton Athletic games – unfortunately for him, always on the wrong side. John

Hodge, the writer, was a genuine and interesting man. He's a doctor as well as a writer, and he was to play for Calton Athletic when we took on a team of English celebrities in 1996. Andy Macdonald is a shrewd businessman, but very generous with it and another good friend of Calton Athletic's.

Just before the premiere everybody at Calton Athletic had been invited to a special screening of *Trainspotting* in the Odeon cinema in Glasgow. We were the only people in the audience. We didn't really know what the film was going to be like. Most of us had read the book, but if we are honest we probably still had reservations about how it would turn out. We sat down, and as soon as the film started and the football scene came on and the players saw themselves, everybody relaxed. At the end we were gobsmacked. We thought it was a tremendous film, and that watching it and seeing ourselves in it was a tremendous privilege. The film sent out a lot of important messages that we could all relate to. All 80 of us stood up to give it a standing ovation.

Some people said it glamorised drugs. Nonsense. It deglamorised drugs. How? It highlighted the HIV issue. The last one in the film to start injecting was the first one to get the virus. These sorts of things happen; I've seen it myself. The film also vividly illustrated the cot death of the baby of two of the drug-addicts. If you look at cot death statistics, a high percentage are children of at least one drug-addict. It also exposed the methadone myth. When Renton is going through his withdrawals and his mum and dad come into the room, he pleads with them, 'Please, get me some methadone,' and his parents refuse. 'No, methadone didn't work the last time.' They are right, methadone doesn't work. And I think that's got to be highlighted to an awful lot of people who think that it's the golden cure. It's not the cure if you want to come off drugs. Even at the end of the film the characters were still ripping each other off. That's addicts for you. Anybody who saw the film and hadn't used drugs before but afterwards said, 'I think I'll start injecting heroin,' must come from another planet. It showed the realities of drug use. It wasn't all doom and gloom. There are the funny bits. There are the kicks. But it took you to the dark side, the withdrawals, the infections and the cot deaths. *Trainspotting* gave Calton Athletic a platform outside Britain and attracted media interest from all over the world. It also proved a real financial bonus for the club. The Trainspotters weren't fair-weather friends and didn't forget us. We were all looking forward to the premiere, and the big night finally arrived.

It would probably have been one of the biggest nights of my life, but I was just coming out of the intensive care unit at the time. I had been in the hospital with heart problems and an infection. I hadn't been feeling well for a couple of years. I'd maybe been in and out of the hospital three or four times. Maybe it was the strain of the work and everything else. The night just before the premiere my wife visited me and told me she wasn't going to go, with me in hospital. She had been involved in the film as well, though, and I told her to go. She went and it was fantastic, so I was told. The Trainspotters laid on a party and they did not spare anything. Everybody from Calton Athletic enjoyed themselves, mingling with the stars. They knew them by this time. They had been working with them. They had been extras. It was good meeting up with them again. Well, for them, not me – I was in the hospital. But they sent us word anyway to the hospital via my wife that they would like to play a football match and raise some more money. I thought this was a smashing idea, and it became a reality. In short, our experience with the Trainspotters in 1996 and beyond was very positive. They're good people. The best.

Ewan McGregor was no exception to this. As I said, when he turned up on our doorstep with Danny, I thought he was an addict. He was right into the role already. It shows how good he is that here was I, someone who had worked with hundreds of young addicts, thinking he was one too. Ewan fitted in so well. He was really eager to learn from our members and always showed great respect for them. You knew Ewan would go on to greater things.

When our School Drugs Awareness team visited Crieff High School in his home town, I wrote to Ewan. When I read *Porno*, the follow-up to *Trainspotting*, I tried to convince Ewan to take the role, although he said he was reluctant to do it. He's the only guy to play Renton for me. I thought Irvine Welsh had once again captured it perfectly ten years on – how cocaine was now the drug.

Ewan is a lovely fellow. He turned out for Calton Athletic in charity games and he has a really nice family. Any guy that is as good to his granny as Ewan is has to be brand new. One night I was watching Parky on telly – Ewan was on Michael Parkinson's chat show – and I just about fell off my seat when Ewan mentioned me, his pal Davie Bryce. Ewan will always be a pal.

Bobby Carlyle was the biggest headcase in *Trainspotting*. And that's a compliment. His character Begbie didn't take drugs, or, rather, he took one out of a glass, alcohol. What Irvine Welsh caught brilliantly and Bobby did a magnificent job of in the role was that alcohol is responsible for more crime, violence and drug addiction than anything else. Bobby is another helluva nice guy. He did not forget us and came back to turn out for us at Baillieston.

I can't speak about *Trainspotting* without mentioning the main man, Irvine Welsh. He's a great writer and I've read all his stuff from *Trainspotting* to *Porno*. An accolade for Irvine is that he has changed a word in the English language worldwide. You mention 'trainspotting' anywhere and people will immediately think of the book and the film, not some guy in an anorak with a flask in a railway station taking doon train numbers in a notebook. It's a modern classic.

More importantly for me, he is a good friend. I respect his work and his insight into the drugs scene, but respect him even more as a person. Like myself, Irvine got involved in running and started with a marathon, graduated to a half-marathon and then a 10 km run. Some may say that's arse fae elbow, but maybe that's the sort of guys we are. Irvine is a great guy, someone you can count on, and I'm delighted to be his pal. His life has changed tremendously as well, but he has never forgotten where his backside came from. He's a big Hibs fan, but as a bluenose I won't hold that against him. He's a smashing big guy and I hope he keeps that pen going.

CHAPTER TWENTY-FIVE

Sad State of Affairs

Such was Calton Athletic's reputation by now that I was invited to join Scotland Against Drugs (SAD) when it was set up in 1996 by Michael Forsyth, then Scottish Secretary. I was impressed with some of the people on board: Cardinal Winning, John Scott, editor of the *Evening Times* in Glasgow, and Gus Macdonald from Scottish Television, who went on to become Lord Macdonald. However, what I wasn't aware of was that SAD were struggling badly with their credibility, and that was why I was invited on board.

SAD had been coming under attack from across the drugs field, particularly from folk in Edinburgh. It was decided that SAD should go out and win the hearts and minds of communities across Scotland with a roadshow. SAD's director and PR team were very keen that we be involved. I thought this was because they believed in what we were doing. We agreed to join them, although even then I realised it was more a PR exercise than anything else. But I was taken aback at the hostility to SAD when the roadshow reached Edinburgh.

One man in particular shocked me when he stood up and said he had nothing against Calton Athletic. In fact, he said, he had a lot of respect for us, but what he couldn't understand was what we were doing on a platform with the likes of David Macauley, Jack Irvine and David Whitton? Macauley was the director of SAD and Irvine and Whitton were the PR gurus taken on board.

I started taking stock of what was happening at other venues. I had given SAD my total support to start with, but I had been naive. They were inexperienced, the structure was all wrong and there was far too much emphasis on PR. Most of the staff weren't suitable for the job.

SAD had a big budget, but none of it came anywhere near Calton Athletic. As a council member I couldn't really see where the big bucks were going, except on advertising and PR. When we travelled on the roadshow to places such as Inverness, Oban and Edinburgh, we paid our own way, while the SAD officials would be put up in hotels. We'd caught on by now that we were being used. We had tons of credibility and they wanted some of it. The SAD council had started off full of enthusiasm, but, slowly and surely, people had drifted away. One of the first to go was Gus Macdonald. They were discussing the advertising strategy at one meeting and big Gus said he thought Calton Athletic should be used throughout the whole campaign, but his suggestion was never taken up. A lot of good ideas that we passed on were also never acted on, and if they were, SAD would always try to pass them off as their own.

Meanwhile, few of their ideas worked. They started the Challenge Fund, which was open to community drugs projects to apply to for funding. Part of the criteria was you had to find 50 per cent of the money yourself, but it soon became apparent how difficult it was for a drugs group that was already stretched for resources to find even a third of the money. We applied to them, the same as everybody else, to fund our School Drugs Awareness team. With the help of the Robertson Trust we had been able to get a schools coordinator, a couple of full-time staff and nine volunteers. The project we came up with for funding was to turn our volunteers into full-time workers. The three-month pilot scheme would be an ideal opportunity to gauge whether working full-time made them more productive and professional. The scheme was very successful, and we delivered a service to 3,000 pupils. We dished out questionnaires that we had developed. The kids would fill them in, listen to the presentation, get a chance to give feedback and then fill in the second part. We didn't restrict this approach to just schools. We were doing parents talks at night on the same model.

So here was this one project delivering a service for the pupils, teachers and parents. This time we had an evaluation done by Professor Neil McKeganey of the Centre for Drug Misuse Research at the University of Glasgow, and insiders told me it was very positive. I know that Neil McKeganey had applied to the Scottish Office for further funding for the next two years to make the evaluation and the research more meaningful. But for some reason the Scottish Office turned it down. We were halfway through a school term, but the full-time workers had to go back to being volunteers. I had a very difficult job trying to persuade those that had lost their jobs to finish off the school term and still give it their best shot.

I was very upset about this and vented my opinion at a SAD council meeting, maybe expecting to get some financial help from some direction, whether it be the chairman, Sir Tom Farmer, or Marks & Spencer, one of the companies supporting the agency. I got sympathetic words, but that was all. However, the Robertson Trust realised this was an injustice and increased their funding to the end of the school term to allow the original volunteers to remain full-time, and that helped us to carry on and complete our busiest, most successful school term to date.

Meanwhile, Tom Farmer had dreamed up this idea of sending two people 'in recovery' to the South Pole in an expedition made up of young people from all over the world. They would travel to Argentina and then on to the South Pole. On returning to their own countries, they would share that experience with schoolkids as an alternative to drugs. They were looking for two volunteers and put the feelers out for one male and one female. The boy that we put forward, Mark McLaughlin, was an ideal candidate who had been doing very well at the club. He came from the Baillieston area of Glasgow and had been involved in the School Drugs Awareness team as a volunteer and gone on to become a full-time worker. Mark had a special gift. He was a good communicator and had a good appearance that the kids could relate to. SAD accepted Mark onto the scheme and found a suitable girl themselves.

When Mark came back from the South Pole, he was full of enthusiasm. This dwindled, though, when the second part of his appointment – talking about his experience in schools – came to an end after three months, and if it wasn't for the Robertson Trust he wouldn't have been kept on in full-time employment.

Meanwhile the SAD crew would head for the nightclubs, trying to make themselves acceptable to the young people out clubbing. By now I realised how phoney it all was. SAD was there for the wrong reason. It was a PR exercise, and nothing really to do with what the drugs field was about. They were trying to create spin, but instead created a lot of division.

This was a genuine pity, because some of those originally invited onto the council were good people who wanted to make a difference. I enjoyed sitting next to Cardinal Winning, who took me aside one day. He told me he'd been informed I was the David Bryce who used to be the Grand Master of the Orange Lodge in Scotland. 'It isnae me,' I said. We had a good laugh about it, but I started to realise the lengths that some folk would go to to ruin my credibility. The cardinal didn't take long to realise he had been misinformed – if he ever believed it in the first place – but he wanted to mark my card that people were trying to undermine me. I had met Tom Winning before at Cardross in 1986, when Willie Blaney was opening his first Aids exhibition and he came along. He was an archbishop then, but now he was a cardinal. I got good vibes off him, and without his support I don't think we would have got into as many Roman Catholic schools as we have over the years with our schools team. Tom Winning, who is sadly no longer with us, was a good man who cared about the people and communities suffering because of drug addiction. He never caused us any problems, and it was good to get that misunderstanding sorted out about the Orange Order.

I also got good vibes from Gus Macdonald. He was enthusiastic at first about SAD, but Gus wasn't daft. He looked at the make-up of the council and obviously decided he was wasting his time. I wish I had made the same decision at that time, but it took me a bit longer. While Gus was there, he invited us over to Ibrox one night as a guest in his box. It was a smashing night. Rangers were playing Grasshoppers in the European Cup. We had a pre-match meal and I met his wife. We got on, as Sarah's family had been involved in boxing, and my son David was the current Scottish champion in his age group. At the end of the night you got a souvenir, a beautiful tankard.

Big Gus said, 'Davie, you've got three kids, haven't you?'

'Aye.'

'Here, take three of them.'

Fair play, Gus – we've still got them. I was glad to see Gus go on and do well as a government minister, as I was sure he would.

Another smashing guy I met at SAD was big John Scott, the editor of the *Evening Times*. John was involved in these pilot projects and had put forward the Football Against Drugs festival that the *Evening Times* ran for a couple of years. The festival got involved in the Soccer Sevens for schools. There would be regional knockout stages and a final day where all the kids would come and play. It was a good way of pulling young people together and one of the few other things in the Challenge Fund that was successful.

I don't know what happened to all the others put forward to the Challenge Fund, but Calton Athletic's two projects were better than any that materialised. SAD's main priority was supposed to be about prevention, and our School Drugs Awareness programme was staring them in the face. It was the most successful project not just in Scotland but probably the UK at the time, but in spite of the good evaluation we received from Professor McKeganey we were still funding that project by ourselves. There's never been any cash from the Scottish Executive or SAD. We've relied solely on the Robertson Trust. Today the project still stands up to scrutiny and evaluation. Others have not had to put their stuff on the table to be evaluated in the way that we did, but they have received SAD backing.

In 1996 we moved into premises in College Street with the *Big Issue*. A funding opportunity had arisen again through a SAD pilot scheme with the same criterion as before – find private money which would be matched by SAD. The first pilot project had been backed by the Robertson Trust, but this time we were backed by the Trainspotters – Figment Films, GB Posters and Gerry McGinn Construction. College Street was where our new Under-21s project would be based, a step up from the Under-18s. Through founding the Under-18s team we realised there were a lot of people out there in the under-21 age group who weren't getting a service that was more than prevention, but a programme for change. I'd had concerns about the young people in this age group for a number of years, and although it wasn't ideal putting them in beside the older addicts, it was all that we had to offer. Doing so was fraught with problems, though, as the younger addicts could fall under the influence of the older ones, and most of those were infected.

I was determined we'd do something for them, and we came up with the Under-21s project for SAD, which would be quite unique. It would be *for* young people run *by* young people. We had had a lot of good young people coming through the door over the years, and I don't know how they made it, but they did. And a lot more would have made it if we had introduced the Under-21s programme earlier. The project cost £106,000, and we raised £66,000. Instead of a three-month pilot, like the schools team, it would be five months, and it would be researched and evaluated by Rebecca Gordie from the University of Glasgow. Once again we were open to evaluation and research.

Here we were with the School Drugs Awareness team evaluated twice by university researchers, yet nobody else in the field had put their project on the table even once. We weren't worried about putting our Under-21s project up for evaluation. We had nothing to hide and knew it would be successful. The Under-18s football team and project had been a success, and some of the boys who had come through it would be providing the service at College Street. We officially opened the College Street Academy in December 1996. At the opening night Sir Lachlan asked us why I called it the Academy. 'Well,' I said, 'apart from noising some people up, it is going to be an academy of excellence. If young people are interested in football, there'll be a real coach to teach them and we'll give them a lifestyle to match their physical ability.'

It would be an academy of training not just for the football team but also for group workers. We would open the place up to other organisations, who could come and be trained. We would be an alternative to all the harm-reduction training in Scotland at this time. Harm reduction wasn't the be all and end all. There was certainly a place for it, but there had to be a place for prevention and rehabilitation. It was slow in coming, though. To make progress we had to go around making these deals for pilot schemes with SAD. Apart from the responsibility of delivering a service, we were also always having to find funding.

College Street was good for us as it gave us the chance to demonstrate we could provide everything under the one roof. We'd started off as a football team. Then, when we got our first premises on London Road, we were able to put more of our ideas into practice. We were naive enough to think that the people coming to us would be people who had just come out of rehabilitation residential units or prison and who wanted to continue their recovery in an after-care programme, but the reality is it never worked out like that. The people who came to the premises were still using drugs. We had to detox them before we could put them on the programme. Then we'd put them on a rehab programme for three months, but it takes longer than three months to fully recover. There had to be some form of after-care service, and we had to start to create it. After-care service is all fine and dandy, but for true and meaningful recovery it's all about jobs. At the end of 1996, thanks to SAD's funding, we were finally able to achieve that.

It's the best thing that I'd seen going through SAD's system. We were getting to young people before they became infected. There was a myth out there about addiction. In the past people who didn't inject drugs weren't seen as a problem. This was the wrong message to send out. We were telling people to come back when they had needles sticking out of their groins and were infected. But addiction is nothing to do with injecting. People are addicted before they inject. When you stick a needle into your groin, you've already lost control, and it's drugs that make you lose it.

There were many lessons to be learned in this game. When we started off, we thought we could cure the world. Then we realised that the only people you can help are those who want help. Even wanting help doesn't guarantee anything, but at least we can work with people who are committed to being clean. I was confident about the Under-21s service at College Street. I'd be based there to lend my support and supervision to the project, along with the schools team. Ally McCoist did the honours at the official Craigpark opening, where we had a fundraiser which included wine tasting and an auction of football regalia from both Old Firm clubs. The amount of money we raised, Camelot would match pound for pound. We gave the bidding an upper ceiling of £5,000, but at the end of the night we collected £10,000 from Camelot. A lovely gesture – the money was needed and I can't thank the Camelot people enough. Ally's got a smashing personality, and he certainly did the business for us that night. Tom Farmer turned up as well and contributed his £10 for coming in the door. For reasons that will become apparent, I got Tom to sign the tenner. I framed it and stuck it on the wall at Craigpark.

Several months beforehand, Tom had come to our annual dance and awards ceremony. These ceremonies are very moving occasions, and Tom no doubt was touched, the same as anybody else who was there. That night there were Jimmy Boyle, Sir Lachlan, officials from the Health Board and David Macauley from SAD. During the ceremony I called Tom up, along with other VIPs, to present the awards. After Tom had handed one over, he grabbed the microphone. He told everybody how impressed he was with Calton Athletic and how he'd been wondering what he could do for us. And he had come up with the answer. For the next year he was going to sponsor Calton Athletic in a big way. Not Calton Athletic the football team – he was going to sponsor the whole thing. Everybody was gobsmacked and delighted. After all Tom was ranked the second richest man in Scotland in a 'Rich List' that year, and here he was giving us a guarantee in front of everybody.

The next day the media arrived, and we took part in a publicity stunt, jumping up in the air like Kwik-Fit fitters. This was in 1996. Almost ten years later we still haven't received anything from Sir Tom, apart from his tenner, which is why I framed it. Not a bean. I can't understand somebody making statements like that in public and not living up to them. The only excuse or explanation I can give is he must have got carried away with the emotion of the ceremony. Then, when he went into the SAD office on Monday, his advisers probably told him, 'You can't do that with Calton Athletic. Everybody else will be upset.'

They knew Calton Athletic were doing the best work in this field, but they couldn't upset people out there. They were looking after themselves while trying to buy friends with funding and investment in projects that had no chance of success. I still find it hard to come to terms with Tom Farmer's behaviour. I couldn't act like that. I have been to many places, and if I say I'll sponsor people or I will do something, I do it. Tom didn't get any pressure put on him that night. He made the sponsorship offer himself. I'm prepared to give him the benefit of the doubt that he genuinely meant what he said at the time. He was impressed with Calton Athletic. He'd seen the awards ceremony. He'd been the chair of SAD and he was looking for decent projects. Here he had found something that he was going to sponsor, but I believe his advisers couldn't handle it because they couldn't control Calton Athletic.

Still, the opening at College Street was a tremendous night. Four years later Glasgow City Council would try to open 'academies' at Glasgow Green. You bet your life the idea came from Calton Athletic. People were prepared to steal our ideas and never admit they were ours, but they never stole the people who could implement them, which was a mistake. You've got to have the right people to do the job: people who have been trained properly and who have a passion for it.

Another source that helped us to pull it all together at College Street was the *Daily Record*. They were trying to get their street sales up and they had approached Calton Athletic about our young graduates selling the papers. I was a bit offended at first, thinking was this all they thought our young folk were good for – selling newspapers? But they explained they would give them an hourly rate for the job, and they would have to pay tax and insurance. Some of the young ones said, 'Fuck that, I'm no' selling papers. I didnae come here to sell papers.' But when it became known that the club thought it would be a good idea, and if they stuck at it they could save up and maybe come to Jersey with us in the summer of 1997, there was more enthusiasm.

We all had a lot to look forward to in 1997. In the space of a year after opening the College Street premises, we had doubled the amount of people coming through the door, while Craigpark had turned into our women's services base. Going into 1997, we'd completed the full picture.

CHAPTER TWENTY-SIX

Rest in Peace

College Street was a good way to finish off 1996, but there was a personal downside as, on the day it opened, I'd just buried my sister Moira. She was 18 when I was born, and she brought me up. Her heart condition meant she couldn't work, so she stayed home and spoiled me rotten. Moira was one of those people you never heard anyone say a bad word about. She was well liked by everyone who knew her and generous to a fault. But it got to the stage where her heart condition wore her out. Tragically, she passed away, and Moira was not the only relative I lost during this period.

When we opened our first premises in 1991, my sister Wilma had been one of the first to volunteer, and she did the dinners for our women's programme. Wilma had been a sceptic, but she'd become so proud of me, after seeing the change I went through. She volunteered the services of her man, Walter Smith, who I always kidded was blessed with the same name as the great Waldo, the Rangers and Scotland manager. Walter was on our management committee. Wilma had a wicked sense of humour, sarcastic like myself. She was diagnosed with cancer and eight weeks later was dead at only forty-eight. Her main concern in her last days was her man, who idolised her. She put on such a brave face but wanted to see Walter all right.

My mother would outlive all three of her daughters, as Ann suffered from emphysema like myself. Steroids initially helped her, but she died suddenly. The hardest thing I have ever had to do was go and tell my mother that Ann had died. I tried to pick my mother up, but she loved them all so dearly. At her age a woman should have her daughters to look after her. My Jeanette adopted that role.

Ann's death was also very hard on her daughters, who had lost their brother only a few years before. I have to admit it was not easy for me in a six-year period dealing with the deaths of my nephew, three sisters and then my mother. I had to be strong and organise the funerals. I put on a brave face and never really gave myself time to grieve. So much was happening at Calton Athletic, and I was having problems with statutory agencies, but compared to my personal loss all that was easy.

I never thought of drink or drugs to kill the pain, and I am proud of that. It would have been a slap in the face to my mother and sisters if I had been drunk at their funerals. I had to handle it with dignity. It didn't mean I was not hurting. It was hell, but my wife Jeanette was tremendous. She was a rock. She looked after my mother, as my mother had never wanted to go to an institution, and she used to joke, 'Your mum will live to 100.' I couldn't have achieved what I did without Jeanette.

It all took its toll on my health. Twice my emphysema landed me in intensive care – one of those times was when I had to miss out on the *Trainspotting* premiere. I would take time off to rest and then drive myself on, which is why I ended up in hospital. But it was because we were doing good things that I kept going.

CHAPTER TWENTY-SEVEN

London Calling

I'd be lying if I said that recognition for what we were doing didn't give us a lift. We got it from the community, but not from official bodies in Scotland. However, people elsewhere seemed to appreciate Calton Athletic. In 1991 I received the Whitbread Award for Community Involvement. It was a prestigious award, and I guess it was through people like Gordon Brown, Lenny Henry and Ray Stubbs that the committee had heard about what we were doing at Calton Athletic. I was invited down to London to Whitbread's headquarters and was presented with the award by Princess Michael of Kent and Sam Whitbread. It came at a time when we needed a bit of moral support. The Whitbread people treated us marvellously, and there was another strange coincidence. I was there as Scotland's representative, and there were six others from England. One was a Scot, and we got talking. This guy, Jim Wilson, was overall UK winner, for starting a group to stop male violence against women. He was doing it through the power of example. We hit it off and he told me that he'd been trying to get in contact with Jimmy Boyle. Every time he phoned up, he couldn't get him – it was the answering machine. I told him, 'I know Jimmy well. I'll pass that message on to him. Give me your number and I'll contact you and get things sorted out.'

The next morning we were in the foyer waiting to leave our hotel. I'm standing talking to Jim Wilson and who should come walking out of the lift but Jimmy Boyle. Jim Wilson turned to us: 'Christ, Davie, that was fast work.' It was a total coincidence. Jimmy just happened to be passing through London on business, but then again, strange coincidences and Calton Athletic seemed to go together.

Five years later I was nominated for the Unsung Hero Award by the Celebrities Guild of the UK, just as our relationship with statutory bodies in Glasgow was really beginning to deteriorate. I was invited down to a presentation dinner at the Dorchester in London and took my wife and the management committee. This was a big lift to us at the time, as a lot of things were starting to go wrong – not with Calton Athletic, the service was running at a peak – but resentment was building among others in the drug field. Success breeds success, but it also breeds an awful lot of resentment. Our programmes were built on self-generated sources, which only increased envy and resentment. The Robertson Trust was funding us, *Trainspotting* had come out and Polygram was sponsoring us, and we were part of a nationwide poster campaign. We got a lot of media coverage and a lot of visitors from abroad. But sometimes the pressure was an awful lot to bear, and this award relieved it for a while.

As we set off for London, they had still not told us who had nominated us. Whenever we went somewhere, we always tried to kill two birds with one stone, and I set up a meeting with the Stone Foundation in London. Davie Main and I went along to a very grand address in Belgravia, the house of Lady Gosling, who was one of their trustees. One of her colleagues was a Scotsman, Dr Richard Woolman, who had gone to Glenalmond, the same school as Robbie Coltrane, and it went very well. They put their money where their mouth was, agreeing to sponsor a new van for the schools team to travel round the country.

Then we headed for the awards, togged out in dinner suits and evening dress and sat at our table, marked out 'Calton Athletic'. The top table was made up of people like Stirling Moss, David Jacobs,

Harry Secombe, Barbara Windsor and a lot of other well-kent faces. I was impressed and a bit nervous, and I still didn't know who had nominated us. There were six nominees from all over the UK, and a different celebrity to hand out each award. I was told I would be the last one up. I was looking around to see if I could spot who'd put me forward, but although I recognised so many faces, I didn't actually know any of them. Then in walks Lenny Henry with Al Hunter. It was great to see them. I had always known Lenny wasn't a fair-weather friend. I sat back and watched gobsmacked as Lenny went up to make the nomination. I had a lump in my throat when I went up to get the award. It felt good, and it was a welcome respite from the hassles that I was now starting to face in Glasgow. This wasn't hassle from the streets, from drug-addicts or their families, but from the industry that was failing miserably while Calton Athletic seemed to have the Midas touch. Everything we touched was turning to gold. The statutory service seemed to have it in reverse – everything they were touching was turning to shit.

I'd now won two awards in London but nothing in my own city. I did wonder about that. But I believe things will change and, with hindsight, people will see we were right all along.

The day after the awards ceremony I was doing promotional work for Polygram for the video of *Trainspotting* with an interview on Five Live. A representative for Polygram had come with us to the BBC, and I was asked at one point, 'The whole drug field seems insidious – what do you make of that?' Polygram's publicist looked worried. Because of my background she thought I wouldn't know what insidious meant. I replied, 'It might be insidious, but it's not insurmountable. I believe that the drug problem can be tackled.' The publicist seemed so relieved that I knew what it meant. Of course I knew what it meant. I'd had to face it head on. Insidious means cunning, baffling and deceitful, and there's plenty of these traits about, especially in addiction.

CHAPTER TWENTY-EIGHT

Trainspotting in Baillieston

In early 1997 we opened our women's premises in Craigpark. We'd had women at the club from the beginning, but now we were providing a specialised service for women in recovery. The Health Board and Social Work had never acknowledged this, but our service for women was a reality. In the rest of the drug field, women were not coming off drugs, but we were having some success, and other people appreciated it.

Rosemary Harley and Ursula Barclay, lecturers at Strathclyde University, asked if we would be interested in putting on a fashion show with the university. Women in recovery at Calton Athletic would be models on the night, along with the students. A previous show had been a tremendous success, with 900 people at the Barony Hall, and here they were wanting us to be involved. This would also prove a tremendous success.

Meanwhile, Andy Macdonald and the Trainspotters had been in touch about a charity football match with Calton. To make it more interesting we decided to sign up some celebrities for Calton for the match, but we had only two weeks to do it and arrange a venue. This was a great opportunity, though, to help the women's service.

I had a friend up at Baillieston Juniors, and they agreed to let us play there, but the park was in a terrible condition. That wouldn't be a problem, though – people wouldn't be looking at the conditions; they'd be looking at the players. The police invited us down to London Road police station to discuss the logistics of bringing these superstars to Baillieston. We would need extra police at the game and a safety certificate. They inspected the park and weren't too pleased with what they saw, but they promised to come back in another couple of days. The police were afraid that maybe 20,000 people would turn up at Baillieston, so they restricted the crowd to 1,500. Nobody would get near the ground unless they had a ticket. Radio Clyde helped to advertise the match, and in no time the tickets sold out. All we had to do now was get Baillieston Juniors' park in shape for the Health and Safety inspectors. A squad of 60 Calton Athletic volunteers descended on Baillieston, and when the inspectors and the police arrived two days later they couldn't believe it was the same park. We had transformed it, and they gave us the green light.

An advance party of Andy Macdonald, Danny Boyle, Ewan McGregor and Johnny Lee Miller arrived at Craigpark. Polygram were represented by the top man Stuart Trill, who turned out to be very helpful to Calton Athletic afterwards, while Figment Films brought with them a £10,000 cheque. Channel 4 also sent one for the same amount. Richard Branson pitched in with another £10,000. We wondered how Beardie had got involved. It seems he had used a *Trainspotting* poster to advertise his new train set-up without permission. The Trainspotters had contacted him and told him they wouldn't do anything about it if Richard Branson made a contribution to Calton Athletic.

We had £40,000 before a ball had been kicked, and we were charging a fiver at the gate (three quid if you were on the buroo). It came at just the right time. Three years beforehand we'd received funding for the women's service after I had been on Radio 4. After the broadcast Davie Main had said, 'That was smashing, Davie, but who the fuck listens to Radio 4?' Well, John Paul Getty for one. He was that impressed with what I'd said he sent us £36,000 funding over the course of three years, which gave us £12,000 a year to employ a female coordinator. That investment allowed us to put a bit of specialist work into the women's service, and three years later the women were in their own premises up at Craigpark with all their own ideas and aspirations. Unfortunately they had no resources to carry them out, so the football match funds were for them. This £40,000 would allow us to employ two women full-time, Lorraine Fraser and Jeanette Bryce, and they would do a marvellous job.

On the night I arrived at Baillieston Juniors the place was mobbed half an hour before the game. I didn't anticipate what an attraction it would be. Just when I'd got there I'd noticed a big stretch limousine pulling up. The Trainspotters had brought everybody with them: Danny Boyle, Ewan McGregor, Bobby Carlyle, Johnny Lee Miller, Phil Cole, Irvine Welsh, John Hodge and Peter Mullan. Peter was to go on and make *My Name is Joe*, the film about an alcoholic starting a football team, which won the Palme d'Or at the Cannes Film Festival. That looked kind of familiar when I saw it.

In Calton Athletic's celebrity line-up were Tommy Burns, Alex McLeish, Chick Young, Tony Roper and Jonathan Watson. Robbie Coltrane kicked off the game. So many celebrities were wanting to play for Calton Athletic that we had only three of our own team out: Davie Main, my own son Davie and Peter O'Rourke in goal. Everybody at Calton Athletic wanted to get on, but the crowds had turned out to see the stars, the *Trainspotting* stars and the Tommy Burnses of this world. I was emotionally drained at the end. Everybody who came was fantastic, signing autographs and posing for photos. There was a lot of fun on the park. The referee sent Tommy Burns off for missing too many sitters, and as Tommy was walking off the park he got down on his knees and blessed himself. The crowd loved it. It was very hard to get guys like Tommy and big McLeish off the park, or Chick Young for that matter, because they were enjoying it so much.

I had to stress to the Calton team before the game that these guys were big-time players now, so they had to be careful not to injure naebody. It was a fantastic night, as Calton Athletic had brought Hollywood to Baillieston for a night that Glasgow would remember. The after-match entertainment was laid on at Café Cini, Charlie Nicholas's place in the city centre. That night was another demonstration of *Trainspotting*'s commitment to Calton Athletic. But it wasn't just the *Trainspotting* crew. It was the likes of Tommy Burns, Alex McLeish, Chick Young, Tony Roper and wee Jonathan Watson, our pal from Italia '90.

I must mention my other big pal who was playing: big Gerry Collins. Both Gerry and Tommy had stayed up the same close on Soho Street near me as boys. It was great publicity, as the more our name got known the better platform we had to let people know that we were more than a football team. We were a service with a track record for men and women, and our credibility was second to none. As I say, the only problem was the resentment that this was causing.

CHAPTER TWENTY-NINE

Fallout

Despite our success in the eyes of the community and the wider public, the relationship between Calton Athletic and the statutory funders, the Health Board and Social Work, was really turning sour. We'd meet with the key players from each organisation, whether it be Health Board or Social Work, every quarter to discuss the service agreement. At that time the representative from the Health Board was Bill Boyd, and we never had any problems with him. The Social Work rep was Paul Silk, and I've got to give Paul a bit of credit as well. We had no problems with him either. The representative from Glasgow Council of Voluntary Services (GCVS), which was looking after the Health Board's and Social Work's money, was a guy called Bill Welsh, and we did have our moments, but generally he took instruction from Calton Athletic's management committee. It was clearly established that the management committee was in charge of the core funding and could spend it on whatever they saw fit. This included our schools programme, prison work and services for families. However, with the demise of Strathclyde Regional Council there was now a new regime, Glasgow City Council, running Social Work, and a lot of the councillors were jockeying for positions of power. If I thought the experience with the regional councillors had been bad, what would happen with the city councillors would be ten times worse. Even to this day I find it hard to forgive some of the ones who put their tuppence worth into the drugs debate.

I didn't realise the implications at first. Up to this point Dr Laurence Gruer, who was in charge of the coordination of infection and addictions at the Health Board, was no problem. But the council started changing the representatives who would be at the meetings. I also met one of the city councillors at one of our presentation dances, and the first thing she told us was that Social Work was sending somebody in to sort out Calton Athletic. We'd won the hearts and minds of local people, who knew what we were about. But now I was surrounded by people who I was supposed to be negotiating with, who had a conflict of interest with us. They were just waiting for an opportunity to pounce and, in some cases, seek vengeance.

As the previous service agreement ran out, they were starting to flex their muscles and take control of the policy, just as they had done in all the other projects. I remember a staff meeting in which I explained to everybody the reality of the situation. When I'd started to work full-time, I believed I was working for Calton Athletic management committee and had the freedom to direct resources, but the situation had now changed. The Health Board and Social Work were dictating terms, such as that the people they employed should only be working on the day-care programme. They shouldn't be going out to schools. They were also telling me how to run it, and I didn't like that one bit. They even wanted an evaluation started and the individual supervision of staff members. I could see the debilitating effect this would have. They were out to divide and conquer, but we had to carry on, otherwise people would lose their jobs.

Two guys volunteered to leave, and we asked if we could use their salaries for core funding. Then our administrator from the statutory side, Carol Murray, walked out. We were now three down. Calton Athletic had come a long way since the start of the service agreement. At London Road we'd provided a recovery day programme which had evolved into a service that was taking people off drugs, detoxing them in their own community, putting them through rehabilitation, after-care, providing advice and information for parents, prison visits, a whole range of services, but the statutory funders had problems recognising this. However, I was able to fill in those statutory positions because we had a bit of flexibility with staff who were funded by our own resources and under my direction.

One day in early 1998 my administrator told me that we weren't in control of the statutory service. 'What's new? I've known that for a while.' He asked us what I was going to do about it, but I didn't know. We looked after our accounts with the back-up of accountants Scott and Paterson, but GCVS wasn't capable of looking after the statutory funding. They weren't qualified to look after that amount of money, and they handled it terribly. In spite of paying two people off, we ended up with a major overdraft problem at the end of that financial year. Our administrator was never able to get a look at the statutory accounts, which GCVS was handling. With the support of our accountants it was decided to manage them under one system, and that would mean that we would be in charge of the money. There was no need for GCVS. They weren't doing anything for Calton Athletic anyway. However, there was no way the statutory funders were going to sign a new service agreement if they weren't in charge of all the resources.

The Drug Action Teams weren't doing Calton Athletic any favours. Roddy Campbell, who had originally started the Drug Action Teams, was now away. He was replaced by a guy at the Health Board. Meanwhile, Glasgow was hitting record levels of drug deaths. Things had been bad under the Region, but were now disastrous under the City Council and the new Drug Action Teams. Nothing was working, yet more and more money was getting spent on favoured projects. My head administrator told me that he couldn't handle the pressure any more because of the way the statutory funders had set up the accountancy system with GCVS. Now, in the space of a couple of months, we had lost two group workers, the statutory administrator and our overall administrator.

We had to undergo an internal audit. There was nothing amiss, which I know put a lot of people's noses out of joint. The internal auditors apologised to our own accountants for the statutory set-up. There had also been a well-placed leak to the press about the internal audit, but needless to say nothing was printed about the result of that audit. They'd come in expecting to find a mess or irregularities, but there weren't any. They were trying to do what they had done with all the other community projects they'd been involved with – divide and conquer so they could take control of the policy and the management committee. The threat was clear: if you didn't play the game, you'd end up with no jobs or resources. A simple way of solving it would be to fund us in accordance with how many people we had on the programme, as they were doing with other organisations in the city, such as the Crisis Centre, Phoenix House or Red Towers. But Calton Athletic had become a victim of its own success.

The amount of people coming through the door had doubled, but now, in the new financial year, they were going to cut our resources by £6,000. This was a terrible indictment of their attitude towards the most successful drugs project not just in Glasgow but the UK. They were consumed with the idea that Calton Athletic had hidden millions from the funds that came from *Trainspotting*. All the money from *Trainspotting* had been ploughed right back into our services and properly accounted for. The statutory funders seemed to believe that the more we generated, the less they should put in. The situation was becoming unsustainable. But the worst was still to come.

In early March 1998 we were informed by our statutory funders and GCVS that there wasn't enough money to pay the staff. Our management committee had to step in and pay people's wages, and clear the overdraft created by the statutory service. But our committee made certain stipulations: from April 1998 onwards no more of Calton's self-generated money would get used to prop up the statutory service. If there was no money in the statutory account (i.e. no funding from public agencies), there would be no statutory services provided. All this proved that the statutory funders didn't give a shit about the management committee. They had started to take control of the project, just as they had done everywhere else, only this time they were told clearly at the start of the 1998 financial year that Calton Athletic would spend no more of its self-generated funds propping up the statutory part of the service.

Calton Athletic would also not be signing a service agreement.

This was a tragedy, because at the time Calton Athletic was the best known and most successful rehabilitation service in the country. It was not just our rehabilitation programme that was successful – our School Drugs Awareness project was going great guns. We were also providing a service to schools in England, but the statutory side were still creating an awful lot of problems. It was as if they didn't want us to succeed. Tragedy is not too strong a word to use, as people were dying in record numbers from drugs.

CHAPTER THIRTY

Vive la France!

As ever with Calton Athletic it was not all doom and gloom. We had already started saving up for our World Cup hat-trick – France in 1998 – but first we had a return trip to Jersey. Till then male and female members had gone on separate trips. The first women's trip abroad had been to the Canary Island Gran Canaria, but a dozen were now coming to Jersey with the boys. We thought it would work because of the success we'd had the year before, and my friend Jim McFarlane made the arrangements in a beautiful campsite just outside St Helier. The ground rule was the same as usual: nae bevvying. Everybody had to stay sober and straight. I've got to take my hat off to them all, as nobody let themselves down. Jim told us after we'd got there that the people running the camp had got a wee bit iffy when they found out we were recovering drug-addicts and had tried to cancel the booking. But the local police phoned them up and gave Calton Athletic a glowing tribute. It just shows how our name had spread. Still the staff at the campsite were apprehensive. Come the day we left, though, they all turned out to wave us off as our coach headed for the ferry. It proved you can change people's attitudes towards you. As long as you do the right thing, people will accept you. However, we may have caused some resentment by entering the camp's competitions for archery, karaoke, a general knowledge quiz and snooker. Calton Athletic made a clean sweep of it, with every competition being won by one of our members. We were not just good at football. I wasn't surprised at the talent in snooker and singing, but archery? Then again we were from the East End.

Not long before we went to Jersey, we had taken part in a charity walk along the West Highland Way. We'd done it twice already, and each time only half of us had completed it. Even though it was the wettest May in 22 years, everyone finished it this time, as they would again the following year.

Meanwhile France beckoned, and Scotland had qualified for the finals, unlike at USA '94. After our experiences in Italy and America we knew if we looked hard enough, we would get tickets, and that's exactly what happened. Just before we set off for France, a guy approached us who had been an officer in the RAF and had had a bad car crash. He had got invalided out and was cycling to Paris for the eve of the World Cup, raising money for the Head Injuries Trust. Would we support him? It sounded a good idea, and so two of our girls, Kerry Condron and Janice McKendall, plus John Gibson, who'd all done a bit of cycling, set off with him to arrive in time for the Scotland v. Brazil match in Paris.

Jim Farry, the chief executive of the SFA, and a TV crew waved them off from SFA headquarters at Park Gardens in Glasgow with SFA goodie bags and a cheque for £500. On the way down they would stop off at some major Scottish sporting grounds: Parkhead, then Ibrox, next Kilmarnock (Rugby Park) and then Palmerston Park (Queen of the South's ground in Dumfries) before heading into England.

They made it to Paris on time and the BBC was waiting for them. They asked them where I and the rest of Calton Athletic were. Kerry explained we didn't have tickets for the game against Brazil and were heading straight for our base in the south of France before heading up to St Etienne for the game against Morocco. We'd done a bit of planning and preparation. I'd gone over six months before and discovered a place in Antibes, right on the Riviera, with apartments for four at £200 a week. That was fifty quid a week to stay in the south of France, on the Riviera. That wouldn't get you a doss house in the Gallowgate these days, but through planning and preparation we found the perfect venue. There were 40 of us and half were under 21. Our Under-18s had become the Under-21s and were now providing a service as well as a football team. When we went to Italy in 1990, Father Willie Slaven had provided Father Archie as an interpreter. This time we were going to take French lessons, and for eight weeks before we left, big Frank, who was a teacher at St Aloysius' College, came and taught us once a week. Big Frank was smashing. We didn't become fluent, but we all picked up a bit. A new guy arrived at Calton one evening, and he was getting shown around when he walked into a room and we were all speaking French. You could tell he thought, 'What are these guys on?'

We also designed special Calton Athletic football shirts for the World Cup – probably the best T-shirts we'd ever had. For many years we were associated with the famous red T-shirts that we gave people who had graduated from the three-month day programme at Calton Athletic. Our France '98 ones were based on a similar style, only they were in the Scotland colours and had 'Scotland' written on the back. The bus picked us up at Duke Street and we were off. In spite of my fear of flying, when I saw everybody else enjoying themselves I settled down on the flight to Nice. The cabin crew were tremendous. There were a lot of high spirits, but the crew weren't daft. They could see that nobody was ordering drinks. When we touched down in Nice airport, the cabin crew got the captain to announce over the Tannoy: 'Calton Athletic, we hope you have a wonderful two weeks' stay in the south of France.' I'll never forget that. It was an omen for the remarkable two weeks that lay ahead.

We took a fleet of taxis to Antibes ten miles away and spent the first couple of days getting to know the place. On our third day in Antibes we decided to walk along to Grasse to meet Mike Trace, the deputy UK drugs coordinator, assistant to Keith Hellawell. I'd met Mike before when he was over in Edinburgh and mentioned we were going to the World Cup. He was going too, so I suggested we meet up. Mike travelled up from Barcelona with his son and a friend and we met up. They hadn't found accommodation, so I offered him one of our apartments and we bunched up in the others. Big Mike isn't daft, and here were 40 Scotsmen in recovery at the World Cup and everyone was sober – a big, big achievement, and Mike knew it.

The next day we were travelling up to St Remy, where the Scotland squad were based, as we had a game to play. When Kerry and Janice and Gibby had arrived in Paris, they'd met Tom O'Connor from the BBC, who said they wanted a take-on. Kerry arranged with him that we'd meet up in St Remy for Calton Athletic v. the media. The media were there for two weeks and had already taken on the local police and firemen and beaten them, and now they were about to play us. Meantime I'd called Jimmy Boyle, who had a house in Antibes.

Big Davie Main, Andy Curran and I went down to meet him at the railway station. Jimmy appeared in a convertible and drove us up to his house. As we turned into his driveway, I was pretty impressed. His neighbours included Madonna and Diana Ross. 'No bad for a dunce at school, Davie,' Jimmy grinned.

I insisted that Jimmy come down and meet all the boys. He had given us the money for our premises in London Road, never realising that eight years later we would meet in the south of France and Calton Athletic would be a success. We'd got everybody to go up to the rooftop pool and wait. When Jimmy arrived and stepped out onto the roof, everybody clapped and cheered. I swear to God there were tears in Jimmy's eyes as he said a few words. He spoke to the team about the early days of the club, about the premises, the long struggle against all the odds and now meeting us all here. I knew then that both of us were experiencing a miracle. Nobody had given us a hope in hell bar Jimmy Boyle. That team that they said wouldn't last a season had gone on to win the Scottish Cup. We had become the best-known rehabilitation project in the UK and were now in the south of France beside a rooftop pool on the Riviera with the guy who had made it all possible. That first year when we went to Italy, Jimmy had given us a lot of financial support. This time we had done it all ourselves. The boys had saved up the money themselves, behaved themselves and were enjoying themselves. We were all benefiting from the joys of sobriety. France was working.

There was something special about that moment that will live with me for the rest of my life and probably with some of the boys. Jimmy had his son Kidd with him and his nephew Mark, who looked on in amazement. It was a great day. We'll never forget it. Thanks for everything you've done for us, Jimmy. I'm quite sure you'll never forget that day either.

But it was the usual roller-coaster with Calton Athletic, as the very next day we got word from Scotland about an article in the *Sunday Mail*. I got it faxed over, and I couldn't believe what I was reading. Here was us, off on our biggest ever achievement to date, and the *Sunday Mail* had this big photo with the headline 'JUNKIE JUNKET'. The article was twisted to make it look as if we were staying in the lap of luxury at the taxpayer's expense. Nothing could have been further from reality. This trip was completely self-financed. We did not get a penny from anybody. Here we were in France passing our biggest test to date, and here was this article in the *Sunday Mail*, the biggest-selling Sunday paper in Scotland. It was a set-up to discredit Calton Athletic.

It was a low blow, and I found it hard to take but realised we had to go on with the holiday. There were several quotes in the article that enabled me to piece together where the damage was coming from. Scotland Against Drugs was involved in it, as were Mothers Against Drugs (MAD), or Mothers Against Certain Drugs, as they were known. There was a quote from a Councillor Jim Coleman, who thought we had 'lost the plot' going to France. Lost the plot? It was our biggest achievement to date, and he was rambling on with some nonsense about how we would never get tickets. The reality, Jim, and I hope you're reading this, is that every single one of us got tickets.

I was pretty upset, but at least I knew the source of the misinformation. I phoned home and told our administrator to fax the *Sunday Mail*. This was a disgrace. It wasn't the first time the *Sunday Mail* had done this sort of thing. They ran an article about an incident in Marco's Leisure Centre, also trying to taint Calton Athletic. Two young men had had an argument. It was no big deal – these sorts of things happen, even at the *Sunday Mail*, I'm told. Marco's hadn't complained about anything, and the police hadn't been involved. But the *Sunday Mail* seized on it to discredit us, as though blood was flying everywhere, the police were involved and Marco's Leisure Centre had barred us. It was a load of crap. But this should have been a warning to us. I should have been ready for what was happening now. This article about us going to France was complete rubbish. When the *Sunday Mail* ran another article trying to rubbish us a few months later, enough was enough. I took them to the Press Complaints Commission and the PCC upheld in our favour.

Meantime we headed for St Remy, where the Scotland team was based, to take on the media, but this time at football. When we arrived, we couldn't find the venue. I didn't know where Tom O'Connor was, but somebody had told us in the town that the Scotland squad were in the training camp. So we got directions and made our way down, but walked around in circles and ended up back where we started from. We got more directions, but just before we got to the Scotland training camp we noticed a coach driving off with the Scotland players in it. We had missed them by a couple of minutes. If we hadn't got lost, we would have bumped into the players, which would have been smashing. There was a bit of disappointment, as the boys thought the opportunity to see the players had gone. I had a quick chat with them to try to lift morale and reminded them that we had come here to play football – anything else would be a bonus. We were unlucky not to see the players, but we shouldn't let that spoil things.

We made our way up to the town centre, where I phoned Tom O'Connor. I sat down in a café and ordered a Coke. Everybody else was sitting over on the steps of the chapel nearby. Davie Main and Willie Burns were with me. I got through to Tom right away. 'Tom, it's Davie Bryce. We're here in St Remy.'

'I know. I've seen and heard you.'

I asked if there was any chance he could come and meet us to arrange the football match.

'No bother, Davie. When do you want me to come?'

'How quick can you be?'

'I'll be with you in two ticks.'

'Where are you?'

'At the table behind you.'

I hadn't met Tom, so hadn't recognised him in the café. We had a good laugh about it, and Tom said that he would need permission from the SFA to play the match on their training ground, and he would meet us in an hour. It turned out not to be a problem, and we got to use the pitch and the changing-rooms with the SFA's blessing. Again Jim Farry had stuck to his word. Before we had set off to go to France, he gave me two mobile numbers to call him on if there was any bother. I hadn't needed to use them, because Tom came back with the go-ahead. We scheduled the match for two hours' time. Meanwhile we had nothing to do but have a big singsong. There were over forty of us by this time, because we had been joined by a few friends, and we sang for a solid two hours on the steps of that church. The locals were driving up to join in, and film crews arrived. The local police turned up with drinking water for us as they had heard we were playing football. A couple of the Scotland players had gone past as well and noticed us, and I suppose word had spread that Calton Athletic were in town. We spotted Jim Traynor – probably the most well-known football reporter in Scotland. He worked for the *Sunday Mail*'s sister paper, the *Daily Record*, but we wouldn't hold that against him. It had nothing to do with Jim, but we were singing the Jimmy Hill song except to the words, 'We hate the *Sunday Mail*.'

Jim Traynor was having a good laugh, and although it was all fun the *Sunday Mail* had taken a liberty. Jim Traynor wasn't part of the problem, and we knew most of the journalists at the *Sunday Mail* weren't. There are a lot of good journalists at the *Sunday Mail*, and a lot of good people work in the printing shop. I know quite a few. But these articles were an attempt to blacken the name of Calton Athletic. Take me if you can, but leave my men alone. I could take all the flak that SAD wanted to fling at me, but I could not stand by while an effort was being made to undermine our work as drug deaths were reaching record levels up in Glasgow and would keep going up over the next two years.

The kick-off of our match against the Scottish media was approaching, and it appeared both teams were wearing Scotland colours. The press boys had official Scotland strips, and we had our Calton Athletic T-shirts. They asked us if they could strip to the waist, and we had no problem with that – except that by this time it was about 90 degrees. The press boys weren't daft. They knew that, as our team was younger, we'd last the pace. They had Scotland manager Craig Brown's son playing for them, who was a smashing guy. Rob McLean from the BBC was also playing, as was the big rugby player John Leslie, another smashing guy. Mike Trace, the deputy drugs tsar, turned out for them and he was not a bad football player. But Mike had never seen us play, and that day we were tremendous. We adapted to the conditions, and I'm quite sure they'll all remember one of the goals we scored. We were well in front when one of our boys, Derek Colquhoun, got the ball, lifted it over his opponent's head, took it forward, beat the next guy, went towards the goalkeeper, flicked the ball up and headed it in. It was as good as any goal in the World Cup. Derek was showboating, but we all loved it, and the opposition appreciated it too. It was a good-natured game, and the result didn't really matter, but we won, and we always play to win.

The press boys weren't downhearted, and we had a good chat and a photo session after the game. All that was left now was to get changed and go home. But it didn't quite work out that way. We had something to eat and a half-hour to kill before the coach arrived to take us back to Antibes. I was talking to Mike Trace, and he was saying his son was disappointed because he never saw the Scotland players. We decided to go up to the Scotland hotel. His wee boy was excited, and Mike told him to calm down: 'Davie's just taking us up to do his best. It might not happen, so remember that. Don't be disappointed.'

There was a lot of security, but we noticed a woman standing there with two teenage lassies. She was from Blairgowrie and told us she had been there for hours. Nobody had come out. I told her, 'They'll come out now, hen.'

'What are you gonna do?'

'We're gonna serenade them.'

We started singing 'Flower of Scotland' and all the songs that were part of our repertoire. After a few verses big Colin Hendry came walking out of the main building towards the gate. We started chanting, 'Braveheart, Braveheart,' and the closer Colin was getting the more he was growing in stature. You could see the hairs on the back of his neck bristling. Colin was tremendous that day. He was the first player out of the hotel. He couldn't have been any better, signing autographs and making our journey worthwhile. Just as Colin was about to go back in, Simon Donnelly and Jackie McNamara joined him. Simon and Jackie were both at Celtic then, and quite a few of our boys were Celtic fans. Calton Athletic is, as you'd expect, half-Celtic, half-Rangers, but the first club is Calton Athletic. These two young players were tremendous with us as well, and John Collins also came out. We had set off for St Remy to play football, and anything else was going to be a bonus. The Scotland players did a smashing job lifting our morale. The people of St Remy were also marvellous and made us ever so welcome. Locals, as well as the police, were bringing down water for us in the heat that afternoon. Simon Donnelly, in the World Cup column he was writing for the next day's *Evening Times* back home in Glasgow, mentioned his experience of getting serenaded by 40 Scotsmen who were all sober and enjoying themselves. Indeed he had never seen people enjoying themselves as much as this when they hadn't had a drink. Simon's article was much appreciated and also helped to redress the balance after the *Sunday Mail* article.

A couple of days later we set off for St Etienne for Scotland's game against Morocco. Jimmy Boyle's nephew had asked him, 'Do you think they'll get tickets up at St Etienne for the game?'

'Davie's a pretty resourceful guy,' Jimmy said, 'but it's over 40 tickets they're looking for. They have no chance, but at least they'll go up there and enjoy themselves.'

Jimmy was just saying what anyone else would, but we were Calton Athletic and had built up a wee bit of expertise at this sort of thing. When we got to St Etienne, we headed to the stadium. It was four hours before kick-off, and we all marched around the perimeter. It was like Joshua at the walls of Jericho, all of us marching round it and singing, but the walls never collapsed, so we headed to the town centre. I thought that day in Birmingham with the Dutch fans at Euro '96 was a tremendous sight, but when we got into the centre of St Etienne, it was awash with Scotsmen. There were thousands. There was a big screen set up so that people who couldn't get into the game could watch it. We had decided we would go as far as £100 for a ticket. It would be everybody in or nobody in. And that's what we did. We'd collected money on the bus, everybody putting in £100, and we had £4,000 to get us into the game. Meantime in the square we met an awful lot of people I knew. The *Daily Record* had a big bus, and people like Alex Salmond of the SNP and other VIPs were on it, waving down to everybody. Meanwhile our scouts were looking for tickets. Tickets were at first going for £150, then somebody would come back and say they'd seen them for £125. Then somebody would come back and say they had them for £100, and we thought, well, we had agreed £100, let's go for it. By the time I had got to the guy, he was obviously a wee bit frightened, as there were a few of us and we were asking for 40 tickets at £100 a head.

He said he would need to go and see his boss. He came back with a big Cockney guy. The Londoner took one look at our T-shirts and turned to his tout: 'You never told me it was Calton Athletic. I'll take fifty quid a skull.' What a result! We were prepared to pay £100 and here was this geezer from the East End of London telling us because we were Calton Athletic from the East End of Glasgow we would get them for £50. We'd saved £2,000, and everybody was getting in to the game. Everybody got a ticket, and I hope you're reading this, Councillor Jim Coleman.

We set off and joined in the singing with the thousands of people on their way up to the stadium. Scotland had lost to Brazil and drawn with Norway. If we beat Morocco, there was a chance that we could get through. Scotland got beaten 3–0. We might have been disappointed with the result, but as we went 2–0 down I turned to Andy Curran. 'What are we gloomy about? We're going back to Antibes after the game, and a lot of these other people are going straight home.'

Andy took the point: you can't base a World Cup trip around Scotland winning; you've just got to make the most of the situation. We were interviewed on TV after the game. This was our third World Cup, and after St Remy the media knew we were here. People back home could see that Calton Athletic were still alive and kicking, no matter what the *Sunday Mail* said.

When we got on the bus, one of the Under-21s, Alan Mitchell, asked the driver if he could use the microphone. I was wondering what was up. He wanted to thank Calton Athletic management committee and me and Davie Main on behalf of the Under-21s for organising the trip to France. These young ones who nobody had any faith in when we took them to Euro '96 were maturing into young men who could behave themselves. The temptations were all there for any boy to go astray – the excitement of the World Cup, the hot weather, beautiful women and booze everywhere – yet everybody stayed sober.

Back in Antibes we were to take in an excursion to Monte Carlo. It was a unique experience for the boys and a wee bit different from the Gallowgate. As I was strolling along the front, we banged into John Collins, Tosh McKinlay and Darren Jackson. They had a day off from training, and John Collins was staying in Monte Carlo at the time. I'd known John from the video work we had done with the SFA. I also knew Darren and Tosh. Tosh had been up at our premises in Glasgow and Darren had been involved in the Head Injuries Trust cycle photo session up at Parkhead.

It had become a tradition on these World Cup trips to have a meal together on the final night. Jimmy Boyle had recommended Jimmy Chunga's nightclub in Cannes. He would phone and let them know we were coming. I thought that night in Romford at the rockabilly club would never be equalled, but I was wrong. Everyone dressed up in his or her best gear and was looking good with the sun. Jimmy Chunga's is right next to the Marchionette Hotel, one of the famous places on the Croisette. It is usually the haunt of the rich and famous, so some of our boys were a bit overawed. We didn't know there would be a cabaret, which started during the meal with the R. Kelly song 'I Believe I Can Fly'. We were all sitting listening in amazement, because that's how we felt. The singer put the microphone in front of my son David, and I couldn't believe it when he joined in with her. We all joined in then. At one o'clock in the morning we were still there, dancing by this time and helping out with the cabaret, while a queue of millionaires outside couldn't get in. We had taken the place over. It was a perfect finish to the World Cup.

The apartments we were staying in had their own sort of dinner-dance each Saturday night, and the staff asked if we could do a cabaret for them. We didn't have any musical instruments, but Davie Main and Andy Curran got dressed up like Harry Lauder and sang a medley of Scottish songs. Every one of us was gobsmacked, because we never knew they were so good. They had never done it before, but they just put everything into it. The French loved it. I couldn't believe it at the end when the boys gave Davie Main a present in recognition of the great work he had done when he was over there. They bought him a lovely tracksuit, some T-shirts and a pair of training shoes. I was really taken aback when they did the same thing for me. I could maybe see the point in Davie getting it, but I'd pretty much taken it for granted that because I was the leader I did things without getting or expecting any reward. The main motivators behind this gesture were the Under-21s. They were full of gratitude. Davie and I took this to be as good a sign as any that we had made the right decision in developing a prevention approach in the form of our Under-21s and schools programmes.

There was one other way that we did our bit for Scottish football at France '98. We had sponsored a seven-a-side league in Glasgow and arranged facilities at Crown Point sports centre and backed them up with clerical support and some finance. We had a gala day that attracted over 3,000 people to Crown Point. Calton Athletic were in charge of the security, and no motors were broken into for the first time since that day when Lenny Henry was there. Govanhill were one of the winners, and seven years later I was in Morrison's gym when two guys approached me. They were pros with Aberdeen and Airdrie. They wanted to thank me, because they'd been part of that team, and seven of their squad went on to reach the senior ranks. One of them had been Aiden McGeady of Celtic, now rated one of the best prospects in Scotland.

I remembered watching Aiden that day at Crown Point and thinking what a talent he was. He had the chance to go to Paris for a seven-a-side tournament underneath the Eiffel Tower at the start of the World Cup. Arsenal had invited him, as had Celtic. But there was a dilemma. Arsenal had made provision for his father to attend, but he'd have to pay his own way. Celtic had made no provision for his father at all. But we thought it was important his father should go, as Aiden was only 11. I'd have felt the same if it was my boy. Aiden's father was training to be a teacher and was short of money, and the guy who ran the league asked if Calton Athletic could sponsor him. Our management committee approved it, and Aiden and his father went to that tournament with Arsenal.

His father couldn't thank me enough and promised me two things: if Aiden made it, he would never sign for Celtic, and he would never forget us. Unfortunately Aiden's father did forget us, or maybe he cannae find us. But we're still here. Tommy Burns can tell him how to get in touch. I've no problem either that Aiden signed for Celtic. I'm glad he did, as it kept a special talent in Scotland.

I mention this not to embarrass the McGeadys but to emphasise the support we gave to the Soccer Sevens and how it paid off. We also stepped in to sponsor the Scottish Boxing Federation after there was a split in how the sport was being run. We gave them the same opportunity as the Soccer Sevens: a place to meet, clerical support, a phone line and help with their annual review. Again we picked winners, as Alex Arthur, Barry Morrison, Barry Connell and Willie Limmond were some of their boys, and they went on to become pros. We could spot a worthy cause and always appreciated that we'd only got where we were with the support of others.

CHAPTER THIRTY-ONE

Frankie Goes to Holyrood

France recharged our batteries. Despite the backstabbing by SAD and MAD we were still achieving major things. We had been to our third World Cup, and each one had got better. Not long after we returned, it was time to get our heads down and start training for the Glasgow Half-Marathon. We were going to enter our biggest field of 85 Calton Athletic members. We all wore the Calton Athletic T-shirts that day. There were 11,000 runners in that half-marathon, and I'm quite sure every one of them knew that Calton Athletic were in there. I don't think 85 from one group such as ours is a British record; I think it's probably a world record. I don't think it will ever be repeated again that an organisation could have 85 recovering drug-addicts taking part in a half-marathon. In the past, with the older age group, we were just delighted to finish, but now, with the young blood coming through, it was about finishing in good time, setting standards and records. One of our member's time was 90 minutes. We never thought it would be beaten. But things do get better, and it was. The young ones drew better efforts out of everybody, because it was no longer about going round; it was about doing it in the best time you possibly could. And this didn't just apply to the Glasgow Half-Marathon.

Before we had gone to the World Cup, we had taken part in the Glasgow Women's 10 km. The first time we did it, we had two runners, but in 1998 there were twenty-two. That was another record – not just for Calton Athletic. There wasn't another group in the country that had 22 women in the race. Then we entered the Great North Run in Newcastle, second only to the London Marathon. Something like 30,000 take part. It was the weekend after the Devolution vote in 1999, and when we arrived in Newcastle that day we painted our faces with the Saltire and wore our red T-shirts. One of the commentators said, 'There's a striking group of people – must be the Devolutionists down from Scotland.'

We got a fantastic welcome in Gateshead, and I met up with Ray Stubbs again. He was now fully established as the anchor man at BBC *Grandstand*. I met him at the Copthorne Hotel in Newcastle the night before, and we went over old times and the documentary he made about us in 1990.

This was our third time on the Great North Run, and we fielded 50 members for it. That gives a good indication of the popularity of running and its therapeutic value. It is also a great mechanism for letting people know who you are. There are thousands of runners throughout Britain, and we made our name among them.

Yet here we were with a hat-trick of successful events and notable achievements – the World Cup, the Glasgow Half-Marathon, the Great North Run – and poison was being spread about us back home by people who were supposed to be professionals in their field.

Our annual awards presentation dance had been in the Thistle Hotel in Glasgow the previous August, shortly after the World Cup. There were 250 people there. We had come a long way from when we used to have our awards ceremonies in tenement halls in the Gallowgate, where it would be a buffet that we had prepared ourselves. Everybody was sitting down for their meal and there were a few VIPs, among them Frank McAveety, who was then leader of Glasgow City Council and not yet an MSP.

Just before we did the presentations, Frank approached me kind of sheepishly. 'If people ask me, Davie, how will I tell them you paid for this dance?'

The alarm bells went off again. What a stupid question. It was self-explanatory. Everybody had paid good money to be there. If they had paid £2, they could have had a tenement hall in the Gallowgate. Because they'd paid £15, they had the Thistle Hotel. 'In fact, Frank,' I told him, 'the only people who haven't paid for a ticket are you and your wife.'

I think the point was taken. But Frank was asking because the knives were out in the City Chambers. Looking back I think that Frank McAveety was only ever a fair-weather friend, unlike people such as Jimmy Boyle, Lenny Henry, Robbie Coltrane, Danny Boyle, Ewan McGregor, Irvine Welsh, Sir Lachlan MacLean, Tommy Burns and Walter Smith.

That night, though, we had him as guest of honour, hoping to build bridges with the City Chambers. But it appeared that Frank was part of the damage. The awards were not just about the football team but how Calton Athletic was a service for both men and women, and this was the first time we had a chance to honour our Under-21s and Under-18s. We had a Young Person's Example of the Year and a Young Person's Overall Example of the Year award for both male and female members. Example of the Year was for somebody in their first year at Calton Athletic, while the Overall Example was for somebody who had been there for over a year.

There were a lot of photos taken that night, and Frank McAveety is actually in one presenting an award. But Frank took the hump when he didn't get to make a speech. I reckon that was the only reason he had come along. But my card was marked, although I'll stress again that not all councillors were responsible for undermining Calton Athletic.

I still have the correspondence with then Councillor McAveety about the problems we were having with Social Work and our appeal to him to sort it out. I met him on a couple of occasions, but nothing came of it. I didn't know what Frank's agenda was. He was a school teacher at the time, and we were providing a service in Glasgow schools. You might have thought he would have appreciated that.

I think his focus was on getting into the Scottish Parliament, and you never know, he might not have made it if I had stood against him. I considered it in 1999 and contacted the Scottish Office to get the necessary forms. I informed Sir Lachlan at the Robertson Trust that I was going to do it. I even made a statement on the BBC. A couple of days later I got a phone call from Sir Lachlan, and he said that he'd spoken to a couple of the trustees and they thought I would best serve Glasgow by staying at the helm of Calton Athletic. So that's what I did, but I know that if I had stood, Frank McAveety might not have had such a clear run for that seat in the East End of Glasgow. I'm a well-known face, and I had a lot of credibility due to what I've been doing over the last 20 years. I was better known in the East End than Frank at that time, and even though it was one of the strongest Labour seats in Scotland his majority over the SNP was not as high as expected. If I had stood, I might not have won, but I would have taken a lot of votes away from him, and he would have had to sweat.

With encouragement from the Robertson Trust, though, I stayed at the helm of Calton Athletic and Frankie went to Holyrood. I've always thought the best way Frank could have helped sort out the drug problem in his constituency in the East End of Glasgow was by helping Calton Athletic. You have a duty to represent us at Holyrood, Frank. I asked him in the late '90s to help us, and he didn't. I am asking him now to stand up and be counted. He's still our MSP. He's had to eat humble pie, as he is no longer a minister, but, Frank, we're ready to work with you again if you have an open mind.

CHAPTER THIRTY-TWO

Downing Street

Meantime I had to attend another function in London with the Celebrities Guild of Great Britain. They'd asked us if we wanted to take a table. Our guests were the Trainspotters Danny Boyle, Andrew Macdonald and John Hodge. I thought we had been invited to the Dorchester just to make up the numbers, as it was the Guild's anniversary, but when we got there we found out they had invited the most prestigious winners of the last twenty years, and I was one of the six selected. This was a tremendous feeling, as a lot of people with real credibility had won these awards. I hit it off with Lisa Potts, the nursery teacher who had saved the weans in Wolverhampton during an attack by a maniac with a machete. Another of the six was Heather Mills, for her work against landmines.

I'd been sitting there when I noticed this beautiful blonde lassie pointing at me and then at herself. She was mouthing, 'You're with me.' I turned round but there was no one behind me. She gave me a big smile and mouthed it again: 'It's you and me together.' Here I was beginning to think I'd not totally lost my boyish good looks. But then someone came over and said that Dani Behr, the model and TV presenter, would be giving me my award. So that's what she was up to. Dani was going out with the footballer Les Ferdinand at the time, and he was there with her. She introduced us to Les, and he was a smashing guy.

It was a special night, as to win one award from the Celebrities Guild was special, but two was something else. Once again what we were doing was being appreciated and acknowledged down in London at a time when we were coming under all sorts of pressure in Glasgow from the usual suspects.

The day after the Dorchester we set off for Downing Street to hand in a petition. I'd become so concerned about the state of affairs in Glasgow I thought I'd appeal directly to the prime minister. Apart from those who were at the Celebrities Guild dinner, a coach-load from Calton Athletic had arrived from Glasgow and had brought 20,000 of our school questionnaires. We'd done 148 schools and there were also 4,000 questionnaires filled in by parents and teachers. When we got to Downing Street, the Calton Athletic members were already there, faces painted with the Saltire. They were singing our usual songs and the media had descended upon us. At the appointed time we took the petition into Downing Street and had to use a wheelbarrow to carry it. As we were going up the step at No. 10, somebody said, 'What are you doing here, Davie?'

I turned around. It was Gordon Brown. He'd just come out of No. 11. He came over to speak to us and I told him about the difficulties we were having and added we were having particular problems in Fife. Schools in Fife wanted us in, but they were stopped by the local Drug Action Team. They were determined they weren't going to let anybody else into Fife. I hoped this petition would help and that meeting Gordon would maybe be a breakthrough.

The Downing Street meeting went well, and I'm quite sure if Tony Blair ever read any of those questionnaires he would have been impressed with what Calton Athletic were doing. But all of this valuable information that could have been a great research tool wasn't being used. These questionnaires nevertheless gave us a lot of hope because they showed we were making a big impression with young people and teachers. If it's not a credible message, kids will switch off, but the people delivering it had all the credibility in the world. They'd been there, done it and bought the T-shirt. They'd walked the walk and were now talking the talk.

The statistics showed that 92 per cent of the people who had heard our presentation thought it was the best way of passing on drugs information: that is, through recovering drug-addicts. I've got to emphasise the word 'recovering'. Our addicts were not just drug-free but were alcohol-free, and this boosted our credibility because our talks in the schools weren't just about drugs but also about booze, infection and peer pressure. When I was young, I thought peer pressure was somebody twisting your arm up your back. As an adult I know it is more subtle. It is the urge to belong, to be part of the crowd and not to feel left out. All of these things are particularly important for young people, who are at a vulnerable stage in their lives.

Yet back in Glasgow our programmes were getting systematically dismantled. Our management committee had accepted under pressure that they would lose control of the statutory service and Glasgow Council for Voluntary Services would look after it. The statutory funders were only interested in funding the adult day programme, not our prevention work in schools, prisons or with young people. I was also told that if I wanted to do work with the Under-21s programme or the School Drugs Awareness project I would need to do it in a voluntary capacity. It didn't make any difference, as that was what I was doing already. I had never been paid for the schools programme or the Under-21s work. If the statutory authorities were taking control of the adult day programme, we told them quite categorically that no more of Calton Athletic's self-generated income would get used for the statutory service. This statement was made in front of George Smith, Dana O'Dwyer, Iona Conveil and GCVS. Six months later we withdrew from the day programme after farcical mismanagement of the accounts.

The situation had become unsustainable and not because of Calton Athletic. We were doing our best to get as many people through the door and off drugs as possible. We had a record amount of new starters at that time. But our resources had been cut, we were struggling, and I asked them to wind the project down and give everybody their just entitlements – holiday pay, their time in lieu of notice and their redundancy. It wasn't the workers' fault. I had given it seven years, as had my deputy. The group workers had been at it for five years. It was a tremendous blow, which took the shine off all the things we'd achieved in 1998, although it could never take these things away from us – they were part of our track record.

I was determined this was not to be the end of Calton Athletic. We would do what everybody else was supposed to do, and that was get on with the job. The pay-offs were painful, as we'd just lost a quarter of a million in funding. We had to cut our cloth accordingly, but I can say today that every client at Calton Athletic who had come through the door that year and who was still with us at the time of the shutdown continued to receive Calton Athletic's services till they decided to move on. This came at a great expense to Calton Athletic.

Meantime the statutory funders said they would look after our clients. We got them all to phone the council and Health Board, but nobody could get a satisfactory service. They were told they might have a place for them in six weeks. The only place which could see them that day was the Crisis Centre, which dished out methadone. But these were people who were well past the methadone stage. These were people – some young, some single parents, some married – who were doing well on programmes, and who subsequently got their legs pulled from under them. Calton Athletic and our management committee were determined that they continue to get a service, despite what had happened. As the day programme shut down, we took them to Craigpark, although we were under no obligation to do so.

CHAPTER THIRTY-THREE

Behind Bars

Mike Trace, Tony Blair's then deputy drugs tsar, obviously had a different opinion of us to the drug establishment's in Scotland, and we were invited down for a football match in London against Crouch End Amateurs. He'd seen us play in France and realised we were a bit tasty, so just before we came down he phoned and asked if we would mind playing another game against Downview Prison in Surrey. They were some outfit who hadn't been beaten for several years and who played on an artificial surface that used to be at Queens Park Rangers' ground. I think Mike's idea was that they would soften us up so that it would be easier for his Crouch End team on the Sunday. When we arrived, the whole prison had turned out to watch the game, but it wasn't in the slightest bit intimidating for us, although we'd heard it had put other teams off. It was a great game, which finished in a draw. Downey didn't give us respect right away, but we'd earned it by the final whistle.

Danny Boyle was due to play for us at Crouch End, but unfortunately, due to a mix up, he missed his chance. The game started and at first the English boys showed a wee bit of resistance, but as I've said Calton Athletic don't play friendlies. We ended up beating them 14–1. Big Mick and I got the chance to have a gab again about another achievement, taking a team of recovering drug-addicts down to England, being accepted in English prisons and playing the deputy drug tsar's own team.

But being behind bars was nothing new for Calton Athletic. We had been playing in Scottish prisons for years, such as Barlinnie, Shotts, Perth, Longriggend, Polmont, Dumfries Young Offenders, Castle Huntly Young Offenders and Nortonside. We had done a lot of work with Scottish prisons, and several years earlier I'd been invited through to Calton House, the prison service's headquarters, to give a presentation to all the Scottish governors. As I was speaking, I looked up and recognised one of the governors. It dawned on me that he was an old screw who used to be in Polmont when I was doing my Borstal. All these years later he was a prison governor and I was there doing a presentation about Calton Athletic. I'd actually bumped into him in Blairgowrie at a folk festival in the interim. He created a big impression on me as a Borstal boy, and I suppose I must have made some sort of impression on him, because all these years later we were still friendly.

We'd earned credibility not just with governors but with the rank and file of the prison staff. It didn't come overnight – it takes you years – but I remember in the early days being invited to a seminar up in Barlinnie. One of the prison officers told me it would take time, especially with the old guard. A similar thing had happened with Alcoholics Anonymous when they had started in the prison service. We provided a service even in the state hospital at Carstairs. I took two of our workers down with me, and they were nervous. I had been through the Scottish prison system but had missed out on Carstairs, luckily enough. I tried to alleviate the fears of Lorraine Fraser and Archie McCormick, telling them everything would be OK – they'd be with me the whole time.

When we arrived at Carstairs, a prison officer said, 'Davie, you come to this hall with me – you two go to that hall.' We split up and they were terrified, but everything went fine. We met up for dinner and I got introduced to the group. I recognised a couple of them – one was a young man from my own community, Gary Simpson. Gary looked well at the time and he was delighted to see us. There was another young man there, and I knew his family from Blairgowrie. The last time I'd seen him was as a young boy up in Blairgowrie at the berries. He was the same age as my oldest kids, and it was sad to see he had ended up in Carstairs. The prison officer told us not to be disturbed if some people got up and started wandering about during the session. It wouldn't be out of disrespect; it was because of their condition. I started to talk, and an hour later, when I finished, they burst into applause. The feedback went on for a long time, and nobody had got up and wandered about. People sat there listening because they could identify with what I was saying. At the end of the session the prison officer said to them that he could see they had got a lot out of it and would they like the group to continue? He explained that I was a busy guy and I couldn't come back, but that he was experienced in counselling and how would they feel if he took charge of the group?

One of the prisoners answered, 'You're a nice guy, Kenny, and you're good at your job, but you're no as deviant as Davie. You wouldnae understand.' That was some compliment, being called a deviant by a patient in Carstairs. This prison officer had been on courses, and he was good at his job – but he was a prison officer. On the other hand I could empathise with these people, and they could empathise with me. Some of them had been pretty normal till they started suffering from drug-induced mental illness. I found there were an awful lot like that at Carstairs. It's a pity that, after all these years of providing a service in Scottish prisons, a service that was supported through self-generated funds and where we made a big impact, we don't provide it any more.

Don't get me wrong – sometimes we do respond to the odd request, such as from Longriggend remand centre for football. By this time we were concentrating on people under 21. Longriggend and places like it, such as Polmont Young Offenders, are where you can get a chance to reach people who are away from the influence of the street. For a lot of them, the rule applies that if they're reachable, they're teachable. An awful lot of people came to Calton Athletic after hearing us at a prison talk. We planted a seed that maybe things could be different once they got out.

I got to know Clive Fairweather, HM Inspector of Prisons, and had respect for the man, and I believe Clive's got a bit of respect for

Calton Athletic. He came to visit us. I kept up communication with him, and he knows where Calton Athletic stands. He believed that there was a place for Calton Athletic in the prison service, especially at Polmont Young Offenders, the biggest in Scotland. We went down there, and I spoke to 250 young offenders that day. We played football, and I knew by the time I left we had made a big impression on them. The governor gave me a gift of a pen holder, on Polmont slate, with the words 'Polmont Young Offenders' and the date. I looked at it and realised that 30 years ago to the day, I had been in there as a Borstal boy. The structure of the building had changed, but the make-up of the young people was the same.

When I was a Borstal boy, the age of the inmates ranged from 16 to 21, and Polmont Young Offenders had this age range as well. I believe that at various times in the young offenders institutions people do get a chance to think and that good work can be done there, particularly in the rehabilitation service. I also believe that the harm-reduction policy would work best in prisons, where prison officers can ensure there is a 24-hour supervision of the policy. But prison is the only place in which I believe that harm reduction could really work. I also believe there has got to be a place for rehabilitation in Scottish prisons, and the same process should be used as is currently used in the community, thanks to the combined resources of Calton Athletic and government schemes. If prisoners don't want to stop using, they should be offered harm reduction. If prisoners do want to stop using and become drug-free, they should be rewarded for being able to stick to this.

At Calton Athletic if people want to use drugs, we send them somewhere else. We only work with people who are serious. Even then we don't guarantee success. I think the prison officers would have more chance of success if they knew what they were working with and had the clear-cut rules that we have. And I believe that the prison service should start to implement drug-free prisons rather than drugs 'free' in jail. There has got to be a carrot there for people who want to do the right thing. There should be harm-reduction projects for those who want to keep using, but they've got to be separated from those who want off. That's what we did at Calton Athletic. That's when we started to get success.

CHAPTER THIRTY-FOUR

Blacklisted

The Scottish Drug Forum had also joined the various bodies who were seemingly not working with us. I came in one day, and Davie Main told me, 'You won't believe what's happening.' A woman from Aberdeen had called. She'd phoned up SAD to get our number, and they'd said they didn't have it. She'd called the Scottish Drug Forum, and they couldn't give her the number either. Then she phoned the National Drugs Helpline, and they couldn't give her the number. She later phoned back SAD, who finally came up with the number. But she thought it was a disgrace that she'd had such trouble trying to get in contact with a project that was known up in Aberdeen, yet was seemingly unacknowledged or unsupported by these agencies.

It seemed that, as far as the Drug Action Team was concerned, we didn't exist. It was only because she had persevered that she'd managed to get hold of us. I phoned up the National Helpline to ask for Calton Athletic, and they told me that they didn't have them listed. I got a couple of other people to phone as well, just to make sure I was not jumping the gun, and they got the same answer. We decided to contact the director of the National Helpline, who turned out to be pretty helpful. He told us the reason that we weren't on the

National Helpline was he had received a fax from the Scottish Drug Forum to withdraw our details. He was based in Liverpool and thought the request was pretty strange, but as it came from the Scottish Drug Forum he'd complied. The Scottish Drug Forum had made out they had the authority to do this. This was some indictment of them, and I can only speculate on their reasons for doing this. Perhaps, like the other groups, it was a mixture of envy at our success and not liking our attitude.

Another major decision against us soon followed. While I was in France for the World Cup in 1998, Scottish Enterprise were offering drug projects an opportunity to apply for money to get people who were offending and taking drugs into employment. I'd got a letter from the Drug Action Team. There was to be a presentation from Scottish Enterprise in Blackhill and could I be there? On the day of the event they phoned to say could I go instead to a presentation at Strathclyde House that afternoon? When I arrived at Strathclyde House, I was told that I should have been at the morning's presentation.

Fortunately I was able to get hold of the guy who did the presentations. He told me he was surprised that he hadn't seen us at the morning's event, but he was prepared to find a new slot for us. It would have to be done in a couple of days because the submissions had to be in within a week. We weren't really prepared for this, and I was just getting ready to go to France. Still, we put in for an Under-21s project.

Almost a year later Scottish Enterprise arrived at Craigpark with bad news. Although originally we'd been told this was money to get people who were offending and taking drugs into employment, getting them off drugs was no longer one of the criteria. I nearly fell off my seat. Needless to say we never got the money. All the other pie-in-the-sky ideas that came from the harm-reduction projects got it instead. Getting the people they were putting forward off drugs wasn't one of their criteria because they were all on methadone. Scottish Enterprise had had to move the goalposts. Whether they realised that about 95 per cent of them wouldn't be sticking to methadone, who knows, but this would be more good money wasted.

The introduction of the Ecstasy scene to Glasgow was also bringing a different kind of drug-addict to Calton Athletic. They were younger and had started off just having fun with Ecstasy. Then they'd move on to other drugs, like speed and cocaine. Next it was downers to come down off Ecstasy, or worse, they'd start smoking or snorting heroin to come down. They were on the slippery slope, and if we didn't take action to get to these youngsters then the needle and infection were sure to follow.

As this disaster was happening around us, we continued with our schools and Under-21s programmes, while having to deal with the Scottish Drug Forum and now the National Helpline. To give the National Helpline their due, they faxed us that letter from the Scottish Drug Forum that sure as hell did tell them to withdraw our details and replace it with a blank piece of paper. No explanation was given as to why our details were to be withdrawn at a time when drug deaths were reaching record levels.

If the Social Work and the Health Board hadn't been so underhand, I believe we may have been able to prevent some of these deaths. Even one life saved would have been worth it. At least when Calton Athletic were part of the system, we were getting hundreds of people off drugs each year, which gave everybody else hope. That hope had been taken away, as they were trying to create an illusion through the National Helpline and the Drug Action Teams that we didn't exist.

Yet we had given young people hope with our Under-21s programme and School Drugs Awareness team. Our credibility had been such that we had been invited by Rangers to Ibrox to provide a service on drug awareness for the young players. Big Archie Knox, then assistant manager, sat in on it. Craig Moore, who had just arrived from Australia, was there, along with Barry Ferguson. Alex Rae would join us at a later date, and he impressed me with his attitude. When Tommy Burns became Celtic manager, they asked us to do a presentation to their young players. It went down tremendously well. I can't thank Walter Smith and Tommy Burns enough for this. It was in the early days of the School Drugs Awareness team, and inviting us to work with them only increased our credibility. We were also invited to St Aloysius' College, probably the most prestigious Roman Catholic school in the city. I can't thank St Aloysius' College enough either, and Father Henvey, for giving us that opportunity. After all if it was good enough for Rangers, Celtic and St Aloysius' College, surely it was good enough for other schools in Glasgow?

However, we were blocked by the health authorities, part of whose remit was drug education in schools. They'd come up with the idea of Drugwise, an information pack that was going to solve all the problems in schools. At the same time they were pretending that they didn't have a problem in schools. Then there was Drugwise mark two, then mark three, and both were as ineffective as mark one. Drugwise didn't work in schools, and the problem in Glasgow schools got worse. The age group involved was getting younger. Something drastic had to be done, and I believed that the school platform was the best opportunity you could get for changing attitudes.

We only started to get into Glasgow primary schools when Ken Coster was appointed as the new director of education. He gave us the opportunity to do a presentation to the 200 head teachers in Glasgow primaries. We did it with 25 heads at a time. This gave us the opportunity to get rid of the misconceptions that had been created about us, and I'm delighted to say the Glasgow primaries climbed on board. The presentations were in May, and by the end of the term we had already gone out to 16 primary schools. The following year we did around 50. This coincided with a similar amount through in Edinburgh. We were invited to the International Conference Centre in Edinburgh for a seminar on drugs education in schools, and all the best 'practice' in the country were there, such as Drugwise and Police Box. Unknown to us, the presentations were getting evaluated, and in spite of quite a few in the audience being no friends of Calton Athletic I was astounded by the result.

That day also drew attention to my own health problems. Just before I was ready to go and do the presentation, I had gone to the toilet. As time was short, I had to run back up a flight of stairs. When I got to the platform, I was short of breath, and when I started to speak, nothing came out. I took a drink of water, tried again, but nothing was coming out too clearly. I managed to say I couldn't get any breath and I would hand over to our School Drugs Awareness team. I told the audience to just sit back and keep an open mind, and hopefully they'd enjoy it and gain some information.

The schools team were tremendous that day, and in the evaluation they came out tops. The majority thought it was 'very good'. The rest thought it was 'good'. Nobody thought it was 'fair' or 'bad'. Nobody else had percentages like it. On that day we demonstrated for the first time that we were the most effective educational tool, and we were up against stiff competition.

Soon after, I was invited to a seminar about drugs and sport in London. Tony Banks, the sports minister, was there, and in our workshop there were two other English organisations who had both started football teams trying to achieve what we had. Listening to them was just like hearing ourselves in the early days, with the same kinds of problems. We had given them hope, and at least down in London that day we saw groups who were basing themselves on Calton Athletic. We weren't seeing this in Scotland, but English projects had started turning up at Calton Athletic for advice and information.

Unfortunately, this was England, while back home in Scotland the question we got asked more than any other was why could we not have more Calton Athletics up here? I believe that, by this time, Drug Action Teams had given up hope of getting people off drugs. They'd failed, and all they were doing now was coming up with excuses. The favourite was, 'It's so complex.'

I don't think it was complex. I think they were making it complex. I see it as pretty straightforward. You can only help people who want help. If somebody doesn't want help, there's not much that can be done for them. Yet all the resources were getting spent on people who didn't want help. Things needed to change, and they still do. People who want it have got to get relief, and we can get people off drugs. We've proved it time and again.

There is a way of preventing the next generation getting into a drug quagmire, and that's by deglamorising the whole scene. There's nothing glamorous about infection or methadone, destroying your family or finishing up in a psychiatric hospital or becoming a statistic. When I started off using, I didn't know anybody who had died of drugs. Now the list was horrendous – people who I knew personally, friends, neighbours, Cardross residents, people in other rehabs, former prisoners. I don't think I know anybody who knows more young people who have died. I believe an awful lot of them could have been saved. I know when I was looking for help, I wanted to go somewhere that was serious, because I was serious, and I've since discovered that I wasn't unique. I think that's what we've got to start to do. If people want to get off drugs, they should be fast-tracked immediately. We've got to separate them from those who don't want to get off drugs. I believe that when people phone up for help and they want to get their kids off drugs, they should be directed to projects that do exactly that.

In Scotland the questionnaire that people fill in for the National Helpline is different from in England. In England you have to specifically choose between a rehabilitation or a harm-reduction project. In Scotland you don't have to put the policy you want down. When we got removed from the National Helpline, I wrote to the Scottish Executive about the skulduggery and the questionnaire. The Scottish Drug Forum admitted it was flawed and needed to be changed.

If they're a harm-reduction project, people should know they're a harm-reduction project. We're a recovery project. We want to get people free of drugs, and we're proud of it. We ended up being persecuted because of this, but we know that 90 per cent of the people in Scotland want that service for their kids – to get them off drugs, not to keep them on drugs. That's a fact of life.

When I was down in London, I also met Dawn French's mother and was delighted to get a good chance to speak to her. She was involved in a rehabilitation project for women. There was somebody listening that day who invited us to Northumberland. They had been involved in a partnership through European funding with Germans and Spaniards, and, as part of that process, they had a conference in each country. Northumberland invited us to speak at theirs. I wasn't sure how the accent would go down with the Germans and the Spanish, but it went down well with the hosts because we were asked to do our schools programme in Northumberland.

Their chief constable was a guy called Crispin Strachan, who had been the assistant chief constable in Strathclyde, where part of his remit had been drug work. I'd got on fine with Crispin at first. Then I heard about his trip to New York with Kevin Orr, who was the head of the Drugs Squad. Crispin had prepared for it, but when the time came to do his presentation, all that the New York police had wanted to know about was Calton Athletic and *Trainspotting*. Apparently this did not go down too well with Crispin.

Not long after this he got the job as chief constable in Northumberland. I didn't suspect there was any resentment, but people in Northumberland started to tell us they were having problems with Crispin regarding the invitation to Calton Athletic and had we done anything to upset him? Of course we hadn't. The only thing was that he had gone to America to do a talk and the people there wanted to find out about Calton Athletic and *Trainspotting*, because the film had just come out in America.

Meantime it was agreed I was to do a presentation in Northumberland with the deputy drugs tsar present. It went down very well, and nobody voiced any concerns. They appreciated in England that it could work, and soon we were taking our programme to thousands of kids in Berwick, Blyth, Morpeth and down in Doncaster. That one-day seminar achieved more than many years of effort had in Scotland.

Another bonus at this time was that two of our young players broke through into the ranks of the professional game. Alan Mitchell and Derek Colquhoun were part of the original six boys that had come to us along with my son David, and now these two were about to sign professional football forms with Stranraer FC. The manager was Campbell Murray, and he phoned me up and asked if I would act as a witness. I was delighted to do so. He asked if we could meet in Paisley near the Kibble approved school. Did I know where that was? I had to laugh. 'Campbell, I know exactly where it is. That's my old school.' Indeed it was my Alma Mater when I was a young man of 15, and now I was going back all these years later for a different purpose. I was going back to be a witness.

This professional signing wasn't just good for the boys and Calton Athletic, but it let everybody in the community know that if you were good enough, you could still make it through the Calton Athletic programme.

CHAPTER THIRTY-FIVE

Robbie Williams

It was time to kill two birds with the one stone again down in London. I had won the Unsung Hero Award twice already from the Celebrities Guild of Great Britain, and they asked if we would like to nominate somebody for the award from Scotland. They asked us to put forward a young male and a female. I proposed my deputy Davie Main, as he's the biggest unsung hero I've ever seen at Calton Athletic. His work has paid off all over Glasgow, and by this time he had been with us for ten years. The young female was Kerry Condron, who had done an awful lot of work. She had been involved in the cycle to Paris at the World Cup, the School Drugs Awareness team and the Under-21s programme, and had done numerous TV and newspaper interviews.

We had also arranged a fundraising football match for the same day, by coincidence, as the Unsung Hero ceremony. The Trainspotters had come to our rescue again as we had been a year without statutory funding and had made painful pay-offs. We still had an overdraft. It had cost us a lot of money to maintain our services, especially with the older age group, whose funding had been withdrawn. We had decided to keep them on board rather than dump them, despite the statutory funders taking away the money to do the job.

The match also coincided with Scotland's play-off against England for a place at Euro 2000. To make it interesting the Trainspotters suggested that we should make ours a Scotland v. England match, with a host of Scottish stars playing for Calton Athletic. Forty of us set off for London, with the game to be played at Brentford's ground. Polygram had taken care of the cost of the venue. We arrived in London an hour before Scotland were due to play England in the first leg at Hampden. It was a disaster, as Scotland lost 2–0. If we couldn't beat England at Hampden, nobody gave us a hope in hell of beating them at Wembley four days later. Nobody, that is, except Craig Brown and Calton Athletic. We were determined to make amends the next day when we played the English celebrities in what could not be described as a friendly. There was no way we were going to be beaten.

When we arrived at Brentford on the Sunday, the first person I bumped into was Jimmy Boyle. Jimmy was going to be playing for us, and he was pretty excited. 'Thank Christ you've arrived, Davie. You want to see that English team, there's about 20 of them. They all look quite good. They've all got the England strips on, and there's only five Scottish celebrities in the dressing-room, so thank Christ you've arrived.'

We got into the dressing-room to find that Robbie Williams was playing for the English team. He had just flown in from America, and his latest single had gone to no. 1. He had a lot of reasons for not coming, but he turned up, and that made the atmosphere electric.

Our celebrities were John Gordon Sinclair, Jimmy Boyle, Chick Young and Richard Jobson. Chick was down in London to cover the Wembley match for the BBC. He had brought along the cameras, and the BBC were going to film the game and make it part of a special *Sportscene* programme that would be shown on the eve of the Wembley game. We thought this was a nice touch. Robbie Williams was playing, the cameras were there and it would be a souvenir for the rest of our lives.

As well as Robbie Williams the English team had Jude Law, Robbie from *EastEnders* and Stuart Trill, who was now top man at

Universal. He was not a bad player, and this was the second time he'd played against us. The England team looked good.

I announced our team, and Chick Young – being Chick Young – had suggested that I play him in midfield and make it easy for everybody else. I had to laugh at this, but I gave Chick the opportunity to play there, and, to his credit, he had the game of his life. You'd have thought he had written the script, as he scored two goals.

Before they went out, I told the boys, 'This is supposed to be a friendly, but we've got Scotland strips on and they've got England strips, and they'll be trying to win, to gloat. So let's go out and show them what we can do.'

And that's what we did. I put my own son David in midfield beside Chick to help him out and had Davie Main at the back. I've got to say all the celebrities who played for Scotland were tremendous: Richard Jobson, John Gordon Sinclair, Chick and John Hodge. John's a very quiet, unassuming man. He does a lot of walking, and I didn't think he would be too clever at football, but he did a smashing job, as everybody else did.

When the two teams were warming up, I noticed one of the English players going over to talk to my son and Davie Main. It was Robbie Williams. They were gabbing away. Robbie was making himself available to everybody, but after he'd finished he came running over to me just before the whistle. He said he was telling the two Davies that he was going to chair his own first recovery meeting that night. Would it be possible for us to get him onto our team at half-time? Of course it would. We were flattered that a guy like Robbie Williams, who was playing with an England top on, wanted to play for Calton Athletic.

We were 2–1 up at half-time. The first goal came when Danny Boyle pulled down Jimmy Boyle in the penalty box. Chick took the penalty and scored and got another goal before half-time. In the dressing-room I'd forgotten the conversation I'd had with Robbie, but all of a sudden the door burst open. Robbie threw off his England strip. There was no way he was not going to get a game for us. He'd seen us playing and liked our passion. Could he play up-front? One of the English guys butted in. No way could Robbie play for Scotland. He was English. One of our boys shot back, 'What do ye mean, no Scottish? He humped two Scottish birds when he was in rehab. That's good enough fir us.' We all had a good laugh, Robbie included, and he pulled on the Lion Rampant.

If we were good in the first half, we were even better in the second half. Robbie was smashing. I said earlier, that's the first time I'd met him. To be honest I probably thought he would be some sort of wee nyaff, but I found him to be a smashing guy. He's got a fair physique and is not a bad football player. He stayed on until we went 4–1 in front. The fourth goal was a free-kick, thirty yards out. My son David took it and it was a tremendous strike. When it went in, Robbie Williams was first over to congratulate him. When he was leaving, Robbie ran over and shook my hand. 'Davie, we'll meet up again some day.' I hope it happens, and we'll fill a stadium in Glasgow.

Robbie was totally different from what I'd expected. He was just like somebody from the East End of Glasgow, more like a Calton Athletic boy. He fitted in no problem, and although he was English we were delighted to have him. Anybody who can fly in from America to raise the awareness of Calton Athletic when their record has just gone to no. 1 in the States is not a bad guy.

Our friend Mike Trace, the deputy drugs tsar, was also playing for England that day and he had got their strips from the FA. Chick Young had used his influence to get us the Scottish strips. Maybe now, we thought, Scotland would take a lead off us and go in and do the business at Wembley – and that's what they did indeed do.

Calton Athletic had won on the Sunday, and Scotland won on the Tuesday. We all watched Chick's special on BBC *Sportscene* on Monday evening, which showed our game at Brentford. It looked tremendous, and viewers were treated to what they might have thought were slow-motion replays of Chick's goals. The purpose of that game was to fundraise and to create an awareness in England that we were providing a service in English schools, and it succeeded. However, our appearance on BBC *Sportscene* also created further awareness in Scotland. Being on TV for the whole of Britain to see helped to get rid of the illusion that we had shut down. That game was really special, and to round off the day some of us headed for the Four Seasons Hotel in Park Lane, where young Kerry would pick up her Unsung Hero Award.

We had taken a table of 20. All of the guys had on full Highland regalia, and the women looked fantastic in their evening dresses. Danny Boyle joined us as our guest, as did Dr John Reid, who was then Secretary of State for Scotland. John Reid was on the top table that night but made a point of coming over to ours. I've often wished a guy like John Reid was in the Scottish Executive, as I'm sure we would have got a lot more support from them.

Kerry was presented with her award by Keith Michel, who's most famous for his role in *Henry VIII*. Keith has a great actor's voice, and he made a lovely speech. Kerry got her award, and Calton Athletic were ecstatic. Here was a young person from our Under-21s programme receiving a national award. The quality was starting to emerge. A couple of them had become professional footballers, and now Kerry had won this.

We had just completed our most successful year to date in the schools programme, despite statutory funding having ceased the year before. The Under-21s were doing well, and we kept our older ones on board. The only difference was that we weren't taking any more older people on board. Our statistics at the end of that year proved we were still more productive than any other project, in spite of losing the money, which was of course a drain on our self-generated resources.

We had achieved many remarkable things over the years, but to have two events on the one day down in London was special. Both of these could never have been achieved without the Trainspotters. They'd arranged the game in London and donated a few quid so we could take a bigger party down to cheer on Kerry. The Trainspotters had stood by us in our hour of need. Universal and Channel 4 had also been a great help. Without it at that particular time I don't know what we would have done. It wasn't just the financial help; it was the boost they gave to our morale. The only shame was that some of our old Trainspotting pals couldn't make it that night. Bobby Carlyle was over in America for the *David Letterman Show* to promote the Bond movie, while Ewan McGregor was doing his first *Star Wars* film.

CHAPTER THIRTY-SIX

Backstabbing

Back in Glasgow Jim Orr, who was the assistant chief constable of Glasgow, came to see us. I was impressed with Jim and hoped he could help to get rid of some of the misconceptions about Calton Athletic. He was sympathetic and told us to give him a call if we had any problems. I was to take him up on that, but at least here was a visitor from a statutory agency, namely the police, who wasn't hostile to Calton Athletic. He could see what we were achieving. The police knew better than anybody else that Calton Athletic hadn't just stopped people taking drugs, we were helping them change their lifestyles and get away from the thieving and criminality that goes with being a drug-addict. Maybe the police thought we deserved a decent crack of the whip.

I was also impressed with another visitor, Angus McKay. The drug problem came under his remit as a minister in the Scottish Executive. He had set up a Drug Enforcement Agency and was wanting to monitor and evaluate every project in the country. He was young and enthusiastic, and I got the chance to demonstrate to him exactly what Calton Athletic were doing through our computerised database for the schools team. He also met young people who had graduated from the Under-21s programme. Angus was from Edinburgh. We had already done a third of the primary schools there, and I'm quite sure word of that must have filtered back to him. A few of the schools that we had done were in his constituency.

Jim Orr went on to become head of the Drug Enforcement Agency. In early 2000 we were invited to a meeting down in Pitt Street. Strathclyde Police were putting together a drugs awareness campaign, 'Choices for Life', for schools. A record number of 32,000 pupils from Strathclyde were invited to the Scottish Exhibition and Conference Centre in Glasgow for the two-day event, along with teachers and parents. It was decided that there would be a separate programme for the 3,000 teachers. We hoped to be able to encourage most of them to attend our seminar on awareness, but for some reason Calton Athletic were not one of the projects on their programme. Davie Main said to me, 'That's a wasted opportunity – all the teachers here and us no' getting a chance to speak to them.'

We really should have been speaking to them because, by this time, Calton Athletic were doing more schools in Strathclyde than all the other projects put together. It was the usual skulduggery, and SAD had got at the police, who were sponsoring the event. We phoned the police to tell them about the missed opportunity but were brushed off. 'Sorry, there's nothing we can do, the agenda is made up.'

This was a total liberty, so I phoned Jim Orr. We weren't asking for favours, only a level playing-field, and the results would speak for themselves. Jim phoned back in half an hour and told us we had our slot. We were delighted, but the other drug projects were demented. The proof of the pudding would come out in the evaluation, which we were confident about.

Stevie Orr from the School Drugs Awareness team did four different presentations at the conference. He was well received at each and every one of them, but our programme didn't get evaluated. This was a slight oversight. I don't know whether it was a genuine one or not, but we wanted to be evaluated. I'm quite sure the people who attended it knew in their hearts and souls who had done the best presentation that day. It was Stevie Orr from Calton Athletic.

One particular incident epitomises how and why we fell out with

SAD. A young boy, Andrew Woodlock, had died through taking Ecstasy. I had been asked to come to the Hilton Hotel for a press conference. I arrived, and they had Andrew's mother, Phyllis, with them. I felt she was being paraded in front of the media to try to get some credibility for SAD. I found it all extremely distasteful. I knew plenty of people who had lost their kids through drugs. None of them ever got dragged out in front of cameras by Calton Athletic. They were all too devastated. They had to have time to mourn, to get over their loss. I've got to say I found Phyllis to be a nice woman, but I don't think she should have been asked to front it. I think she should have been allowed to grieve in peace.

The good people had left SAD long ago, and the politicians who were running it were not as enthusiastic. It was Michael Forsyth's idea to start it, and the Labour Party inherited it, with Sam Galbraith taking over. At a meeting through in South Queensferry I looked around the room. There weren't many people there that I respected. No progress was being made. Our School Drugs Awareness team had been piloted for funding from SAD, and I knew that none of the others could touch it, yet I was still having to find the money to keep us going. The Under-21s programme was just about to go through the pilot, and I knew the same thing would happen. I started to pick up my papers, as I couldn't take any more of the nonsense, the negative vibes and the hostility. A couple of meetings previously I'd fallen out with 'Proddy Roddy' Campbell. He didn't like what I'd said at a SAD council meeting, but that's what I was there for – to give an honest opinion based on my experience. Roddy reminded me who funded us. I took this as a red flag and let him know. Unfortunately I've never had the chance to speak to him since, as Roddy also left SAD and the Drug Action Teams not long after. Although I had a falling out with him, I respected him, and I knew he was under pressure from the rest of the Drug Action Teams.

I'd also had a falling out with Jack Irvine, which I didn't regret. Word had got back to me that Jack was going about referring to us as 'the boys from the Gallowgate without an O level between them'. That made me pretty angry. I pulled up Jack before the meeting and told him I was one of 'the boys from the Gallowgate without an O level' that he'd been talking about. If he continued to badmouth us, he had me to deal with. Take me if you can, but leave my men alone.

At that point he tried to point his finger at me. I told him if he didn't take it down, I would bite it off. He took his finger down sharpish and began to bluster. I invited him outside if he wanted to continue our conversation. There were a lot of people about, but I didn't care. I was angry.

So I walked out of that SAD council meeting in South Queensferry and told Sam Galbraith and the rest that I wouldn't be back. No matter how much they badmouthed us, we would rely on our work in the field and word of mouth to keep going. As I walked out of the meeting, Margo MacDonald came running after me and asked me to go back in. She told me not to chuck it. I'd be better fighting it from the inside. I told her I wasn't chucking anything. There was no point in fighting it from the inside if people didn't want to listen. They could stay in their talking shop, bolster their careers and salaries and waste public funds on PR and advertising. I intended to reach as many schools as possible and keep as many young people off drugs as we could.

The final fallout with our statutory funders hadn't happened yet, but this was all part of the process. I never went back, but a couple of weeks later Tom Farmer approached us with David Macauley. He told us that if I didn't resign they could put our Under-21s project through for £50,000. That sounded good, although it meant we had to find £50,000 from our own self-generated resources. I agreed to it, and from that pilot scheme we opened the academy in College Street. Tom Farmer came along and saw that it was a success.

I may not have liked what I saw with Phyllis Woodlock, but worse was to come. MAD had just come into being after a young boy died in Cranhill. They went on a march and milked it for publicity. Gail McCann, a Glasgow councillor, was using her influence to try to drum up support. MAD had now got involved with the families of two people who had recently died. At least with the first one they'd got somebody's parents on board. For the second one, they never did anything for the poor mother of the boy. They made the excuse that she was a drug-addict. She might have been, but she was that boy's mother and she was hurting. The boy's granny was also hurting. But they got pushed right out of the picture as MAD took over. At this time they didn't even have a constitution, nor any clear aims or objectives, yet within a very short space of time MAD had money, serious money, and the project they were going to deliver was a methadone programme. To justify it they said they were going to have acupuncture as well, as if that would make any difference to people who didn't want to stop using drugs. The last thing Cranhill needed was a methadone programme.

During the MAD campaign a journalist from *The Times* came up to do an article. He arrived in Cranhill and asked some local youngsters if they could get any drugs. Yes, methadone. They disappeared for five minutes and came back with it. The boys told him it was easier to get methadone in Cranhill than a pint of milk. MAD had become 'Mothers Against Certain Drugs'. They certainly weren't against methadone because they were getting resources, and that was what it was all about for them – getting resources for jobs. They were no different from the other parent groups before them. The Glasgow Family Association had sold out and were supporting methadone. They were housed in the Crisis Centre, the main distribution point for methadone in the city. The East End Drug Initiative had been managed by the parents of drug-addicts, who swore they would never do methadone when it first started. As soon as the pressure was on Calton Athletic, they switched the goalposts and became the biggest prescribers in the East End. These were mothers who said they would never get involved with methadone. Family support groups also started calling themselves 'social inclusion' groups. This was to get resources, and no doubt they'd sell their souls to the harm-reduction policy to get them. Their kids were still using drugs, so they'd found a way to justify it. This was all at the expense of people who wanted to get their kids off drugs without getting involved in this harm-reduction policy. A lot of these groups were once friendly towards Calton Athletic. A lot of them we gave money to. A lot of them we gave support to. We took a lot of their kids in and had a go with them, but that didn't matter. When the city council turned the screws on Calton Athletic, they just stood by and watched.

I feel bad for these people and how they allowed themselves to be manipulated by the Social Work department. These groups weren't ordinary people from the community. They were people who had social workers because their kids were using drugs. Once Social Work got their claws into them, they took over. That was their policy, and that's what they've done to every single group in Glasgow. We resisted it, and it cost us our funding. We didn't start Calton Athletic to dish out methadone to people. We saw that the best way to help was to get people off drugs, and now, more importantly than ever, we had to prevent the next generation from getting into drugs.

These harm-reduction groups thought they were serious challengers to Calton Athletic in schools. Their idea was to replace us and get people who were on methadone to go in. This would have been a disaster, as it would have sent out the wrong message. It would have told kids that you could make a mess of your life, still continue to use drugs and get a job while you were doing them, so really there was nothing wrong with drugs. That's not what it should be about in schools.

Those parents maybe thought they were doing their best for their own, but they should also have had the interests of the community at heart. Maybe one day they'll realise the folly of what they've done. They don't represent the parents of Glasgow. We are in contact with parents all the time who come looking for help. Most of them are hard-working people. The only problem they've got is their son or their daughter is using drugs. They're demented with worry and looking for help, and we're there. By and large the people who come through our door are decent people. They don't want the Social Work department in their lives. All they want is for their kids to get off the drugs. We can respond that same day and give them the best advice and information possible. If their son or daughter wants to get off drugs, we'll do it as quickly as possible and get them on the programme. And we're also taking another prescription off the black market.

Calton Athletic have not sold out. We've stuck to everything we've believed in and done our best. Let's not forget either that our relationship with SAD had started on a friendly basis. We were more than happy to help.

The propaganda against us at times was bonkers. Joan Burnie of the *Daily Record*, one of Scotland's leading columnists, did a piece about her trip with the prime minister on the battle-bus during the Devolution Referendum in 1999. Tony Blair had just announced he was appointing a drugs tsar for the UK, so they were discussing the Scottish drug problem. In her column she said the prime minister need look no further than Calton Athletic in Glasgow and Davie Bryce for the new drugs tsar if they were serious about changing things. I had a smile on my face when I read it. I knew it would wind up a lot of people. A few days later I phoned Joan up. She was delighted to hear from us, and when I thanked her she said, 'Davie, I want to tell you about a funny phone call I got.'

The caller was anonymous but sounded like a professional person. He asked Joan was she not aware that I was running the Glasgow underworld? Joan said surely the police would know if Davie Bryce was running the Glasgow underworld, but the caller said that I had them in my pocket. Joan replied, 'Then surely the procurator fiscal would know about it?' The caller explained that I had him in my pocket too. Joan laughed about it, but what struck her was that it's hard to get her mobile number, so this wasn't just some headcase off the street.

Around the same time I got a phone call from Dana O'Dwyer, who had chaired the quarterly meetings for the Health Board when we met with them and Social Work. Dana told me that somebody had informed her I had her address. I told her I didn't have her address, I wasn't interested in where she lived and what would I want to know that for? Obviously Dana had been getting fed the same black propaganda and was phoning me up in a terrified state. It was utter nonsense, and I was surprised she believed them, but these were the lengths that people were going to in their attempts to discredit Calton Athletic.

They made out that we intimidated people, frightened drug-addicts into coming off the drugs. You can't frighten drug-addicts to come off drugs, but maybe they thought that's what our secret was. If only it was that simple. But this conspiracy against us was serious, not because it blackened our name but because it prevented us from helping people who we could have saved but who ended up being another drug-death statistic.

The final fallout with David Macauley came in Edinburgh at a seminar. He asked if Kerry Condron could go down to Downing Street as a guest of the prime minister in recognition for the work she had done in schools. I told him it would be fine for Kerry to go, but she wasn't going down with SAD. She would be going down with her mother and me. Kerry's achievements in the drugs field made her a perfect representative of Calton Athletic. She was 21 at the time. She had come to us looking for help at 17, showed a bit of gratitude and progressed to working in the School Drugs Awareness team, and because of this she was getting called down to Downing Street.

I don't know who exactly got her the invitation, but maybe they hoped they could manipulate her. Kerry, though, was solid. The day came for her to go, and David Macauley still tried to poach her, right up to the last minute. I had to put him in the picture.

When Kerry and I went down to Downing Street with her mother, we did a couple of TV interviews. I wasn't going into Downing Street myself. I had already met Tony Blair several years before in the Calton. I had been invited to a conference at St Alphonsus chapel by Father Willie Slaven, head of the Scottish Drug Forum. Tony Blair, who wasn't the prime minister then, Jack McConnell, who was general secretary of the Labour Party in Scotland at the time, and John McFall, MP, were all with him. There were a couple of other drug groups there too, and Tony Blair was asking us all different questions. Calton Athletic was the only one that was aimed at getting people off drugs. All the rest had already been involved in this 'harm minimisation', as it was called at the time. The other groups felt a wee bit uncomfortable as they couldn't give the prime minister their usual spiel because I was sitting there.

Before Kerry's meeting with Tony Blair we went to Millbank for a television interview. I was in a waiting-room when, just as Kerry started to speak, a group of people came in. Among them were Gerry Adams and Martin McGuinness. The Sinn Fein leaders stood watching Kerry doing the business on the TV. The two of them had been with Tony Blair that morning. When Kerry finished, Martin McGuinness asked us if we would be prepared to come to Derry. I said we would. We had provided services in Belfast twice already, once in east Belfast and the other time in west Belfast. When we'd

228

been in west Belfast, big Eamon Doherty was giving the talk, and Gerry Adams had come walking in. I was told he was very impressed with what he heard. He recalled that day as we were watching Kerry.

I was impressed with both Adams and McGuinness. I had seen them on TV over the years. They struck me as sincere and serious guys, and I believe in my heart and soul after meeting them that they have a true desire for peace. I told people as much when I got back to the East End of Glasgow.

We had photographs taken with them and shook hands, wishing each other all the best. It was a treat bumping into them. This wasn't the first time we'd had contact with the Irish outside the Emerald Isle. A couple of groups from Belfast had visited us: mixed groups of former prisoners – Republicans and Loyalists – along with community activists. They loved what they saw at Calton Athletic, and what took them a bit of time to really get used to was how we managed to get the Protestants and the Catholics sitting down together. Glasgow's a divided city as well, but they were amazed at how we could get Rangers and Celtic supporters sitting down together, never mind getting them off the drugs. We had our bigots in the early days, but they're not tolerated at Calton Athletic. This service isn't just for men and women; it's for Catholics and Protestants, people of any religion or no religion, and of any colour. Nobody's discriminated against at Calton Athletic. These people from Northern Ireland were good communicators. Probably the only wrong route that the former prisoners had taken in life was standing up for a cause they believed in, and during their long years in prison their attitudes had changed. A bit of self-realisation came along and change had come into their lives the same way it had come into mine. I wished them all the best. It doesn't matter what side of the religious divide you're on in Northern Ireland; as long as you're making serious attempts towards peace that's fine by us. The Troubles have done a lot of damage, and a lot of young people have turned to drugs.

We hope that we're able to pass on the experience we've gained, and not just for people from Northern Ireland. We've had an awful lot of groups up from England, as well as people from Canada and media interest from Japan, Germany and France. One programme we appeared on was *The World of Football* on the satellite channel. That programme went out to 140 countries. So people who saw it in these 140 countries would have known more about Calton Athletic's Under-21s than the Scottish Drug Forum did, or the Scottish Executive and the Scottish Parliament.

CHAPTER THIRTY-SEVEN

Shame and Blame

I felt vindicated when Davie Main attended a seminar funded by the Robertson Trust in November 2004 addressed by Clive Fairweather, the former inspector of prisons. It was to announce the outcome of research about jails being awash with methadone by Professor Neil McKeganey of Glasgow University, one of Scotland's foremost experts on addiction. Professor McKeganey's research showed that 60 per cent of addicts entering treatment wanted to come off drugs through abstinence. Only 1 per cent were looking to use drugs safely. Professor McKeganey stressed the need for balance in services, instead of methadone being the only game in town.

Here he was putting his finger on the issue that brought Calton Athletic into conflict with the Health Board and Social Work department six years earlier in 1998. Fears we had expressed for a decade had materialised. It was clear from Professor McKeganey's research that the majority of school pupils wanted recovering drug-addicts to educate them about prevention. Glasgow University's research in 2004 was again echoing what Calton Athletic had been saying throughout the '90s.

Neil McKeganey's report undermined the credibility of the

government's £7 million methadone programme. He found that drug-addicts were less likely to commit crime and more likely to find work if they went through 'cold turkey' withdrawal than those who did not. His research revealed that half of the addicts who take methadone are likely to offend, compared with less than a third of those on abstinence programmes. It also found that those who went cold turkey were twice as likely to try to get a job. The research showed that many methadone users were topping up their prescriptions with illegal drugs and committing crimes to pay for their addiction.

'If you think of it as a race between these two approaches to get into employment, it is clear that the abstinence approach is ahead,' Professor McKeganey told the media. 'Methadone is not a magic bullet that removes all offending behaviour. Work we have carried out with recovered addicts has shown that recovery has been about building an entirely new life that is not based around drugs and association with other drug-users, and that is what the abstinence programmes are about. Methadone can leave damaged people dependent on powerful drugs for ten to fifteen years.'

Familiar, isn't it? This is much the same message I've been banging on about throughout this book. It was not news to us. It was what 'the boys from the Gallowgate without an O Level between them' had been trying to tell the Scottish Office and Scottish Executive and all the statutory agencies for over a decade. Our research had been done on the job, out in the field working with junkies and seeing friends and loved ones die. Previous research by Professor McKeganey also backed us up that most addicts would prefer the cold-turkey approach to long-term addiction to methadone. He also said, 'We need many more agencies that have an explicit abstinence focus that will work with you from day one to take drugs out of your life.'

Here I should explain how hard it was since we got our funding cut in 1998 for people to find their way to Calton Athletic. Paul was 20, came from East Kilbride and had been involved in drugs, starting off on the dance scene and ending up on heroin. He went to his doctor, who gave him methadone. It worked OK for a while, but he started using other drugs with it. The only thing the doctor suggested was the Glasgow Crisis Centre. His family took him, and while they were in the waiting-room they were offered heroin three times. When they saw a counsellor, he suggested putting Paul back on methadone. He didn't want to go on methadone. He had already done it, and it hadn't worked. He was wanting direction, but the Crisis Centre couldn't help him. Then the counsellor asked him, 'Have you ever heard of Calton Athletic?'

'Is that the football team?'

'Yes, but they're more than a football team. I used to go to Calton Athletic, and it would be ideal for you. You're only 20, and they've still got a service for Under-21s. I'll give you their number but don't tell anybody. I'll phone them up and tell them to expect you.'

He'd told the boy not to tell anybody that he'd recommended us because he might have lost his job. Six months later Paul had come through our Under-21s rehabilitation programme and had received his red shirt from Calton Athletic. His family were delighted.

Alex was 35 and had been using drugs for 15 years. His younger brother had come to Calton Athletic two years earlier. Alex wasn't daft. He saw how his brother came off drugs, got a job and had a family. But Alex couldn't come to Calton Athletic because our programme for adults had stopped, so he had had to go through 'official' channels. If you phone for help, you have to wait six months for a rehab. If you don't want off the drugs, they'll put you on a methadone programme. Six months is an eternity to wait. Alex got the chance to detox in Parkhead Hospital, as he was struggling from drug-induced mental illness – schizophrenia. They took him in for five days. After detox they had to discharge him, because it was a drug-induced mental illness.

They gave Alex tablets which didn't take the withdrawals away but which helped to carry him for the next 12 days. He then had his first meeting with the drug worker from Parkhead Hospital. He was now 14 days off heroin. His brother went with him. While they were in the group session, a client appeared and apologised for being 20 minutes late. He got told he wasn't 20 minutes late, he was 2 days late. Nevertheless he was allowed in. All of the clients were under the influence of drugs except Alex. The drugs worker said to him, 'You look an ideal candidate for the methadone programme.' What could have possessed any drugs worker to suggest to somebody that they're an ideal candidate for the methadone programme after they have been completely detoxed from drugs for 14 days? Alex told her he didn't want it. She then suggested he was an ideal candidate for Red Towers – funding had just become available and they would send him to the respite centre down at Helensburgh. It's a respite, but not for people who have come off drugs. They'll keep you on drugs while you're in Red Towers. He said he didn't want to go to Red Towers, but she was insistent: 'It'll help you get a house if you go.' He was totally disillusioned, but his brother phoned and asked if it was OK if he brought him to us. Although officially we'd stopped taking people over 21 since they withdrew the funding, we still took people if they had the right attitude, and this guy was committed. He stuck in at Calton Athletic, and within three months Alex had done his first 10 km run, although he'd been in a terrible physical condition when he'd arrived.

The reason I'm mentioning these two is that these are the sort of hurdles people have to get over to find us. But they aren't unique. There are hundreds of people out there in Glasgow who are screaming out for Calton Athletic. If people want to use drugs, sure, let them go to the Crisis Centre, but if people want to come off drugs they should be directed to Calton Athletic. It's a miracle these two boys got to Calton Athletic, and it wasn't through officialdom.

The National Helpline had also not got its act together, despite reassuring us we would be put back on their list. A woman had phoned looking for help for her 15-year-old son. The National Helpline directed her to a project in Drumchapel. This project, however, told her that she wasn't in their catchment area. She should go to one in Anniesland. Anniesland offered her three telephone numbers for counsellors who would do it in a private capacity. The woman never took up the offer. Although she was middle class, articulate, intelligent and could afford private treatment, she rightly wanted the services that she was directed to by the National Helpline. Confused and angry she called the Scottish Drugs Forum, the coordinating body for projects in Scotland. She told them her dilemma about getting referred to Drumchapel and then Anniesland, and they suggested she phone a project called Resolve. The woman phoned up Resolve, only to find out that they were in England. They said, 'Why don't you phone Calton Athletic? You're nearer to them and they've got a good reputation.' The woman was astounded. It had taken someone in England to give her the phone number of Calton Athletic.

She came to see us with her son. He was smoking cannabis, only it wasn't joints. His mother had found his apparatus in the bedroom: the plastic bottle cut in half and used with a bucket of water to force the smoke straight into the lungs. It is the most extreme way you can take cannabis. When you start to do 'buckets', you don't go back to smoking joints. Joints are like throwing fairy cakes to an elephant compared with the buckets. The boy was intelligent. He didn't smoke fags. He played rugby. His parents were sound. The young man had counselling and we got him on the right path. An anonymous donation of £300 arrived soon after. We found out it was from this woman. She told us she wasn't going to let the issue rest with the National Helpline. She told them what she had had to go through to get to Calton Athletic. What was the reason for it? They couldn't give her one. We phoned up ourselves, and sure enough they couldn't give you advice on Calton Athletic, even when you asked for it specifically. After we had been reassured the year before that it had been rectified, the same thing had happened again. When we contacted them, they couldn't apologise enough and admitted that the mistake was theirs. I thought for this to happen twice was too much of a coincidence.

People shouldn't have to go around the houses to find a service. There should be clear signposts. We're not a threat to other groups, and they've got to realise that. Once they do, they won't feel intimidated. Their jobs are quite secure. That seems to be their priority. Meantime there are thousands of people out there who are infected. There are also thousands out there who are not yet infected, and we should be given the opportunity to make sure that this doesn't happen.

We've had hundreds of infected people at Calton Athletic who are leading drug-free lifestyles now. Meantime people with hepatitis C aren't going to get treatment because they're on methadone, which counteracts the drugs used to treat the infection. But they need help.

We would never turn our back on anybody who is on methadone. It's just that when they're at Calton Athletic they'll not be using it. That was the same for me. I never got into recovery until I put the methadone down. I'm not against methadone used the right way – when you know you are going to come off it, and that you'll get withdrawals when you do. But for too many it prolongs or just continues their drug habit. With the right attitude, it can be a means to an end, as they gradually reduce your doses to make it slightly easier for you to stop. After all I was somebody who benefited from it, but I did it the right way and that is how I made it. If other people want to make it, they've got to do it properly. The rest is just paying lip-service, and the drug-addicts out there know that.

But perhaps the most damning statistic of the Scottish Executive's policy is that more people were dying through prescribed drugs in Glasgow in 2005 than through illegal ones. We now had state-sponsored junkies. The state, through the Health Service and pharmaceutical companies, had become the biggest pushers. At the beginning of 2005 there were 8,000 people in Glasgow on methadone, yet people are still dying. It's not stabilising people's lives but costing them. Some people do well on methadone, but they are in a small minority. The jails are awash with it, and government policy is not doing anything to take people off it. They have now even introduced 'retox' in prison. Prisoners are introduced to methadone and build up their tolerance to it before they go out, in the misguided belief that they will not use other drugs on the outside.

If you want to do something positive about your addiction, be it to heroin or, now more popularly, to cocaine, you have not a hope in hell. If you want off drugs, they will tell you there is rehab but you have to wait for months. Meantime if you want to stabilise your habit or addiction they will put you on prescribed drugs. In those 18 months you could end up in jail, hospital, infected or even pay with your life.

In 1997 the authorities had almost given up hope of getting people off. I know you can't get everybody off, but people who want off have to have a service. Record amounts of money were being poured into the drugs service, but still they were not getting people off drugs. First people need the opportunity and then help. Will-power is not enough in most cases. Addicts have to change their lifestyles, and they need help and support to do so. We don't need to reinvent the wheel. Calton Athletic have been getting people off drugs for 20 years by changing attitudes and lifestyles. It's the only way. But things will not change until more services are opened up. It is not a question of just throwing money at the problem. Too many people working in harm reduction do not understand the nature of addiction. Meantime, with more young people on cocaine, there'll be no service till they have needles hanging out of their groins. That is unacceptable.

I've looked at the Dutch experience with the coffee shops where you can purchase cannabis semi-legally, and we should learn from this in Scotland. The average age of the heroin user in Holland is 35. In Glasgow it is 19. The Dutch are doing something right, and you don't see young Dutch kids walking about with joints hanging out of their mouths. They are a cultured, talented people. They're also good at football, and most of them can speak English. Young Dutch kids don't fall into drugs, because it's there and it's legal. They can make an informed choice, with excellent drugs education, and choose not to take them. There's a lot of nonsense talked about cannabis by the likes of the zero-tolerance mob. Nobody's saying it's harmless, because if it was it would be compulsory rather than illegal. But without a doubt it's the least damaging of all the drugs that are out there. Alcohol and tobacco are more dangerous. I know; I suffer from emphysema. If you go into schools and start speaking nonsense about cannabis, the kids will think the rest is nonsense. You've got to give them a credible message.

There is a myth about cannabis being the gateway drug. It's alcohol. Our school surveys proved this. We found in primary schools in Scotland that 3 per cent of kids had tried illegal drugs. This was in Primary 7. Of those same Primary 7 kids 60 per cent of them had tried alcohol and most of them had got involved with drugs when they were under the influence of alcohol. In secondary schools 95 per cent of the kids had taken alcohol.

Scottish people, particularly support groups in the drugs field, have got a problem accepting this, because most of them are still drinking. If you take a drink and you want to talk down to young people about cannabis, they'll switch off. That's a hypocritical message. After all, booze and fags are the biggest killers in Scotland. Kids aren't daft.

The cannabis issue is a red herring. The real threat that comes from cannabis occurs when young people buy it. The dealers are selling other drugs and, just like me all those years ago, if there's no cannabis you may try something else. You've already started with the booze and the cannabis, and there were no problems there, so maybe you'll be able to handle these other drugs. There has to be a middle ground between the zero-tolerance lot, who nobody is listening to, and the other lot, who want to legalise everything.

I am against legalising everything. I go with my experience of cannabis, which tells me that that particular drug is doing very little damage when you compare it with the other drugs. I think the government would have more credibility if they realised there are millions of people out there smoking cannabis and not experiencing the problems that these fanatics from zero-tolerance groups say they are. But the other camp is perhaps just as extreme, wanting to legalise Ecstasy, cocaine and anything else. No Class A drug should ever be legalised.

In the last five years I've seen more people getting into heroin through Ecstasy than anything else. When we said this in the '90s, it was pooh-poohed, but then they were saying that if you had a drink of water you'd be OK. That was before the Ecstasy deaths. The real damage with Ecstasy is caused after the dancing, when you take other drugs to come down. Your tolerance to the other drugs builds up, the same as your tolerance to the Ecstasy. Nobody starts off taking six tabs at a time. They start off with half a tab, then a full tab. Then it's two tabs to do what a half used to do. As your tolerance builds up, you're looking for more drugs to come off it. You start taking Temazepam and Valium and build up a tolerance to them. Temazepam can be expensive, and some people were having to take about ten to come down. Christ, that's 30 quid to come down. You soon realise that all you have to do is buy a fiver bag of heroin and smoke it, believing that if you smoke or snort it, you won't get addicted.

This is the same propaganda that I heard 20 years ago, and people are still falling for it. It doesn't matter how you take heroin; whether you snort it, chase the dragon, inject it or stick it up your backside, you'll become addicted, and it happens very quickly. And when you become addicted, you lose control.

By 2000 most of the young people coming through the door at Calton Athletic had started on Ecstasy. Then they'd been introduced to amphetamines, cocaine, a cocktail of drugs, the downers. And next thing they were smoking heroin, and they weren't dancing any more and there were no nice clothes. They'd end up like the people they used to look down on and said they'd never be like. The only positive thing was that most were still snorting or chasing the dragon, rather than injecting. But if we didn't get them early, they'd build up a tolerance and start injecting, the same as the other 8–10,000 out there in Glasgow on methadone, and when they started injecting they'd become infected.

I've seen an awful lot of people start on heroin through Ecstasy. The only thing that has changed over the years is the drugs. Actual prices on the street have come down in the last 15 years, making it easier and more affordable for young people to get involved. Meantime there are at least 8,000 addicts on prescriptions every day in Glasgow, of which 6,500 are for methadone, the rest codeine or Valium. Mostly it is snorting or smoking it as crack. Do we have to wait till they start injecting big-time before we will offer help? Bear in mind that people are addicted long before a needle gets near them. If you wait till they inject, the horse has already bolted, and it is not just addiction we are talking about but the spread of infection. You can get rid of addiction with a lot of hard work and the right guidance, but you can't get rid of some infections. Incurable infections are with you for the rest of your life, with the possibility that you will infect your wife, husband or partner through sex, or friends by sharing a needle.

In the late '70s and early '80s the drug explosion took place in the schemes and the inner cities, the so-called deprived areas, but now in the twenty-first century it's right across the board. Young people from all sorts of backgrounds are into cocaine, such as affluent young professionals like sportsmen and women, bankers, accountants, lawyers, media folk. Cocaine is the most social drug, as it is associated with having a good time. When I was younger, there was very little of it about. Now it is 'cool'. It's the designer drug and part of the music scene, whereas heroin came to be seen as naff and for losers. Young people who are not into heroin think cocaine and Ecstasy are different. But we have a saying at Calton Athletic: 'They come in on different ships but they finish up in the same boat.' They start off on different drugs, but the end product is the same.

Cocaine as a Class A drug is more subtle than heroin. I have heard so much nonsense about cocaine from so-called experts on TV saying it takes seven years before you get addicted to cocaine. Ask Richard Pryor or Elton John how long it takes. It's Class A and can be every bit as insidious as heroin. The problem with cocaine is that you don't realise you are getting reeled in. But if you're taking cocaine for seven months, you have a problem. Forget the dummy experts. Listen to people who know about addiction.

One place where Calton Athletic needs to become active again is in schools. We started providing a service in schools 12 years ago. There was very little drug abuse in primary schools, and in secondary schools the main drug was cannabis, with very little Class As. But in the dance scene Ecstasy was all about having a good time, as was cocaine in wider circles. Designer drugs don't have the same stigma as smack. Young people want to look good in nice clothes, and Eccies and Charlie also make you more sexually active. With heroin you just want to sit in a corner and gouge.

This is not a moral judgement between the two drugs, though, because the reality will sink in that cocaine addiction is no different from any other addiction. You lose control, and who knows where that will take you. I know parents who have gone looking for help and been told their child's drug use is quite normal. There are 10,000 injecting while your kid is only taking a bit of Ecstasy or cocaine.

But it is every parent's nightmare that their child will or has become addicted. Parents have to be vigilant about the realities of drugs, not just the fun side but infection, crime, family break-ups, violence, courts and your children being taken away. Drugs have to be deglamorised, and prevention is the best form of cure.

Calton Athletic was the most effective service, but it has never been supported by the Scottish Executive, although it has been obvious since 1997 that this is a route which should be followed. I believe this could have prevented thousands of young people from becoming addicted and infected. Official research suggests addiction and infection go hand in hand. Out of 50,000 addicts receiving treatment in Scotland today, as many as 86 per cent are infected, if not more.

The need for a credible policy should be no. 1 on the drugs agenda. But the state of play today is that anyone wanting treatment will have very little chance of getting abstinence-based treatment. What they will be offered is harm-reduction counselling and a substitute drug on prescription, namely methadone or something similar – that is, if they are injecting drug-addicts. The vast majority of these people will be infected with hepatitis C and maybe HIV.

The reality is they only test drug-addicts for hepatitis C – and not HIV – when entering treatment. You have to be off all opiates for eight weeks before they can test for HIV. Not testing for this virus is a culpable act in itself. The only reason they test addicts for hepatitis C, meanwhile, is to take them off any treatment drugs they may be on and put them on methadone. As I've said, the drugs which treat hepatitis C counteract the effects of methadone. But the last thing a drug-addict with this disease needs is methadone. Hepatitis C can't be cured, but it can be treated. We pointed this out to the Health Board in 1997. At that time there were only 800 addicts on methadone. Since Labour came to power, we now have around 8,000 in Glasgow. Drug deaths have risen year on year, reaching record levels in 2003, with a slight decrease in 2004, but it is still at a level far higher than in 1997.

The scene and the manner of drug deaths have changed dramatically since 1997. Before 1997 most of those who died were addicts not receiving treatment. Addicts were dying in the toilets of high-street stores and fast-food restaurants, OD-ing on heroin with a needle in their groin. Now most drug deaths are of people receiving a drug service. The streets are cleaner, as they are dying in their own beds in a scheme or inner-city tenement from a cocktail of mainly prescribed drugs. This is because they are addicts, who cannot keep control or be stabilised. We live in the information society, an age of statistics, yet while drug deaths are recorded there is no information given out about how many of these addicts were infected.

For the last few years most of the drug deaths in Glasgow have not been heroin overdoses but death through a cocktail of drugs. Methadone is usually part of the cocktail. What was disturbing was when people with hepatitis C died, they were tested for HIV. Why were they not tested for HIV at the same time as hepatitis C? Meanwhile it has never been revealed how many of the 99 people who died in 2000 in Glasgow, a record year, were infected with HIV.

Harm reduction may sound good, but for somebody who's got hepatitis C it's like giving them the tools to kill themselves. The first thing that's attacked by hepatitis C is the liver, and methadone is deadly for the liver. It's very hard for the liver to break it down. There is no cure for hepatitis C, but there is treatment. You can't get this treatment if you take methadone, because, as we know, the two medications are counteractive. So the drug-addict has a choice, but the drug-addict is weak and will go for the easy option of methadone. When they choose methadone, they don't get the choice of hepatitis C treatment. But treatment can prolong their life.

It costs £10,000 a year to treat people who have hepatitis C, and if Glasgow has got 10,000 injecting drug-addicts and, according to the Health Board's figures, 86 per cent of them have hepatitis C, do the arithmetic. It would cost a massive amount of money to treat them.

I believe that the Scottish Executive have gone for the cheaper option with methadone. Let drug-addicts choose, and they'll choose methadone, and they'll end up paying for this decision with their lives. The only way the deaths are going to stop is that addicts start to change their lifestyles and their attitudes. Even if you have hepatitis C, if you've got the right lifestyle and attitude, anything's possible with treatment.

What also surprises me is how many people don't realise how strong the link is between drug addiction and prostitution. It's a vicious circle. Many girls get into prostitution to pay for their habit. Then again, many take drugs because prostitution is a lousy way to make money. There is much debate over safe areas for prostitutes, but how can there possibly be safe areas when infection from hepatitis C or HIV is almost at a level of 100 per cent among street prostitutes in Glasgow? I am almost certain that this is the same in

242

Edinburgh, Aberdeen and Dundee. It is certainly not a safe area for the punters who are going with the prostitutes.

The solution is to take a tip from the Dutch and legalise it. On the streets of Glasgow there are between 1,000 and 1,500 prostitutes. I would say that 90 per cent are injecting drug-addicts, and almost all of the 90 per cent will be receiving drug treatment, namely methadone. Giving them prescribed drugs has not made them give up prostitution. Most addicts will have sex without a condom if the price is right. Infection is spread to punters, who may pass it on to wives, partners and casual girlfriends. In 2002 in Glasgow High Court a man received a six-year sentence for knowingly passing on infection, yet no one seems to notice we have got over 1,000 prostitutes doing the same thing every night of the week. The number of prostitutes working on the city streets has trebled since 1997, with the girls involved getting younger year on year. Now we have schoolgirls doing it – girls who have become infected before they are old enough to leave school.

Throwing resources at the problem has not worked. Millions of pounds have been poured into services for Glasgow prostitutes since 1997, with no visible signs of any of them quitting their trade. In fact, as I pointed out, this has increased by 300 per cent. Throwing resources at treatment services has not worked either. All it has produced are record deaths and infections. It is a sad state of affairs when you have a better chance of living if you do not get in contact with a drug service. The services' own research has proved this, not Calton Athletic's, although we were aware of it.

If someone has the guts to look closely at the drug deaths since 1997, they will discover that most of the people who died were receiving drug treatment, and most of the people who died were infected. This is not an indictment of addicts but of those services that were meant to save lives. Please God, things have to change. We have to accept that we have lost a generation, but we must try to save the next one.

Who is to blame? No one seems prepared to meet this issue head on. But you have to look at the people who are managing the problem. The same people were coming up with excuses in 1996, when I was a member of Scotland Against Drugs. They are the drug advisers to the Scottish Executive. The Executive are not experts, but

243

they must take the blame for implementing their advice.

One thing I have learned over 20 years is that expertise is not gained sitting behind a desk, putting together seminars or coming up with pathetic excuses. Expertise is gained through experience, not on courses. I have not seen any of these advisers working in the field. These people have induced the Scottish Executive to implement an infection policy, not a drugs policy, which has only perpetuated the problem.

Let's look again at the people who manage the problem, not just their advisers. The director of the overall coordinating body, the Scottish Drug Forum, is David Liddell. I first came across David Liddell when Father Willie Slaven was coordinator of the Scottish Drug Forum and he was his assistant. I had no problems with Father Willie, who regularly referred people to us. In fact we got more referrals from Father Willie Slaven than all the other agencies put together. When Father Willie resigned and David Liddell took over, all his experience had been gained in an office, but he advises the Scottish Executive on a policy that doesn't provide for people who want to come off drugs. All the eggs are in the one basket. A big industry with good wages has grown up running projects and advising executive ministers, while drug deaths continue.

Glasgow's Health Board have twenty-six projects, and their manager started as a clerical worker eight years ago. Her experience in the field was earned behind a desk. This isn't good enough, having bureaucrats and administrators deciding policies that affect people's lives.

Meanwhile I predict you will see more deaths from cirrhosis emerging over the next five years, brought about by infection with hepatitis C. The only problem is they will not be put down as drug deaths but as cirrhosis. Your chance of cirrhosis increases when you are on a methadone fix every day and consuming alcohol or other drugs. A lot of these deaths are preventable. Agencies may criticise Calton Athletic, but the people running these services are just not trained to get people off drugs. It takes a certain type, and you don't get that experience sitting behind a desk or at a seminar or on courses.

I am not afraid to point the finger, as I am not a careerist. These bodies include: the Scottish Drug Forum; Scotland Against (certain) Drugs; Mothers Against (certain) Drugs; parent support groups;

English charities funding services in Scotland such as Lifeline, Crisis Centre and Phoenix House; the Health Education Board; the Social Work department; the Health Board; and the Scottish Prison Service.

There are examples of good practice, such as Castle Craig, the Priory and some church-funded projects. The reason for their success is they are autonomous and are not part of the harm-reduction camp. These projects work but funding is always precarious.

What's needed? The no. 1 priority is effective and credible drugs awareness and prevention services – not just a credible service, but credible people delivering it. The singer is every bit as important as the song, but there are few credible singers or songs in Scotland. This is criminal neglect, when thousand of young people can be saved. Drug-addicts need quicker access to treatment – and by treatment I mean treatment to keep people off drugs and criminality, not treatment to stabilise their drug use and cut down on criminality. One offence is one offence too many. This can be done, as we achieved it in our last year when we were providing a service for the Social Work department of Glasgow City Council. Calton Athletic's official figures show that we had 300 drug-addicts looking to come off drugs completely when we were receiving minimal funding.

Official research shows that this market is bigger than ever. The addicts that Calton Athletic have dealt with didn't have to wait three to six weeks for an appointment but were seen that day. If they met the right criteria, they could be on a rehabilitation programme within a week. One hundred people entered the programme in 1998 and 75 per cent completed it. Most of these referrals were self-referrals, and the vast majority had never been in contact with any other drugs services. It is so important to attract into services these people who are willing to change their lifestyle through abstinence.

As I've said, statutory funding was withdrawn from Calton Athletic. We have spent millions more since then, yet there are fewer people coming off drugs today. The service we provided was a life-saver – let's make no mistake about that. The closure of our service – adult day programme, women's service, Under-21s, School Drugs Awareness – coincided with a record rise in drug deaths in Glasgow year on year. I don't claim that Calton Athletic could have saved them all, but we would have certainly saved the ones who would have come looking for help, as we did year after year from 1992 to 1998. In spite of all we achieved in the drugs field in Scotland in prevention, rehabilitation programmes, Under-21s services, women's services and family services, we were never truly appreciated by the statutory funders.

Yet we have been appreciated by private bodies, such as the Robertson Trust, Figment Films, Polygram, the Stone Foundation, John Paul Getty Trust, Merchants House, Trades House, Gateway Exchange, BP, Comic Relief and about 150 schools throughout Scotland who independently invited us to speak to them.

I've met many politicians over the years who have always supported us in private, but it is about time they stood up in public. Among them are Tony Blair, Gordon Brown, Brian Wilson, Glenda Jackson, Michael Forsyth, Willie McKelvey, John McFall, Tony Worthington, Jack McConnell, Alex Salmond, David McLetchie and Annabel Goldie.

When he heard I was doing this book, a well-known Glasgow GP told me there was a groundswell of support for Calton Athletic's approach from GPs in the city. He said that we have the right policy. These GPs have got to stand up and say it in public.

I have twice written to Jack McConnell, the first minister, asking for a meeting. I met one of his civil servants, Colin Cook. I believe that Jack is the one person in Scotland who can bring about change. Jack knows who we are. I met him at St Alphonsus chapel with Tony Blair and Father Willie Slaven a decade ago. I also once appeared with him on TV. Jack comes from an education background, so maybe he can appreciate our prevention message to schools. Bridget, his wife, also knows who we are. We have two lets with her. She is convener of culture and leisure on Glasgow City Council, and we use their services. We play football at Glasgow Green and used to at Crown Point before it was shut down. We also train at St Mungo's. The Green is a great facility and your people, Bridget, will tell you we've been there for 20 years and there's never been any trouble and we are well liked. We appreciate the service and treat it with respect.

Jack McConnell gave an interview in *The Sun* during the 2005 general election in which he expressed his dislike of drug projects which propped up the junkie lifestyle. Calton Athletic definitely do not do that. We know rehab is all about being drug-, alcohol- and crime-free and changing your lifestyle. We can do it. We need your help, Jack.

CHAPTER THIRTY-EIGHT

God Bless You All

People ask me what made me do it. Why did I start Calton Athletic, and why have I not chucked it, especially with all the hassle? When I came off drugs in 1982, I went to Alcoholics Anonymous. I attended meetings for about a year, and then I had my spiritual awakening. I decided to carry the message that recovery was possible to the addicts out there, who were still suffering. Over the last 20 years, Calton Athletic have helped over 3,000 people to recover from drugs. Not everybody made it. A lot of them paid with their lives; a lot of them went back to using drugs. Alcohol took more people back than anything else. It's the oldest drug known to man. Most drug-addicts use alcohol the same way they use drugs, only they take it out of a tumbler, and it can have the same effects.

The struggle has taken its toll on my health, and twice I've had spells in intensive care. When I was diagnosed with emphysema in the mid-'90s, I didn't have to look any further than all the smoking I'd done. I had been at it for about 38 years, mainly Capstan Full Strength and Woodbines. I was thinking that if I didn't do something I wouldn't be around to see the best days at Calton Athletic. I decided that if I was struggling with my health, what better thing to do than a day programme at Calton Athletic? And that's what I did. I gave up smoking, went on the day programme, went to Marco's three days a week and had my meetings. I was improving, and four weeks later I had a go at the Strathclyde Park Run. I was the last one to finish in the group, but my son and his girlfriend came running back for me, and we finished together. I know it was only four miles, but for me it was a full marathon. I thought my days were numbered, but this programme had got me to a level where after four weeks I was doing four miles. Six months before that I couldn't walk to the toilet without being out of breath. I had been seriously ill, and here I was taking part in the Strathclyde Park Run.

A few years later, however, I had an X-ray, and there was a spot at the bottom of my right lung. It was quite a big one, and that's when I decided that I had to get the story of Calton Athletic down in case anything did happen to me. So that's what started me off on what has been a remarkable story.

I returned to the spot where we had our famous World Cup trip in the south of France. I found peace. When I was not putting down my thoughts, I was out running or in the gym. I'll never lose my emphysema, but I'm not smoking today: fags or dope. I also celebrated an important anniversary in France, and maybe that was another good reason for coming. I stopped drinking in May 1977. This was May 2005, and I'd never once taken a drink. It was 22 years since I'd taken drugs. I've also not gambled for 15 years.

Meantime this football team that I'd started and no one thought had a hope in hell of succeeding had drawn in £1 million of self-generated resources over the years. We lost all our statutory funding about ten years after getting kicked off the East End Drug Initiative, but we've kept going. The team is still a force to be reckoned with and people are still reaching us by word of mouth.

People still talk about us winning the Scottish Welfare Cup in 2001, a team with no resources except the ones we raised ourselves. The final was against Peppes from Stirlingshire and was played at Dunipace Juniors' ground in Denny. We were two down after ten minutes but fought back to two all and the game went into extra-time. I was wondering who was going to stand up and be counted, and with a few minutes to go Davie Main came running up from the

248

back, ignored the flying boots and threw himself in for a header and scored. It was a fantastic moment.

Mainie has always been a stalwart who we have been able to rely on, but young blood has also come through, such as Eddie Roxburgh, who is today's team captain. Eddie could hardly kick a ball when he came to us he was so knackered by drugs, but he has gone on to prove himself as a role model. He worked on our School Drugs Awareness team and now, as the football-team captain, takes training each week.

Craig Cameron and Colin Martin are another two who have proved themselves. Craig went back to work after he had gone through our programme, but seven years later he's still with us as a Calton Athletic player. Colin came to us at the same time as Eddie. He worked part-time on the schools project and then went back to work, but he has also stayed with the team.

We had 30 people pass through the club in 2005 and receive their red T-shirt. We helped them get clean, and we sincerely hope they stay off. Our Thursday night meetings at St Ann's chapel have a hard core of 25. We have never had stronger characters involved, and most are in full-time jobs. Alex Morrison offered help with a premises in Parkhead, but we would be inundated and could not handle it on a voluntary basis. I don't have the energy to run it without funding, but if anyone in the Scottish Executive is listening and funds suddenly become available I would make our School Drugs Awareness project the priority. Prevention is better than cure.

Today our operation may be low-key, but it's similar to Alcoholics Anonymous, and no one is better than them at getting people off the booze. No one is better than Calton Athletic at getting people off drugs. Even without resources we can still produce success.

Looking back there have been so many high spots, such as *Alive and Kicking* and *Trainspotting*. I've met so many tremendous people from all walks of life. We went from the Gallowgate to the Dorchester for the Celebrities Guild and to Downing Street to meet the prime minister. That's not a bad achievement, and I would like people to judge us on it, not on the gossip, the myths, the rumours and backbiting. We've come a long way. There have been many kicks in the teeth, and they were painful, but we have learned from them.

Without my family's support I would never have made it. Jeanette, my wife, has been tremendous and my kids have turned out well. They're a credit to us. My mother stood by us in the early days at Calton Athletic, with both moral and financial support. She loved what I did at Calton Athletic.

There have been so many stalwarts at Calton Athletic. Willie Burns and me go way back. We'd been bunk boys together in Borstal, and the two of us came off heroin together. I was sober, but Willie was still drinking. Annette, the housekeeper at Craigpark, made sure it was like the Dennistoun Dorchester. Elspeth Hirst, our schools coordinator, did a marvellous job. I was sorry to lose staff like Christine McCafferty, an invaluable, trusted friend. She left to work at the university but still did our accounts every month in a voluntary capacity. Christine, you were a tower of strength.

Big Archie Main and his wife, Anne Main, are special. Stevie Orr and Janice McKindall were a godsend. I owe a special thanks to my management committee. Derek Connell, a former player, was another rock. He was the first boy ever to kick a ball for Calton Athletic. Shuey McGuire arrived in the early days, just out of jail. He showed his gratitude by staying at Calton Athletic. Bert Wilson, our treasurer, was originally from Blairgowrie. Several years ago I helped his son, but I had already known Bert for years. He's a trusted friend, who stood by us through everything. I also need and want to thank chairman James Alston. He was a player at Calton Athletic over a decade ago, one of the Baltic boys (from the Baltic area of the East End). James lost two close friends: Jamie Gillan and Steven Lynch. It was in memory of them that he stayed with Calton Athletic.

We've helped so many people, but so many people have also helped us, such as Walter Smith, the Scotland manager, and his assistant Tommy Burns, both East End boys. There is something about the East End that gives its inhabitants a feeling for life that enables them to bring out the best in other people. Tommy and Walter have that gift. Neither had it easy as young men, and it's good to see East End success turned into national success. Both also have a great sense of humour, another East End trait.

Walter was the manager of Rangers when they achieved the nine-in-a-row League titles. He gave us the opportunity to go and speak to the young players at Ibrox, which added vital credibility to our School Drugs Awareness team. Walter is a gem of a man. He wasn't a fair-weather friend either. When he moved to Everton and had his testimonial, he decided he wanted to give something to Calton Athletic. He invited 26 of us down to Liverpool for the game against Manchester United. He arranged a meal for us when we arrived and met us before the game. Unfortunately Everton got beaten, but Walter came to the hotel afterwards to see us with his wife and a couple of friends. He arranged for the young players to be taken to Cream discothèque, which is one of the best-known clubs in Europe. Walter also picked up our hotel tab but told me, 'I'll pay for everything, Davie, except the blue movies.'

'Our boys are good laddies, Walter,' I told him. 'They don't watch blue movies. But if they do, the first five minutes is enough, and you don't pay for that.'

Prince Naseem, who went on to become the featherweight boxing world champion, was another visitor to our premises at Craigpark, where he had his press conference prior to his fight in Glasgow. The arrangements were made by Alex Morrison, the well-known Glasgow boxing promoter. Alex had been a friend of ours for a few years. In 1995 he had invited me to a boxing night in the Thistle Hotel, where they had a raffle with the proceeds going to Calton Athletic. I went along with one of the boys, expecting to pick up the proceeds of the raffle and was met by Alex's daughter Catherine. She led us in and walked us through all of the tables. I wondered what was happening, and she ushered us up to the top table. I couldn't believe what was happening. Alex had put us at the top table, alongside former world and European boxing champions. That wasn't the first time that big Alex had helped us, and he has continued to do so. One time I phoned my son from holiday and he told me, 'Since you've been away, big Alex's been chairing the meetings.' David was joking, but he half-meant it because Alex was showing a lot of interest in the boys.

Lenny Henry has been smashing over the years. When about 50 of us went to see him at the Pavilion Theatre, I arranged to meet him the next day at the Hilton. I picked him up from there and took him down to our premises at Craigpark. Lenny had a cup of tea, got the photos taken and chatted to everybody on the women's services. As I was taking him back to the Hilton, I asked him if he could come up to the hospital with us, the Glasgow Royal Infirmary. My mother was in there for a hip replacement. She had just lost two of her daughters and her spirits were down. Big Lenny said it was no problem. We arrived, and my mother was sitting with her back to us. I came round behind her and said, 'I've brought somebody to see you, Ma.'

When she turned around, there was Lenny Henry. She couldn't believe her eyes. She loved the big yin. The rest of the ward was buzzing. The whole hospital was buzzing. Here was a superstar to see an 88-year-old woman. He lifted her spirits, and I'm glad to say, Lenny, that that was a very special day for her. She told me later that after the visit all the doctors and nurses started treating her as Mrs Important.

What a character Robbie Coltrane is – another who wasn't a fair-weather friend and who lent his personal support at the first School Drugs Awareness presentation in 1995 that we were doing for VIPs.

Al Hunter, the guy who wrote the TV film *Alive and Kicking* and was Pit Bull in *London's Burning*, is another special friend.

Danny Boyle, Andrew Macdonald and John Hodge at Figment Films have all been tremendous. Through their support since *Trainspotting*, they have raised £400,000 for Calton Athletic. That £400,000, along with £600,000 from the Robertson Trust, has made Calton Athletic what it is. The Trainspotters introduced us to Robbie Williams, Bobby Carlyle, Ewan McGregor, Johnny Lee Miller, Ewen Bremner and all the rest of the gang. And what a man Irvine Welsh is – still a true friend.

The Robertson Trust gave vital support to the School Drugs Awareness team. Many, many thanks to Sir Lachlan Maclean and his chairman Ian Good.

Whenever I look back I can never forget the ones we've lost. Italia '90 was a learning process, and we played a semi-professional team called Genoa 90. One of the boys that day was young Thomas Grant. I thought he had tremendous skill. He was 18 at the time. He left Calton Athletic, and the day he died he was just out of prison. I have special memories of Thomas, and I still think of him often. I'll always remember his contribution in that game and his wasted life. His mother had died through drugs, and his dad was doing an 18-year prison sentence at the time. He came from a wild part of the East End, and his granny was doing the best she could for him, but it's hard in these areas. It's hard when you think you've got a reputation to live up to. He was my daughter's boyfriend when they were about 15, and he wasn't involved in anything at the time. Thomas was a good boy, and, given a level playing field, I'm quite sure he could have made it as a professional football player. I hope somebody's looking after you up there, Thomas.

The first boy in my community who died from using drugs was James Smith. He was the boy I'd taken down to Cardross all those years ago, and it was just after Cardross had shut down that James had died. This was in the early days of Calton Athletic. James liked a drink, and when he returned to the community it took him back to other drugs. He was the first person to die. His family was devastated. They were good people and cared for him deeply. We produced a memorial cup in his memory and played for it every year.

Tam Gorman was our first goalkeeper. He was only 17 when he came to Calton Athletic, the best goalkeeper we'd ever had. But Tam liked a drink and thought he could handle it. He couldn't, and the drink took him back to drugs. Tragically, Tam went.

Duncan McManus stayed down the stairs from us. Now he's gone. Danny Lorimer was another. Danny had just finished a long-term sentence when he died. Not long before he had come down to Calton Athletic with his sister. He was trying hard to recover but struggling badly, and he never made it back. Shuey Fairfield had just finished a long-term sentence. He was a bit older, but he wasn't an old man, only about 35 when he died.

Then there was young Tony Drummond and Roseanne Bullock. Roseanne was from a good family too, a lovely-looking lassie. Danielle Donaldson was a beautiful-looking young lassie as well, tragically killed.

There was James McGinn, or Jimmucks, as we called him, Albert Ferrier, or Albie, and Andy Hewitt. Andy liked a drink and thought there were a few dances in him, but the Ecstasy scene drew him back into heroin. A lot of people at that time had got off heroin and other drugs, but the new Ecstasy scene saw them finish up back on the smack, and many paid for it with their lives.

Shuey O'Neil from Possil was probably one of the best players we had. He liked a drink, and that took him to Ecstasy, which led him back to heroin.

Another Baltic boy was Sticco – Stevie Lynch – another great player. In a way he resembled Tommy Burns – a good football player from a good family. Jamie Gillan had done well at the club. He had gone to Jersey and then settled in London and died down there. I believe if Jamie had stayed in Glasgow or come back home he would have returned to Calton Athletic. Andrew Dippolito, who was our goalkeeper in the *Trainspotting* game at Brentford, went on to take his own life.

An awful lot of people died whose families are all still friends with Calton Athletic. Many of them tell us their happiest times were when their son or daughter was at Calton Athletic. They've got fond memories as their children usually achieved something and we had photographs to prove it. It's been good handing these back to the parents. It's good being there for them when they need it, and it's reassuring they never blamed Calton Athletic and that they still hold us in high regard.

It's been painful speaking about this because there are many more families and I hope they don't feel offended if I've not mentioned them. Running Calton Athletic has never been just about the highs; it's as much about learning to handle the deaths. The hardest thing for me has always been going to see somebody's parents. I've been to see too many of them, and they often ask themselves, 'Where did we go wrong?' Everybody looks for someone to blame, and too often they blame themselves. I tell them that it's not their fault, that they weren't calling the shots. They did the best they could and would have gladly swapped their lives if they could. And I've told them it's hard, it's tragic and it's not natural. We're not meant to bury our kids; our kids are meant to bury us. I've now seen hundreds of parents in the East End who have had to bury their kids and live with it. These are good people. You never forget, but they tell me that time is a healer, or it makes it a bit easier. I speak to a lot of these parents, and a lot of them have continued to help the club over the years. God bless you all. At Calton Athletic we still hold them in high regard, and it's because of them and the memory of their children that we keep on going the way we are. God bless every one of you.